AF480874

Practical guide to forming simulation

RAKESH KUMAR

PRACTICAL GUIDE TO FORMING SIMULATION

First edition. June 2021.

Second edition. December 2023.

Third edition. December 2025.

ISBN: 979888772641

Written by Rakesh Kumar.

DEDICATION

This book is dedicated to my beloved wife, Mrs. Rakhi Sharda, whose unwavering love and encouragement have been my constant source of strength. Her belief in me, even during the long hours of writing, played a crucial role in bringing this work to completion.

The journey to write this book was sparked by a desire to push beyond the ordinary. Inspired by literature on value creation and entrepreneurship, I realized that true professional growth comes from sharing knowledge and solving complex problems for others.

Practical Guide to Forming Simulation is the manifestation of that realization. I am deeply honored to express my gratitude to the mentors who guided my career, and to every colleague who shared their wisdom along the way. Thank you for helping me turn this experience into a resource for the engineering community.

Disclaimer

DISCLAIMER OF LIABILITY The information provided in this book, Practical Guide to Forming Simulation, is intended for educational and instructional purposes only. While the author has made every effort to ensure the accuracy and reliability of the information within, the content represents the author's professional experience and personal methodology. It does not constitute a formal engineering standard or a guarantee of manufacturing results.

Simulation vs. Reality: Readers should be aware that Finite Element Analysis (FEA) and forming simulations are approximation tools. Real-world results may vary due to material inconsistencies, press conditions, lubrication variability, and tool wear. The author, Rakesh Kumar, and the publisher assume no liability for any errors, omissions, or for any damages (financial, physical, or operational) arising from the use or interpretation of the information contained herein. Physical validation and prototyping are always required before mass production.

TRADEMARK NOTICE All product names, logos, and brands are property of their respective owners. All company, product, and service names used in this book are for identification purposes only. Use of these names, logos, and brands does not imply endorsement.

HyperWorks®, HyperForm®, and Altair® are registered trademarks of Altair Engineering Inc.

Any other software or hardware trademarks mentioned are the property of their respective owners.

INDEPENDENT PUBLICATION This book is an independent publication and has not been authorized, sponsored, or otherwise approved by Altair Engineering Inc. or any other software vendor mentioned. The views and opinions expressed in this book are those of the author alone.

ACKNOWLEDGMENTS

The professional world becomes a better place because of those dedicated to developing others. I am deeply grateful to the mentors who generously shared their time to guide my journey. This book would not have been possible without their inspiration.

To everyone I have had the privilege to lead or observe—thank you. Your examples have been the foundation for my understanding of professional excellence. You have shaped my perspective, and it is through your influence that this work was conceived.

I extend my heartfelt gratitude to the peers and team members at the organizations I have been a part of. Without your shared experiences and unwavering support, this book would not have come to fruition. The opportunity to collaborate with such incredible individuals has been both humbling and inspiring.

A special acknowledgment goes to the circumstances that first allowed this book to be written. The challenging times of the past few years provided the unexpected gift of time, allowing me to dive into writing—a passion I had long kept hidden.

Bringing an idea to life is no small feat. I owe a great deal of thanks to my wife, whose unwavering support and belief in me were vital to making this reality.

Finally, a huge thank you to my seniors and employers who provided me with opportunities for growth throughout my 18+ years in the industry. Thank you for being the kind of leaders I trust and respect. It has been an honor to learn from you.

Contents

1. An introduction to Finite element analysis (FEA)

Finite element analysis (FEA) is the use of calculations, models and simulations to predict and understand how an object might behave under various physical conditions. Engineers use FEA to find vulnerabilities in their design prototypes.

FEA uses the finite element method (FEM), a numerical technique that cuts the structure of an object into several pieces, or elements, and then reconnects the elements at points called nodes. The FEM creates a set of algebraic equations which engineers, developers and other designers can use to perform finite element analysis.

Frequently, the physical experiences of a product -- such as its structural or fluid behaviour and thermal transport -- are described using partial differential equations (PDEs). Finite element analysis emerged as a way for computers to solve both linear and nonlinear PDEs. However, it is important to note that FEA only provides an approximate solution; it is a numerical approach to finding the real results of partial differential equations.

Using finite element analysis can reduce the number of physical prototypes created and experiments performed while also optimizing all components during the design phase. Finite element analysis software emerged in the 1970s with programs such as Abaqus,

Adina and Ansys. Now, it is common to find virtual testing and design optimization integrated into the product development cycle to improve the product quality and reduce the time it takes to enter the market.

Finite element analysis (FEA) is the process of simulating the behavior of a part or assembly under given conditions so that it can be assessed using the finite element method (FEM). FEA is used by engineers to help simulate physical phenomena and thereby reduce the need for physical prototypes, while allowing for the optimization of components as part of the design process of a project.

FEA uses mathematical models to understand and quantify the effects of real-world conditions on a part or assembly. These simulations, which are conducted via specialised software, allow engineers to locate potential problems in a design, including areas of tension and weak spots.

With the use of mathematics, it is possible to understand and quantify structural or fluid behaviour, wave propagation, thermal transport and other phenomena.

Most of the processes can be described using partial differential equations (PDEs), but these complex equations need to be solved in order for parameters such as stress and strain rates to be estimated. FEA allows for an approximate solution to these problems.

FEA is the basis of modern software simulation software, with the results usually shown on a computer-generated color scale.

While some theories state that FEA has its roots in the 16th century work of Euler, the earliest mathematical papers directly detailing the technique date back to Schellbach's work of 1851. FEA was developed further by engineers from different industries around the world in order to solve a large number of structural mechanic's problems, primarily in civil engineering and aerospace. The first development of FEA for real world applications began in the mid-1950s and was further developed over the next few decades.

How Does Finite Element Analysis Work?

The simulations used in FEA are created using a mesh of millions of smaller elements that combine to create the shape of the structure that is being assessed. Each of these small elements is subjected to calculations, with these mesh refinements combining to produce the final result of the whole structure.

These approximate calculations are usually polynomial, with interpolations occurring across the small elements, meaning that values can be determined at some but not all points. The points where the values can be determined are called nodal points and can usually be found at the boundary of the element.

What is Finite Element Method (FEM)?

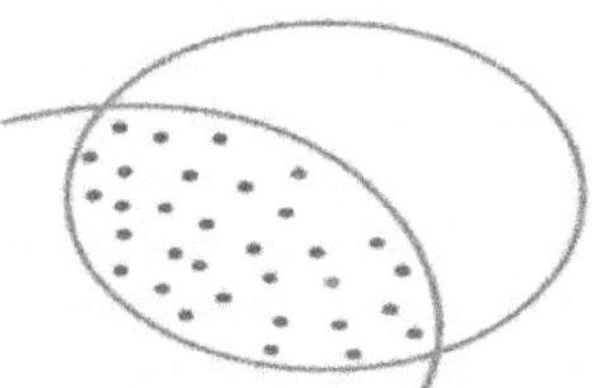

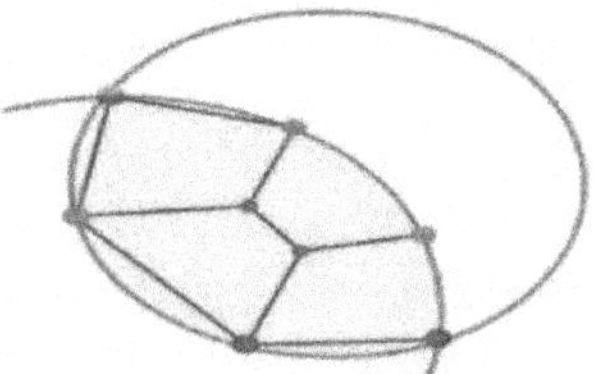

FEM (Finite Element Method)

- A numerical method.
- Mathematical representation of an actual problem.
- Approximate method

The Finite Element Method only makes calculations at a limited

(Finite) number of points and then interpolates the results for the entire domain (surface or volume).

Finite – Any continuous object has infinite degrees of freedom and it is not possible to solve the problem in this format. The Finite Element Method reduces the degrees of freedom from infinite to finite with the help of discretization or meshing (nodes and elements).

Element – All of the calculations are made at a limited number of points known as nodes. The entity joining nodes and forming a specific shape such as quadrilateral or triangular is known as an Element. To get the value of a variable (say displacement) anywhere in between the calculation points, an interpolation function (as per the shape of the element) is used.

Method - There are 3 methods to solve any engineering problem. Finite element analysis belongs to numerical method category.

How the results are interpolated from a few calculation points?

It is ok that FEA is making all the calculations at a limited number of points, but the question is how it calculates values of the unknown somewhere in between the calculation points.
This is achieved by interpolation. Consider a 4 noded quadrilateral element as shown in the figure below. A quad4 element uses the following linear interpolation formula:

$$u = a0 + a1x + a2y + a3xy$$

FEA calculates the values at the outer nodes 1, 2, 3, 4 i.e. a0, a1, a2, a3 are known.

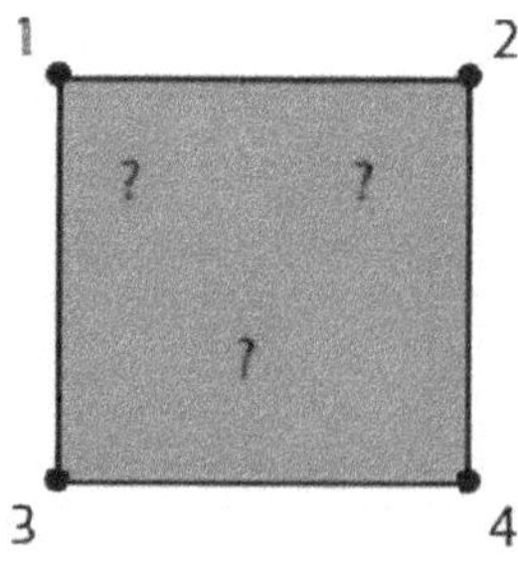

4 noded (linear) quad

The value of the variable anywhere in between could be easily determined just by specifying x and y coordinates in above equation.

For an 8 noded quadrilateral, the following parabolic interpolation function is used:

$$u = a0 + a1x + a2y + a3xy + a4 x2 + a5$$
$$y2 + a6x2y + a7xy2$$

What is DOF (Degree of freedom)?

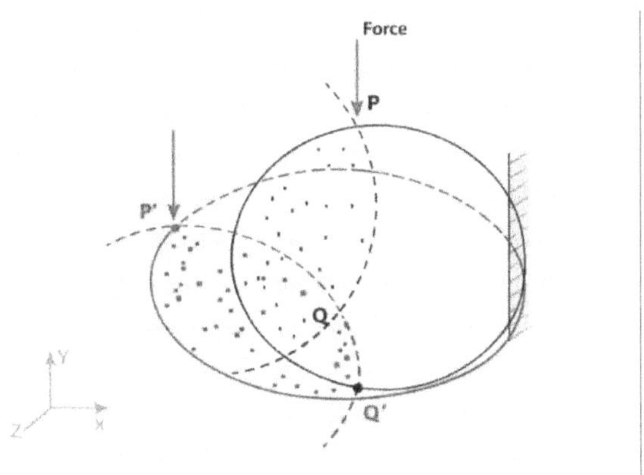

In the example above, an object is fixed at one end and a force is applied at the point "P". Due to the force, the object deforms and Point P gets shifted to new position P'.

When can we say that we know the solution to above problem?
If and only if we are able to define the deformed position of each and every particle completely.

The minimum number of parameters (motion, coordinates, temp. etc.) required to define the position of any entity completely in the space is known as a degree of freedom (dof).

Consider the following 2-D (planar) problem. Suppose the origin is at the bottom left corner and is known. To define the position of point A completely with respect to the origin, we need two parameters i.e. x_1 and y_1, in other words 2 dofs (translation x and y).

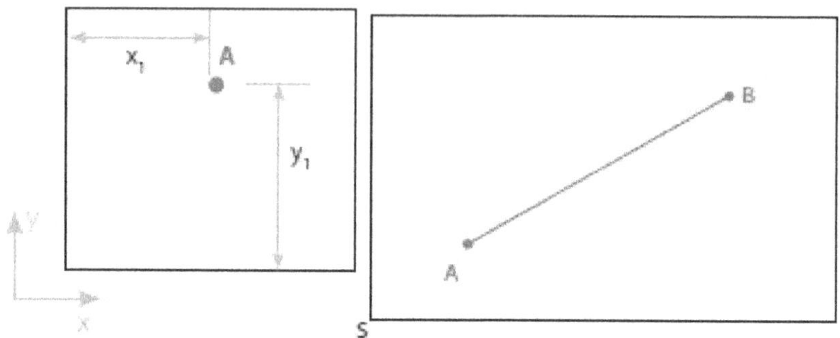

Consider that the point A is a part of a line, now one angle should also be defined in addition to the two translations i.e. 3 dofs (two translations and one rotation).

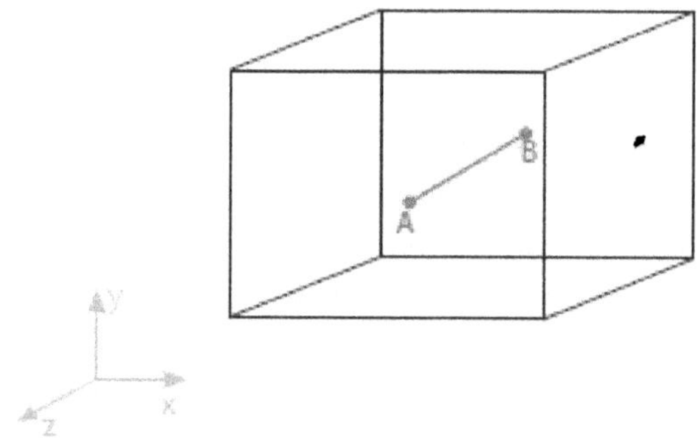

Suppose points A and B are shifted out of the plane and the line is rotated arbitrarily with respect to all of the three axes. The minimum number of parameters to define the position of point A completely would be 6 dofs {3 translations (U_x, U_y, U_z) and 3 rotations (θ_x, θ_y, θ_z).}

Dof is a very important concept. In FEA we use it for the individual calculation points. The total dofs for a given mesh model is equal to the number of nodes multiplied by the number of dof per node.

Use of finite element analysis in manufacturing

Finite Element Analysis (FEA) is a critical computational tool extensively used in the manufacturing industry to enhance product design, optimize manufacturing processes, and ensure product reliability. FEA breaks down complex structures into smaller, manageable elements, allowing detailed analysis of physical phenomena like stress, heat transfer, and fluid dynamics. This method provides significant advantages in various stages of the manufacturing process.

One of the primary applications of FEA in manufacturing is in the design and development of products. Engineers use FEA to simulate and evaluate the performance of a product under various conditions before physical prototypes are built. This simulation capability helps in identifying potential design flaws and optimizing the design for durability and efficiency. For instance, in the automotive industry, FEA is used to analyze the structural integrity of vehicle components, ensuring they can withstand operational stresses and impacts, thereby enhancing safety and performance.

FEA also plays a crucial role in process optimization. Manufacturing processes such as machining, welding, and casting involve complex thermal and mechanical interactions. FEA helps in modeling these processes to predict outcomes and optimize parameters for improved quality and efficiency. For example, in casting, FEA can predict how molten metal will flow into a mold and solidify, allowing for adjustments that minimize defects like porosity and residual stresses.

Moreover, FEA aids in failure analysis and maintenance planning. By understanding how and why components fail, manufacturers can improve their designs and maintenance schedules. FEA enables detailed analysis of failed components to identify the root cause, whether it be material fatigue, excessive stress, or manufacturing defects. This information is invaluable for developing more robust products and effective maintenance strategies.

In summary, FEA is an indispensable tool in manufacturing, offering detailed insights into product design, process optimization, and failure analysis. Its ability to simulate real-world conditions and predict performance helps manufacturers produce high-quality, reliable products while reducing development time and costs. The integration of FEA into the manufacturing workflow thus fosters innovation and efficiency, driving advancements in various industries.

The term CAE (Computer Aided Engineering) includes the following types of analyses:

1.1) Linear static analysis

1.2) Non-linear analysis

1.3) Dynamic analysis

1.4) Buckling analysis

1.5) Thermal analysis

1.6) Fatigue analysis

1.7) Optimization

1.8) CFD analysis

1.9) Crash analysis

1.10) NVH analysis

1. 1 Linear Static Analysis

- **Linear:** Linear means straight line. In linear analysis, the FE solver will therefore always follow a straight line from base to deformed state.

- **Static:** There are two conditions for static analysis:

The force is static i.e. there is no variation with respect to time

(deadweight).Equilibrium condition Σforces (Fx,Fy,Fz) and ΣMoments

(Mx,My,Mz)=0.

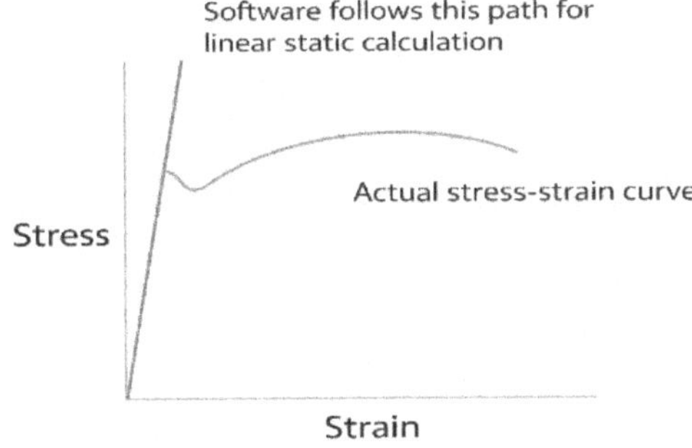

Use of linear static analysis

Linear static analysis is a fundamental type of Finite Element Analysis (FEA) used to determine the response of structures under static loading conditions. It assumes linear material behavior and small deformations. This analysis helps engineers assess stresses, strains, and displacements in components, ensuring they meet safety and performance standards. Commonly applied in fields like civil engineering and automotive design, it aids in optimizing structures for strength and stability.

Non-linear analysis

Material based non-linearity: Force (stress) vs. Displacement (strain) curve is non-linear (polynomial)

Geometric non linearity: In real life the stiffness [K] is a function of displacement [d] (remember: for linear Analysis [K] is constant, independent of[d]). This means in a geometric non-linear analysis, the stiffness K is re-calculated after a certain predefined displacement.

Contact non-linearity: In Contact analysis, the Stiffness K also changes as a function of displacement (when parts get in to contact or separate). Non-linear analysis deals with true stress and strain (unlike engineering stress and strain in linear static analysis)

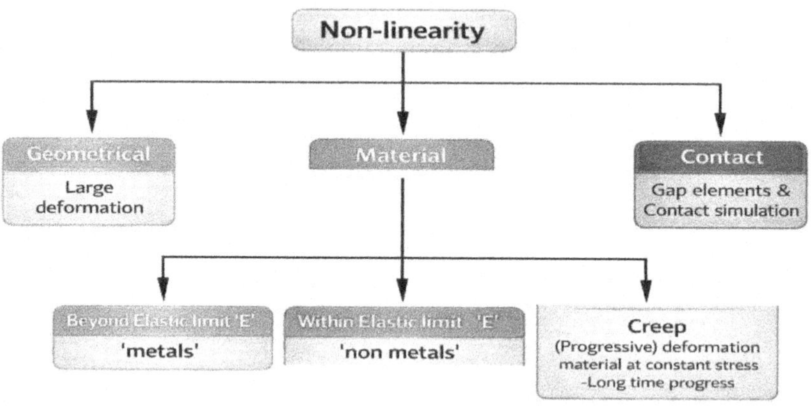

1.2   Dynamic Analysis

Dynamic analysis definition: Dynamic analysis is a method used to evaluate the behavior of structures and systems under time-dependent or varying loads. Unlike static analysis, it accounts for inertia, damping, and the effects of motion. This analysis is crucial for understanding how structures respond to dynamic forces such as vibrations, impacts, and cyclic loads, ensuring their performance and safety in real-world conditions. It is widely applied in fields like aerospace, automotive, and civil engineering.

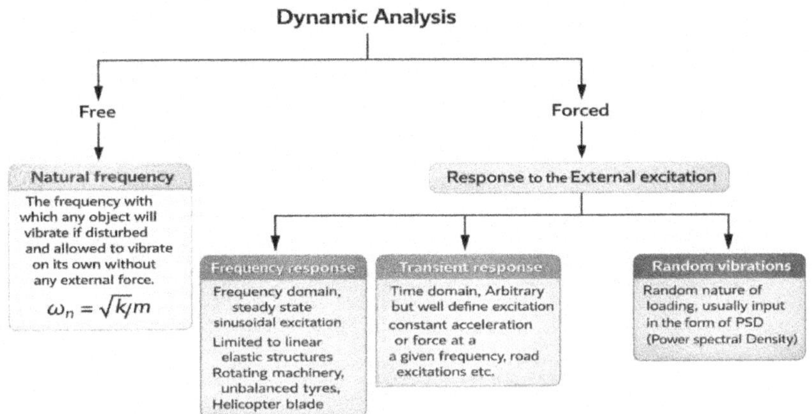

Practical uses of dynamic analysis

Dynamic analysis has practical applications across various industries. In civil engineering, it's used to assess buildings' and bridges' responses to earthquakes and wind loads. In automotive engineering, it evaluates vehicle dynamics for crash safety and ride comfort. Aerospace engineers use it to analyze the impact of aerodynamic forces on aircraft structures. Additionally, it's crucial in designing machinery and equipment subjected to vibrations and dynamic loading to ensure durability and performance.

1.3 Linear Buckling Analysis

Some key aspects:

- Applicable for only compressive load

- Slender beams and sheet metal parts

- Bending stiffness<<<Axial stiffness

- Large lateral deformation

 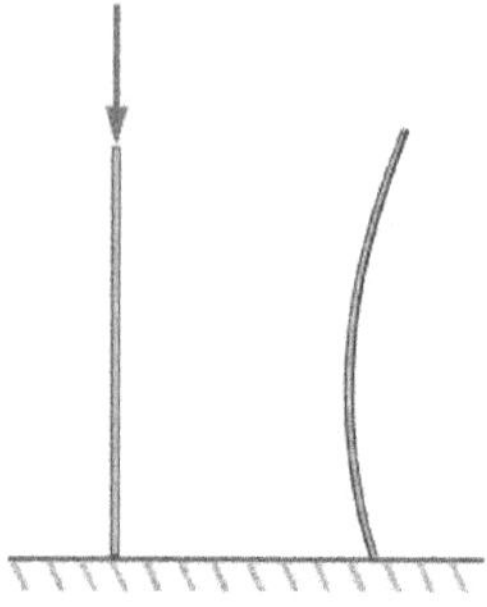

Define linear buckling analysis

Linear buckling analysis is a computational technique used to predict the critical load at which a structure becomes unstable and buckles. It assumes linear material behavior and small deformations prior to buckling. This analysis helps identify the load factors leading to buckling, enabling engineers to design structures that can safely withstand critical loads. It is commonly used in designing slender structures like columns, beams, and aerospace components to prevent failure.

Practical use of linear buckling analysis

Linear buckling analysis is practically used in the design of columns, beams, and other slender structural elements to ensure stability under compressive loads. In civil engineering, it helps prevent structural failures in buildings and bridges. Aerospace engineers use it to design lightweight yet stable components, such as aircraft fuselages and wings. Additionally, it is applied in mechanical engineering to optimize the design of load-bearing components, ensuring safety and reliability.

1.4   Thermal Analysis

Define thermal analysis: Thermal analysis is a computational technique used to study the temperature distribution and heat transfer within a system or component. It evaluates how structures respond to thermal loads, including conduction, convection, and radiation. This analysis helps engineers design components that can withstand temperature variations and manage heat effectively. It is crucial in fields like electronics, automotive, aerospace, and building design, ensuring thermal performance and preventing overheating or thermal failure.

Practical use of thermal analysis: Thermal analysis is practically used in electronics to prevent overheating of components by optimizing heat dissipation. In the automotive industry, it ensures engine and brake systems operate within safe temperature ranges. Aerospace engineers use it to manage thermal loads on spacecraft during re-entry. Additionally, in building design, thermal analysis helps in creating energy-efficient structures by analyzing heat flow and insulation effectiveness, ensuring comfortable and sustainable living environments.

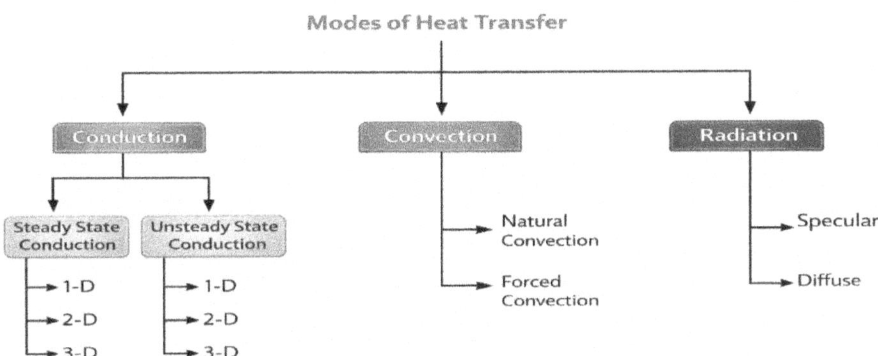

1.6 Fatigue Analysis

Fatigue analysis is a method used to predict the life and performance of materials and structures under cyclic loading. It evaluates how repeated stress and strain cycles can lead to the initiation and growth of cracks, eventually causing failure. This analysis helps engineers design components that can endure long-term usage without failure. It is essential in industries like aerospace, automotive, and civil engineering, where durability and reliability are critical.

In materials science, fatigue is the progressive and localized structural damage that occurs when a material is subjected to cyclic loading. The nominal maximum stress values are less than the ultimate tensile stress limit, and may be below the yield stress limit of the material. Fatigue occurs when a material is subjected to repeated loading and unloading. If the loads are above a certain threshold, microscopic cracks will begin to form at the surface. Eventually a crack will reach a critical size, and the structure will suddenly fracture. The shape of the structure will significantly affect the fatigue life; square holes or sharp corners will lead to elevated local stresses where fatigue cracks can initiate. Round holes and smooth transitions or fillets are therefore important to increase the fatigue strength of the structure analysis.

1.7 Optimization

Define optimization in finite element analysis: Optimization in finite element analysis (FEA) involves adjusting design variables to achieve the best performance according to specified criteria, such as minimizing weight while maximizing strength or stiffness. This process uses FEA simulations to iteratively refine and improve designs, ensuring they meet desired performance targets efficiently. Optimization helps in developing cost-effective, high-performance products in various industries, including automotive, aerospace, and civil engineering.

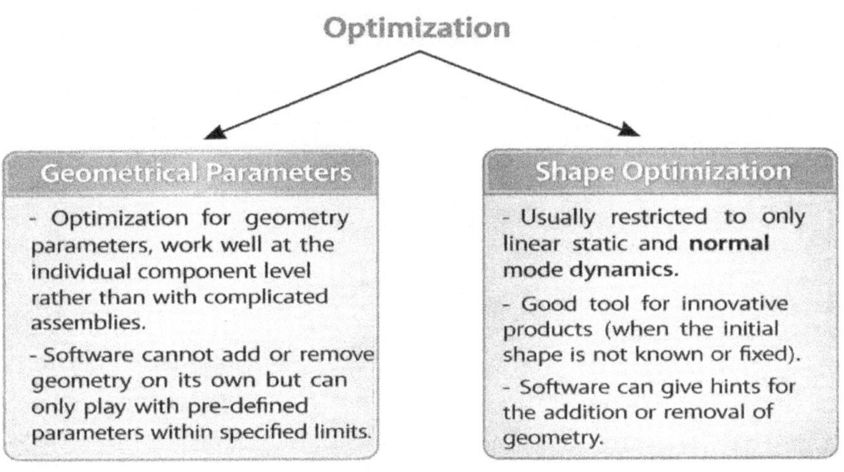

1.8 Computational Fluid Dynamics (CFD)

Define computational fluid dynamics: Computational Fluid Dynamics (CFD) is a branch of fluid mechanics that uses numerical methods and algorithms to analyze and solve problems involving fluid flows. CFD simulations provide insights into the behavior of liquids and gases in various scenarios, such as aerodynamics, hydrodynamics, and heat transfer. This technology is crucial in industries like aerospace, automotive, and civil engineering for optimizing designs and enhancing performance through detailed fluid flow analysis.

A fluid is a substance that continuously deforms under an applied shear stress regardless of the magnitude of the applied stress. Gas and liquids are both fluids. Fluid mechanics deals with the study of fluid, its properties, and its behavior. Computational Fluid Dynamics (CFD) is the branch of fluid mechanics which uses numerical methods to analyze fluid dynamics problems. It is based on the Navier –Stokes equations (Mass,

Momentum, and Energy conservation equilibrium equations).

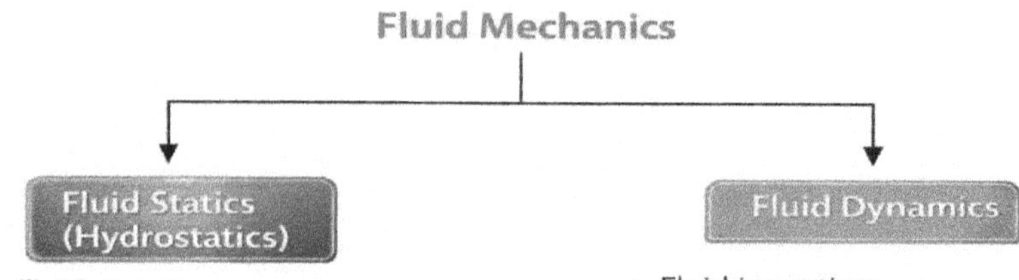

1.9 Crash Analysis

Define crash analysis: Crash analysis is a method used to simulate and study the effects of collisions on structures and vehicles. It involves using computational models to predict how materials and components behave under high-impact conditions. This analysis helps engineers design safer vehicles and structures by evaluating crashworthiness and identifying potential failure points. It is crucial in the automotive and aerospace industries to enhance safety features and comply with regulatory standards.

Practical application of crash analysis: Crash analysis is practically applied in the automotive industry to design and improve vehicle safety features, such as airbags, crumple zones, and seat belts, ensuring passenger protection during collisions. In aerospace, it assesses the crashworthiness of aircraft to enhance structural integrity during impact. Additionally, crash analysis is used in civil engineering to design safer roadside barriers and guardrails, minimizing injury and damage in vehicular accidents.

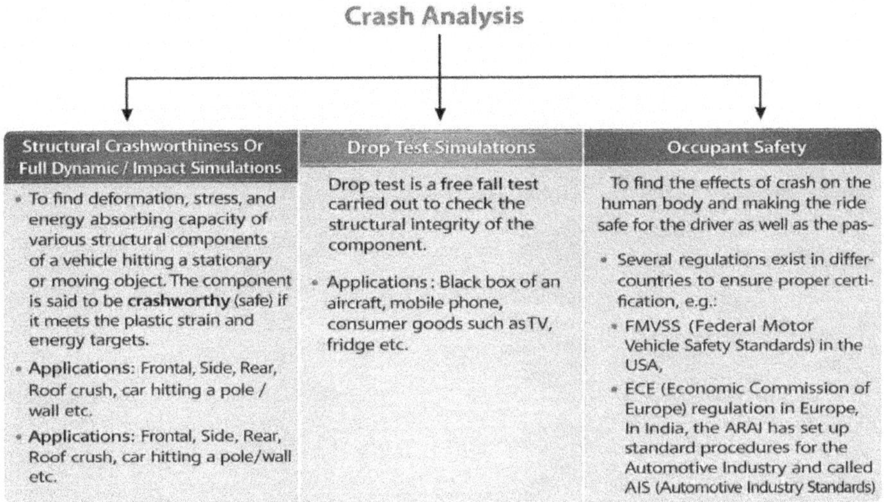

1.10 Noise Vibration and Harshness

Noise, Vibration, and Harshness (NVH) analysis is the study of unwanted sounds and vibrations in vehicles, machinery, and structures. It aims to identify and mitigate sources of noise and vibration to enhance comfort, performance, and durability. This analysis is crucial in automotive engineering to improve the driving experience by reducing cabin noise and vibrations. It is also applied in product design to ensure quieter and smoother operation of various mechanical systems.

PRACTICAL APPLICATIONS OF NOISE VIBRATION AND HARSHNESS ANALYSIS: Noise, Vibration, and Harshness (NVH) analysis is practically applied in the automotive industry to enhance passenger comfort by minimizing engine noise, road noise, and vibrations. In aerospace, it improves cabin comfort and reduces structural vibrations. Industrial machinery benefits from NVH analysis by ensuring quieter, smoother operation, and increased longevity. Additionally, NVH is used in consumer electronics to reduce operational noise and enhance user experience in devices like laptops and household appliances.

<table>
<tr><th>Sound Radiation Or Scattering Or Uncoupled Problems</th><th>Coupled Or Vibroacoustics Problems</th></tr>
<tr><td>

- This predicts how much sound pressure level is felt by a vibrating source at a certain distance as a function of the solid angle. A typical example is how much sound level is felt due to a horn or a silencer vibrating at a certain distance.

These are solved by Boundary Element Method

Boundary Element Method

</td><td>

- This is when there is a clear interaction of a structure and fluid cavity. A typical example is when there is a noise level felt at the driver's right ear due to the engine vibration in an idle condition.

These are solved by Finite Element Method

Finite Element Method

</td></tr>
</table>

2. Forming Limit Diagram (FLD)

FORMING LIMIT DIAGRAM (FLD) OR FORMING LIMIT CURVE (FLC)

FLD, often known as Forming limit diagram is used to predict the forming behavior of sheet metal complex parts or deep drawn parts and it attempt to provide a graphical representation of the material failure tests or some lab experimental database. To measure the material failure (Crack), the round blank is deformed/drawn to make a Dome, with which two axis – Major and minor axis are derived from the repetitive tests on different specimen of same material coil.

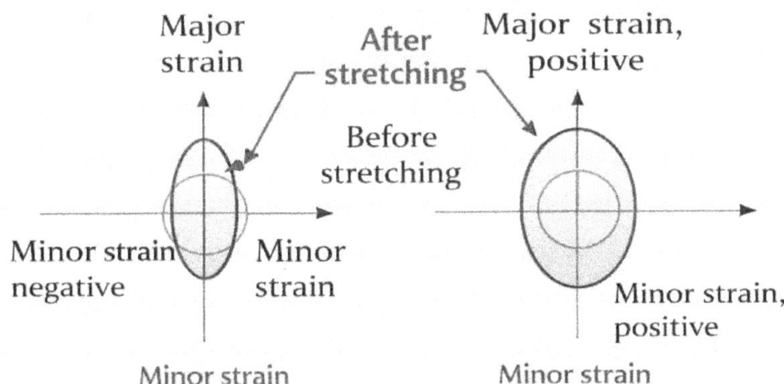

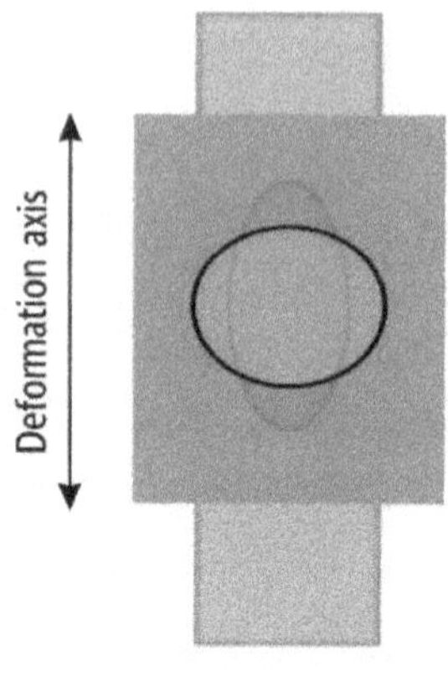

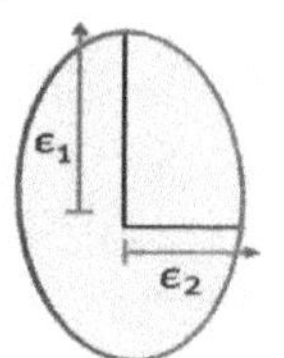

Definition of the deformation axes in forming limit diagram measurement

The ellipse in forming limit diagram consisting of two axis known as major and minor axis, used to predict the behavior of material under different forming conditions, where the role of geometry/shape has a vital significance. In the above geometry, there is a vertical forming, represented by major axis as well as horizontal stretching representing minor axis. The forming limit diagram in derived from the overall forming operation under the given conditions. Where there are multiple variable factors, out of which more important are - the material properties particularly N and R value and shape of the geometry you are going to choose as a stage to achieve the final goal, that is your product.

N = Strain hardening exponent, which measures the stretch ability of the material

R = Plastic strain ratio, measures the draw ability of the material

When the material is formed, both axis in combined form generate the Forming limit diagram.

Main components of FLD/FLC

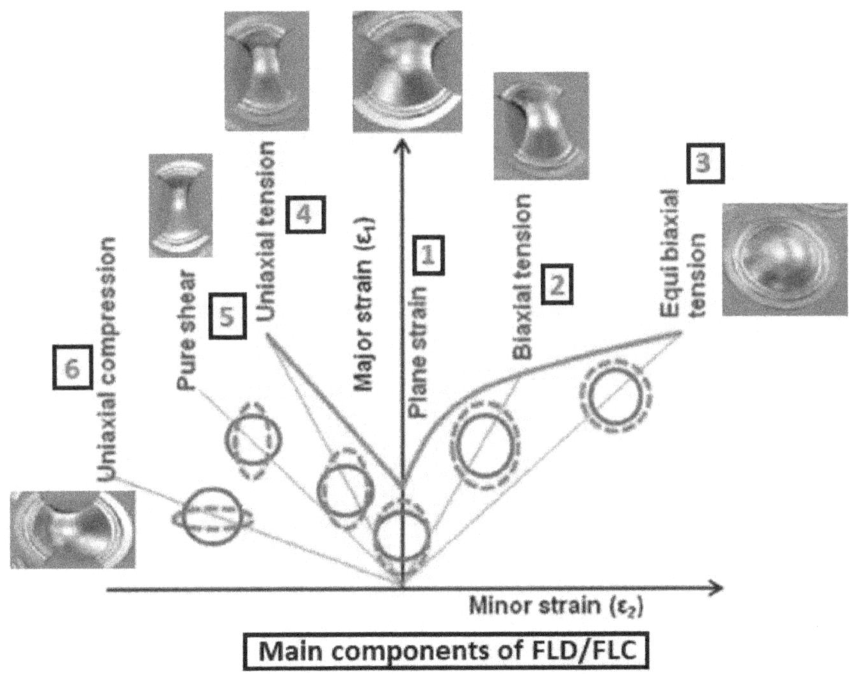

Please be noted that the major strain e1 will always reamin +ve, however minor strain can be both +ve and –ve. Furthermore red line denotes the limit, beyond which the material will tear or crack.

1. **Plane strain** : To fully understand the pain strain, let's do some experiment. Itch the pain sheet with circles, then form it. You will notice that the circle that are expanded in one direction, Major strain e1, with zero deformation along minor strain e2. No crack or tear will happen under red line, forming limit and material will crack beyond

that.

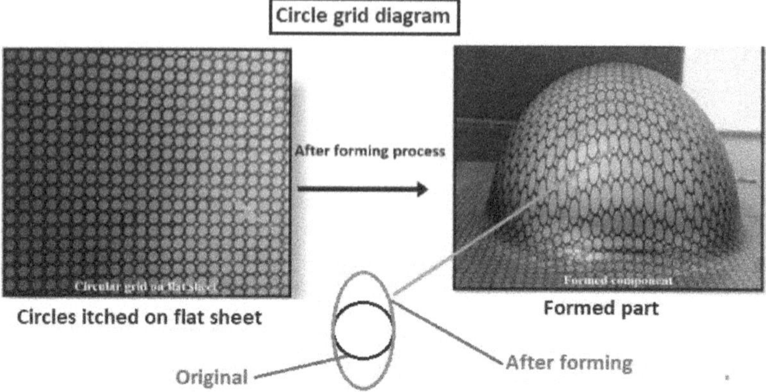

2. **Biaxial tension** : It is the point on the axis, where there is a higher stretch along major axis e1 and less strecth along minor axis e2. The similar points that of marked one are the examples of biaxial tension.

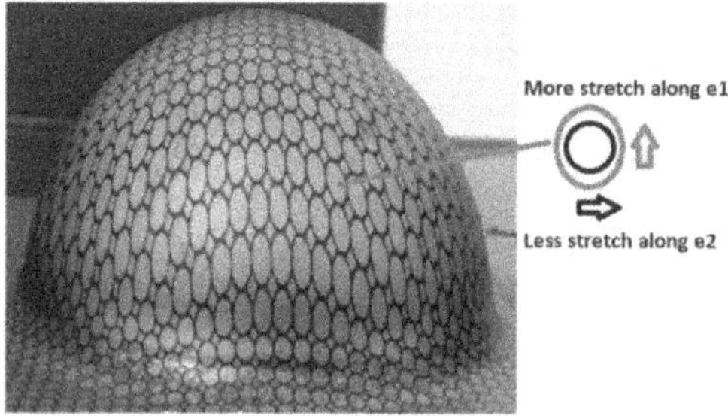

3. **Equibiaxial tension :** It is the point on the axis, where there is a equal stretch along major axis e1 and along minor axis e2. The similar points that of marked one are the examples of equibiaxial tension.

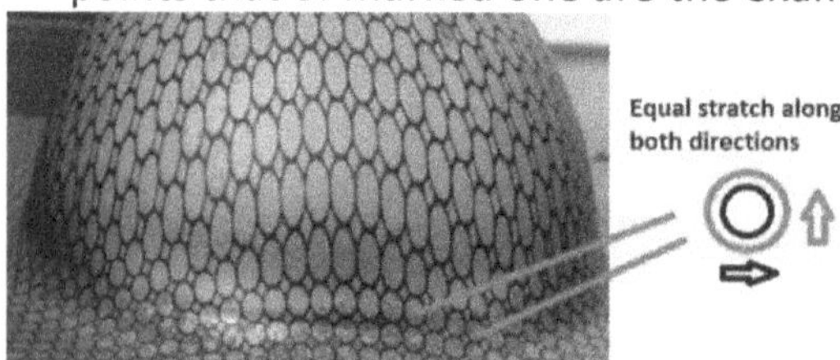

4. **Uniaxial tension:** It is the point on the axis, where there is a high stretch along major axis e1 and –ve stretch or compression along

minor axis e2. The similar points that of marked one are the examples of uniaxial tension.

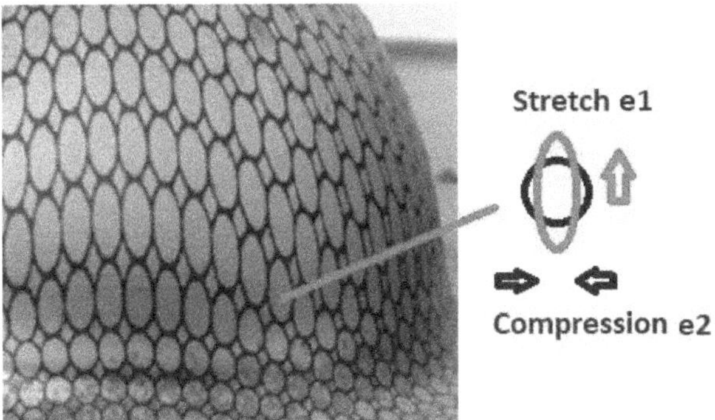

5. **Pure shear** : It is the point on the axis, where there is a equal stretch along major axis e1 and equal amount of −ve stretch or compression along minor axis e2. The similar points that of marked one are the examples of pure shear.

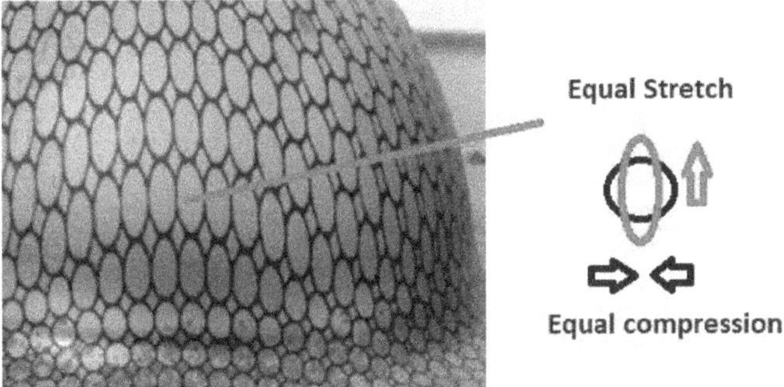

6. **Uniaxial compression :** It is the point on the axis, where there is a -ve stretch along major axis e1 and high amount of −ve stretch or compression along minor axis e2. The similar points that of marked one are the examples of uniaxial compression.

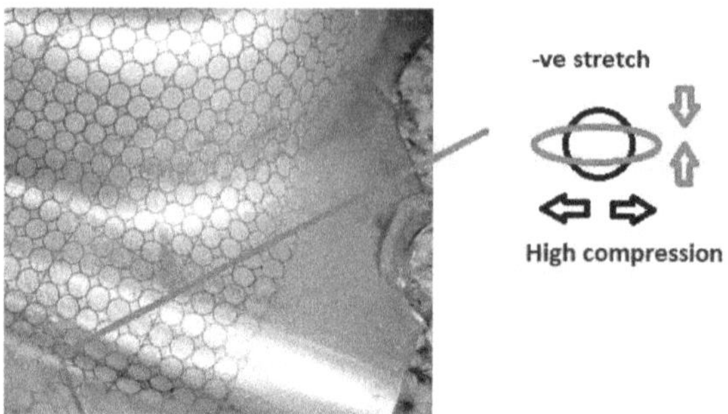

From the below two examples, you can have an estimate that compression may lead to high tendency of wrinkles.

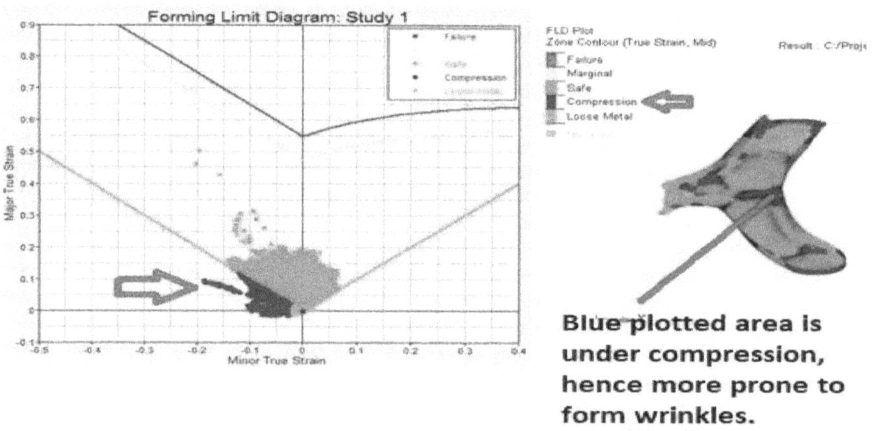

Blue plotted area is under compression, hence more prone to form wrinkles.

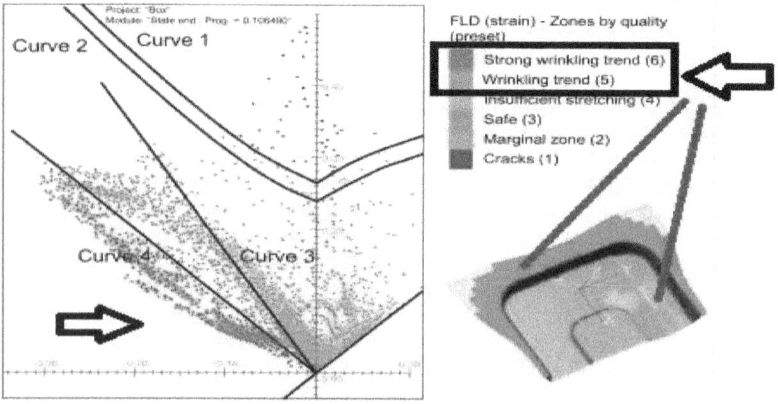

The material defects such as cracks and thinning are predicted by the major axis and winkles are predicted by the minor axis. The experimental data of the Forming limit diagram is used by the many

FEA (finite element analysis) software's to predict the forming behavior of different material under different geometrical conditions.

Different Material Grades have Different Forming Limit Diagram (FLD)

Different Materials have variable values on Cupping Dome test, which are shown in the under-given table. The three main categories of materials are derived –

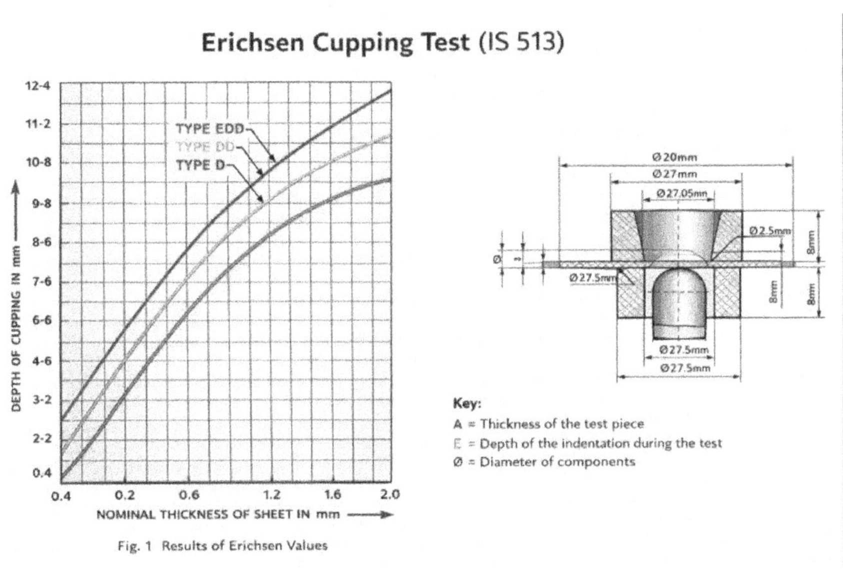

Fig. 1 Results of Erichsen Values

1. Type EDD (Extra deep draw quality) : used for lower thickness and more deep drawn shapes.

2. Type DD (Deep draw quality) : used for lower thickness and Intermediate deep drawn shapes.

3. Type D (Draw quality) : used for Heavy thickness and Less deep drawn shapes with draft angles.

Mechanical properties of the material Affecting Forming Limit Diagram (FLD)

The certain mechanical properties like Strain hardening exponent and plastic strain ratio are greatly influencing the Forming limit diagram (FLD) curve.

E = Young's Modulus

YS = Yield Stress of material

K = Strength coefficient (power law equation $\bar{\sigma} = K\left(\varepsilon_0 + \bar{\varepsilon}\right)^n$)

ε_0 = Pre-strain coefficient

n = Strain-hardening exponent (measures stretch ability/work hardening of material)

r = Plastic strain ratio (measures deep draw ability of material)

Usually greater the n-value (Ranging from 0.14~0.24), the material is more stretchable and more prone to deep draw.

How Forming Limit Diagram (FLD) is generated

History of forming limit diagram : In earlier 1970's Keller and Goodwin conduct some experiments and plotted the forming limit diagrams. They used different material grades repeatedly and different geometries to gather data for analysis.

Keeler and Goowin experiments

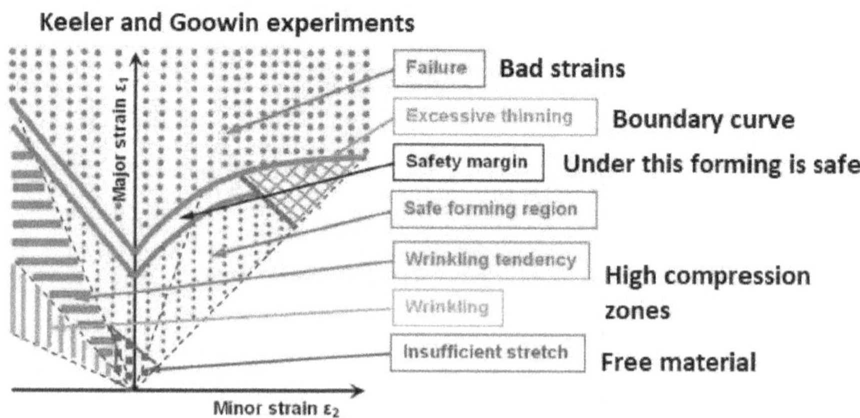

They found that :

1. Failure points were termed as bad strains.
2. Safe points, even with exessive thinning are connected to form a curve.
3. Under that curve, one safe zone curve marked, under which material forming is safe.
4. The high compression zones were marked as wrinkle zones.
5. Some material slips from blank holder, therefore termed as insufficient stretch or free material.
6. Two properties, Strain hardening exponent **n** and matrial thickness **t** are important irrespective of the shape and material grade. Higher value of n and t, the FLD curve will shift higher.

Normally steel manufacturer provides the Forming limit diagram (FLD) curve data for their materials, other sources are outside NABL approved laboratories. The specimen from the same heat are taken under observation and test is repeated at least three times for repeatability, the data is analyzed and the final curve is obtained from the average method. It's experimental data of the companies obtained after years of homework and quite confidential. These days some software companies working on Finite element analysis packages, are using the essential research database to capture the results of final sheet metal cold formed try out results to co-relate with the virtual results obtained in the software in order to increase the accuracy of the results.

Why Forming Limit Diagram (FLD) is important for Industry

Some Engineering service providers are using this data for generating input Forming limit diagram (FLD) curves for their FEA software packages such as LS Dyna, Autoform, Pamstamp, Hyperworks etc. More accurate is FLD data is, more precise the results are. These software's are helping the industry with pre-determination of results are often called Virtual analysis i.e the draw process prediction in the cad stage right before mfg. The defects such Wrinkles, Cracks, Thinning, Thickening are analyzed in advance, helps to boost the development and lowers the cycle time as well as money investment.

I have personally used these Cad packages to solve the process related problems by designing for virtual process before going forward directly to tooled up process, therefore eliminating the number of trials from 15 to 3 numbers for more complicated parts and from 4 to 2 or 1 number for less complicated geometries.

Common Sheet Metal Defects arrested by FORMING LIMIT DIAGRAM (FLD)

It calculates very clearly the material yielding areas such as spitting, necking/thinning, material compression (wrinkle or folds). The forming limit diagram (FLD) analyze data and plot the graph of each element's strain in both major and minor axis and compare the limits of the material to determine whether there are any such defects will probably be there while actual die try out.

Wrinkles Wrinkling in a draw are series of ridges form radially in the drawn wall due to compressive buckling. Practically these are due to low blank holder pressure due to which material slips and wrinkles formed. The optimum blank holding pressure is the key, however in certain cases it doesn't work. Then draw beads are the solutions, the location and shape of draw bead is the challenge, which can be analysed with FEA prior to process design.

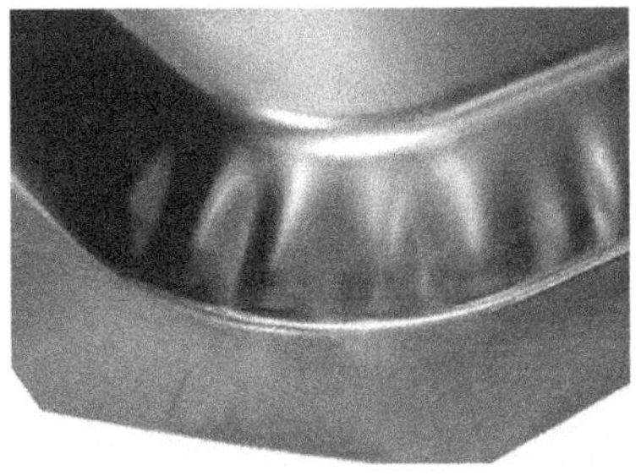 

Cracks

Crack in the vertical wall due to high tensile stresses, some small radius blocks the material flow and results in excessive thinning at that point usually more than 40% of the sheet thk. result in cracks. In some cases, it may happen due to excessive blank holder pressure, which restrict the metal flow. Somewhere it might be due to wrong process design, like try to make a deeper draw in a single stage, which otherwise feasible only in two stages.

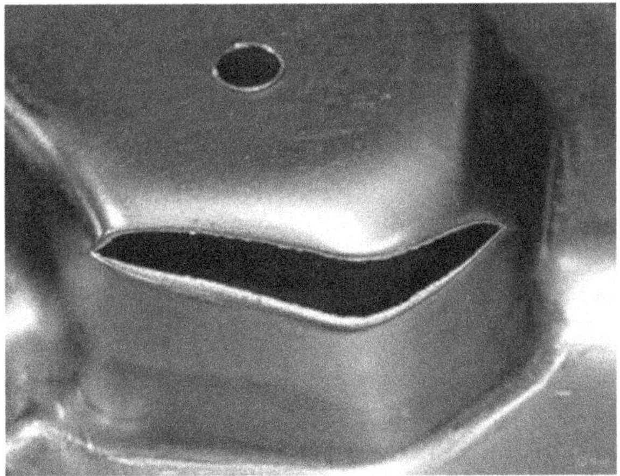

Thinning

Excessive Stretching in the vertical wall due to high tensile stresses cause thickness reduction specifically on the small radius in the metal parts. The image highlights the thinning portions, however up to 20% thinning is allowed due to process limitations.

How FEA Helps by using Forming Limit Diagram (FLD)

The ultimate objective of the Forming simulation is to study the behavior of the material under given shape and forming conditions prior to stamping die manufacturing, that means up to 85% result prediction can be granted during design stage, saves valuable time and money invested in longer try out's. Nowadays FEA software's such as LS DYNA, AUTOFORM, HYPERFORM, PAMSTAMP are very good for virtual process simulations prior to product manufacturing. The defects such as Wrinkles, thinning and cracks can be seen in the design stage right just before the process design, results in correct process selection and reduction in lead time and save valuable money, which otherwise invested in hectic manufacturing iterations.

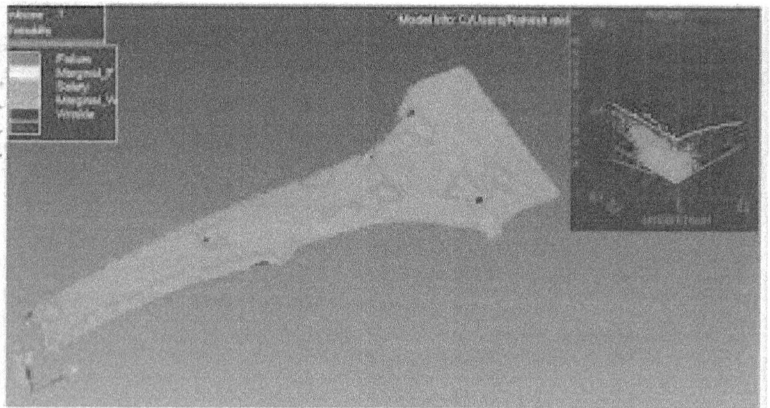

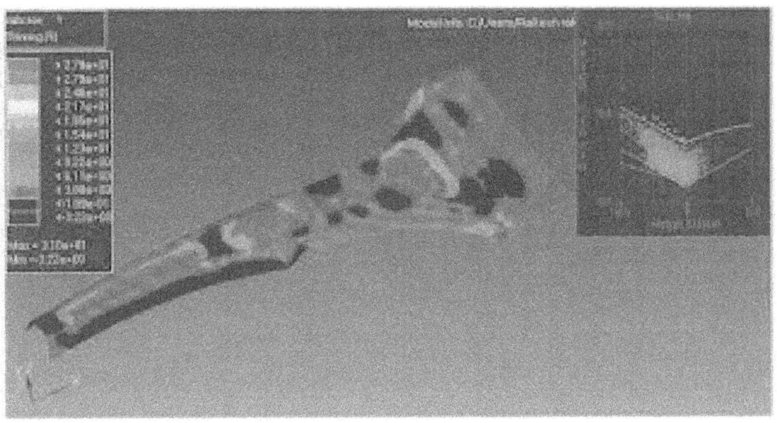

More accurate the input is, more accurate the results are. The mesh quality and size of the elements in the blank and rigid elements is quite more important, the other variants are the material properties assigned to the blank, the blank holding force, the ram speed, ram pressure. Apart from that there are other factors such as selection of right method, the coefficient of friction, the die punch and blank holder movement. The possible error in input may deteriorate your output results by 30%, the max. Possible 85~90% accuracy is matched with the actual try out samples, when all inputs are furnished at expert level professionals.

3. Geometry cleanup

Geometry clean up

In this chapter, you will learn about preparing the geometry for meshing. This process involves organizing, editing, and creating missing surfaces to make the model an enclosed volume. The enclosed volume of surfaces is used to create solids. The solids can then be connected to each other by creating the shared surfaces. These connected solids can be meshed either manually or using Plate Meshing Wizard inside the Polymer Extrusion template.

Geometry clean-up is a crucial step in the finite element analysis (FEA) process, aimed at preparing the CAD geometry for accurate and efficient simulation. It involves various techniques and procedures to address issues such as geometric inaccuracies, complexities, and inconsistencies that may affect the quality and reliability of the FEA results. Here's a detailed look at geometry clean-up in FEA:

1. **CAD Model Import**: The first step in geometry clean-up is importing the CAD model into the FEA software. CAD models are typically created using computer-aided design (CAD) software, and they may contain imperfections such as gaps, overlaps, or small features that need to be addressed before analysis.

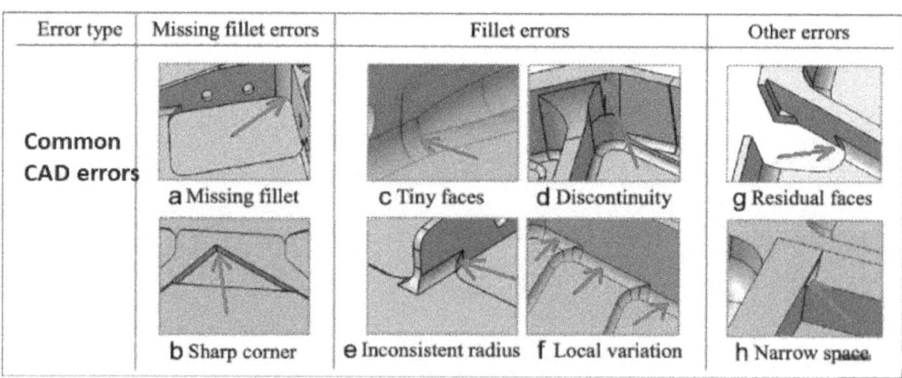

Common CAD Errors

2. Geometry Simplification: Complex CAD models may contain unnecessary details or features that are not relevant to the analysis. Geometry simplification techniques, such as removing small features, filleting sharp edges, or simplifying complex surfaces, help reduce the model's complexity without sacrificing accuracy.

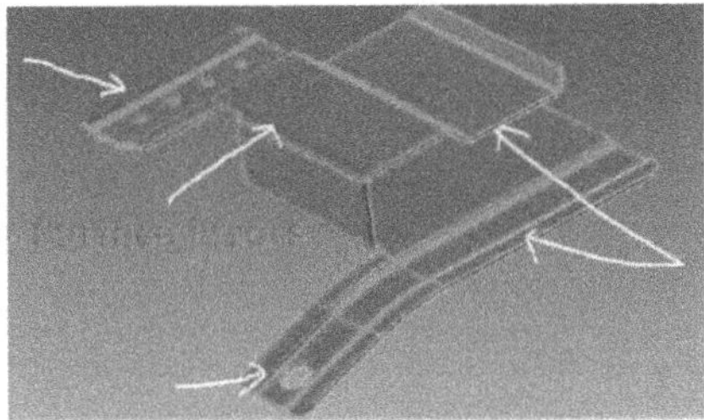

Geometry simplication

3. Mesh Generation: Once the CAD geometry is cleaned up, the next step is generating the finite element mesh. The mesh divides the geometry into small, discrete elements for analysis. Geometry clean-up ensures that the meshing process proceeds smoothly by resolving issues such as narrow regions, sliver surfaces, or intersecting features that may lead to meshing errors or poor quality elements.

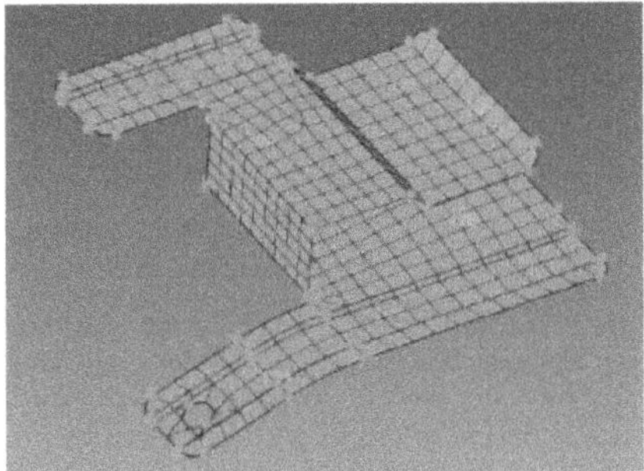

Mesh generation

4. Mesh Quality Improvement: Geometry clean-up also involves improving the quality of the finite element mesh. This includes refining the mesh in regions of interest, optimizing element shapes and sizes, and ensuring a smooth transition between different mesh densities. High-quality meshes are essential for obtaining accurate and reliable simulation results.

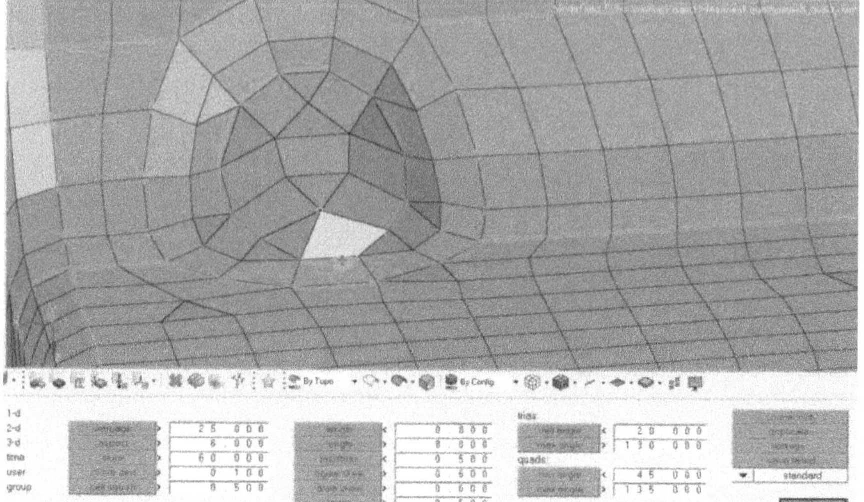

5. Boundary Condition Definition: Geometry clean-up extends to defining appropriate boundary conditions for the analysis. This involves identifying and specifying constraints, loads, and contact conditions that accurately represent the real-world behavior of the structure or component being analyzed. Proper boundary condition definition ensures that the simulation captures the expected response under given loading conditions.

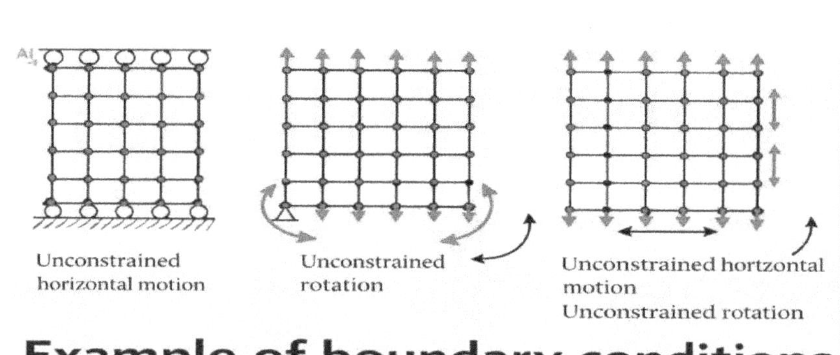

Example of boundary conditions

a. Fixed Support (Zero Displacement)

All degrees of freedom (DOFs) are constrained.

Example: A cantilever beam where one end is fixed.

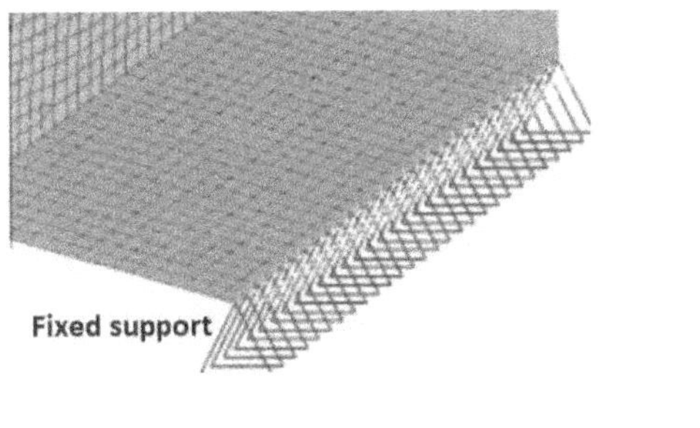

Pinned **Roller** **Fixed** **Spring**

Boundary conditions

b. Pinned Support (Hinge)

Allows rotation but restricts translation in X and Y directions.

Example: Bridge supports.

c. Roller Support

Allows movement in one direction but restricts perpendicular motion.

Example: A bridge expansion joint.

d. Symmetry Boundary Condition

Applied when the model is symmetric to reduce computational cost.

Restricts displacement normal to the symmetry plane.

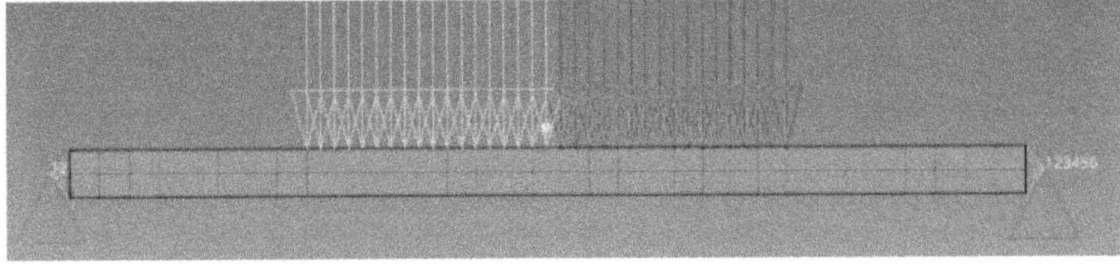

Boundary Condition - Symmetry

e. Force or Pressure Load

A force applied on a surface or point.

Example: A car tire applying pressure on the road.

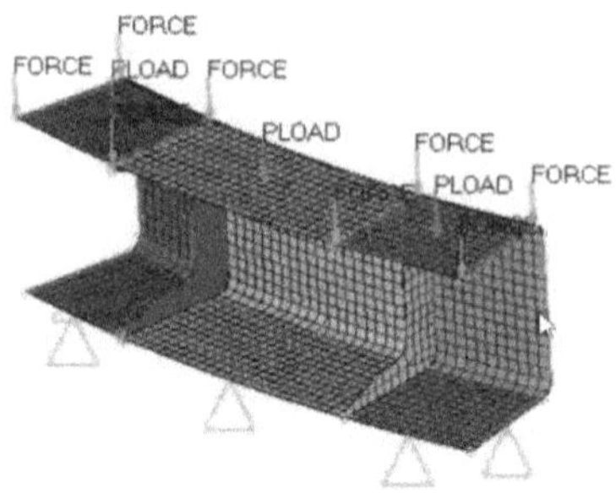

boundary conditions - Force or Pressure Load

f. Displacement Constraints

Restricts movement in a specific direction.

Example: A beam subject to thermal expansion where one end is allowed to slide.

Displacement Constraints

6. Validation and Verification: After completing geometry clean-up, it's essential to validate and verify the FEA model to ensure its accuracy and reliability. This involves comparing simulation results with analytical solutions, experimental data, or benchmarks to confirm that the model accurately represents the physical system and predicts its behavior within acceptable tolerances.

To summarize, geometry clean-up is a critical pre-processing step in finite element analysis that involves preparing the CAD geometry for accurate simulation. By addressing geometric inaccuracies, simplifying complex features, improving mesh quality, and defining appropriate boundary conditions, engineers can ensure that the FEA model produces reliable results that reflect the real-world behavior of the structure or component under analysis.

Benefits of geometry cleanup in finite element analysis

Geometry cleanup in finite element analysis (FEA) offers several benefits that contribute to the accuracy, efficiency, and reliability of the simulation process. Here are some key advantages:

1. Improved Mesh Quality: Geometry cleanup helps in creating a high-quality finite element mesh by resolving issues such as gaps, overlaps, or small features in the CAD geometry. A well-structured mesh with uniformly sized and shaped elements improves the accuracy of the analysis and reduces numerical errors.

2. Enhanced Simulation Efficiency: Cleaned-up geometries lead to faster and more efficient mesh generation processes. By eliminating unnecessary details and simplifying complex features, the meshing algorithms can operate more smoothly and produce meshes with better element quality in less time.

3. Reduced Computational Cost: Simplified and cleaned-up geometries result in finite element models with fewer elements and degrees of freedom. This reduction in model complexity translates to lower computational requirements, shorter solution times, and reduced memory usage, making simulations more cost-effective and scalable.

4. Improved Convergence: Clean geometries contribute to better convergence behavior during the solution process. Meshes generated from clean geometries are less prone to distortion, element distortion, or numerical instabilities, resulting in smoother convergence and more reliable solution outcomes.

5. Accurate Results: Geometry cleanup ensures that the finite element model accurately represents the physical geometry and features of the structure or component being analyzed. This accuracy leads to more reliable simulation results that closely match real-world behavior, facilitating informed engineering decisions and reducing the need for costly physical prototypes or testing.

6. Facilitates Complex Analyses: Cleaned-up geometries enable engineers to perform more sophisticated and detailed analyses, such as nonlinear, dynamic, or multi-physics simulations. Complex features and geometric complexities can be effectively handled and accurately captured in the finite element model, allowing for comprehensive investigations of structural behavior under various loading and environmental conditions.

7. Ease of Model Interpretation and Modification: Simplified and cleaned-up geometries are easier to interpret and modify during the analysis process. Engineers can quickly identify and address geometric issues, refine the model, or make design changes as needed without compromising the integrity of the simulation.

To sum up, geometry cleanup in finite element analysis offers numerous benefits, including improved mesh quality, enhanced simulation efficiency, reduced computational cost, better convergence, accurate results, facilitation of complex analyses, and ease of model interpretation and modification. By investing time and effort in geometry cleanup, engineers can ensure the reliability and validity of their FEA simulations and make more informed engineering decisions.

Geometry cleanup is done to achieve the following:

Correct any errors in the geometry from import

Create the simplified part needed for the analysis

Mesh a part all at once

Ensure proper connectivity of mesh

Obtain a desirable mesh pattern and quality

Practice Exercise
Get free video tutorials along with CAD files on Author's website

https://sharmarakesh.co.in/index.php/tutorials/

Password : Forming2025

10.2 Auto cleanup geometry:

First of all, import the geometry from the CAD file, as explained in the previous chapters.

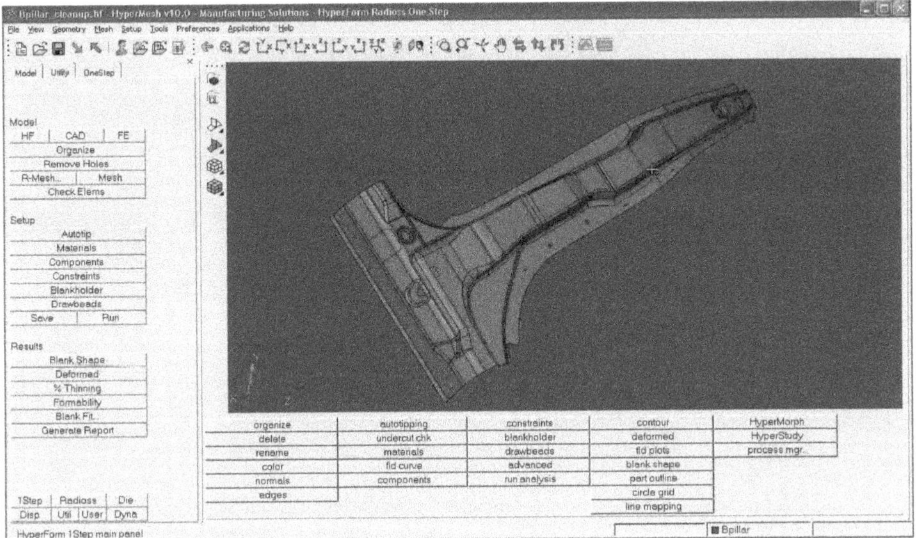

Press F11 to see the defects in the surface, as shown in the below image:

From geometry select the Auto cleanup 1st option to remove the splits (red lines) and duplicate surface (yellow lines).

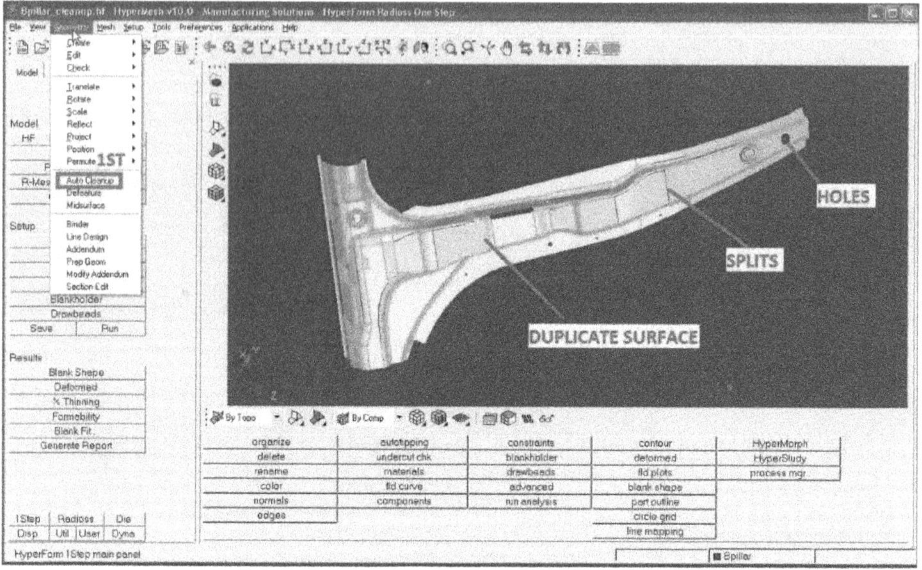

Select the Surface option marked 1st from the below image, from the pop up window pick "Displayed 2nd " followed by "autoclean marked as 3rd " and return 4th from the command.

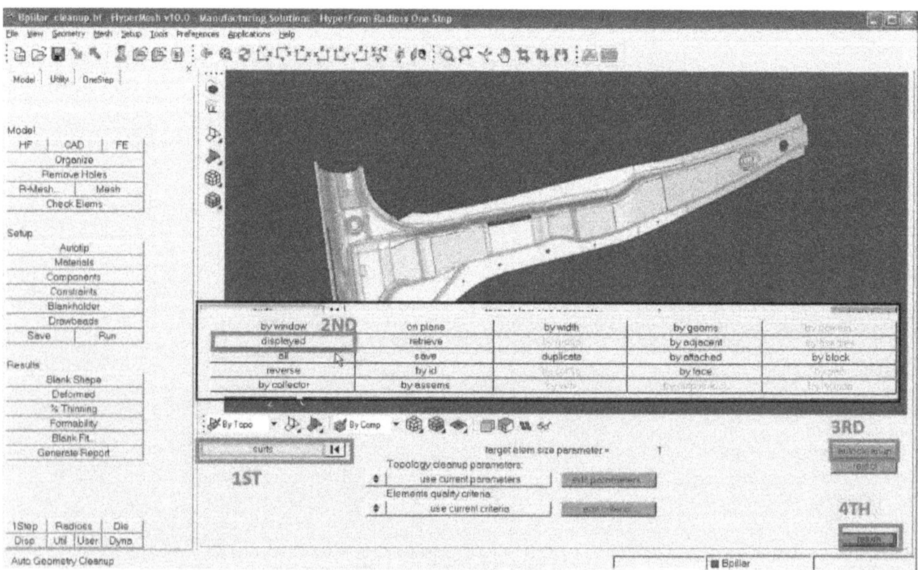

The geometry after Auto cleanup will look like.

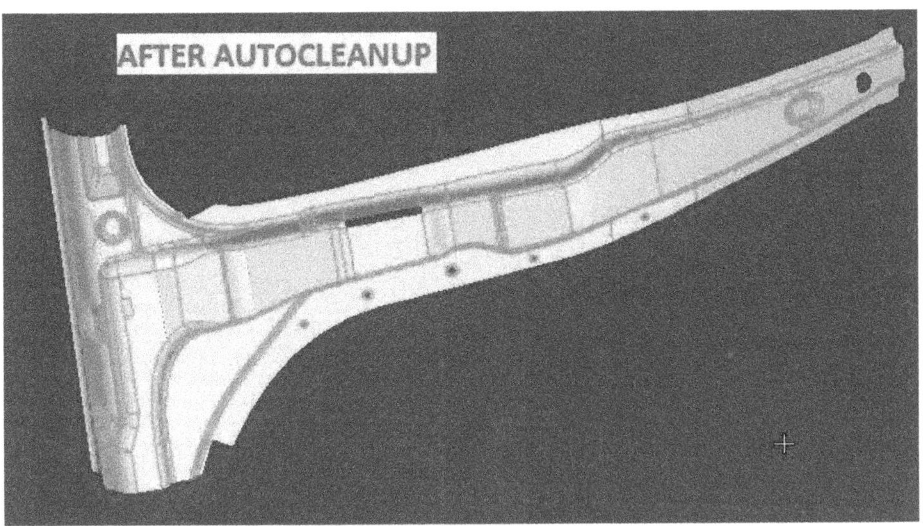

10.3 Fill the surface and holes:

From the geometry, open create dropdown "1st" and pick "surfaces 2nd ", as explained in the below image.

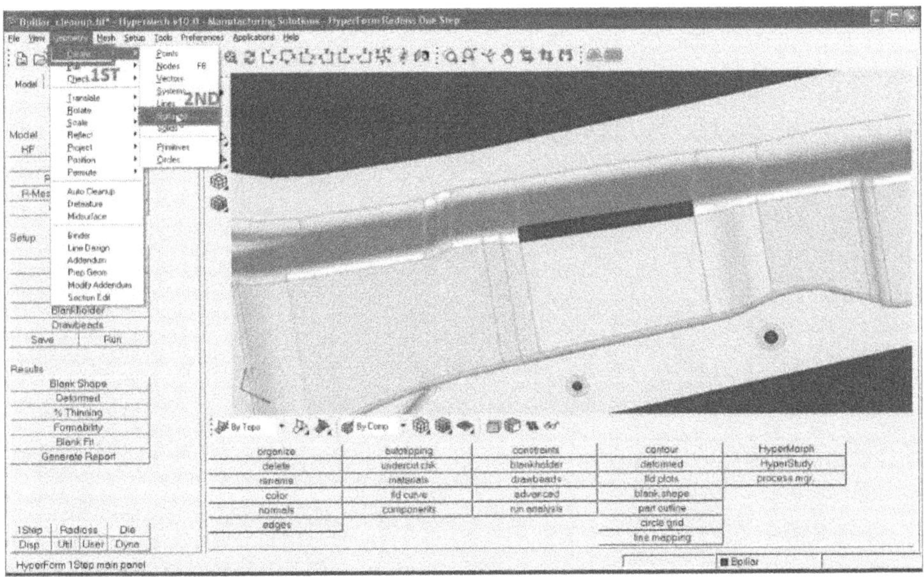

Spline/filler marked as 1st is used to fill the empty surface or missing surface with all tangencies maintained. From the 2nd marking, options dropdown, select lines and keep other as shown.

Pick at location with 3rd marking as shown and return from 4th option.

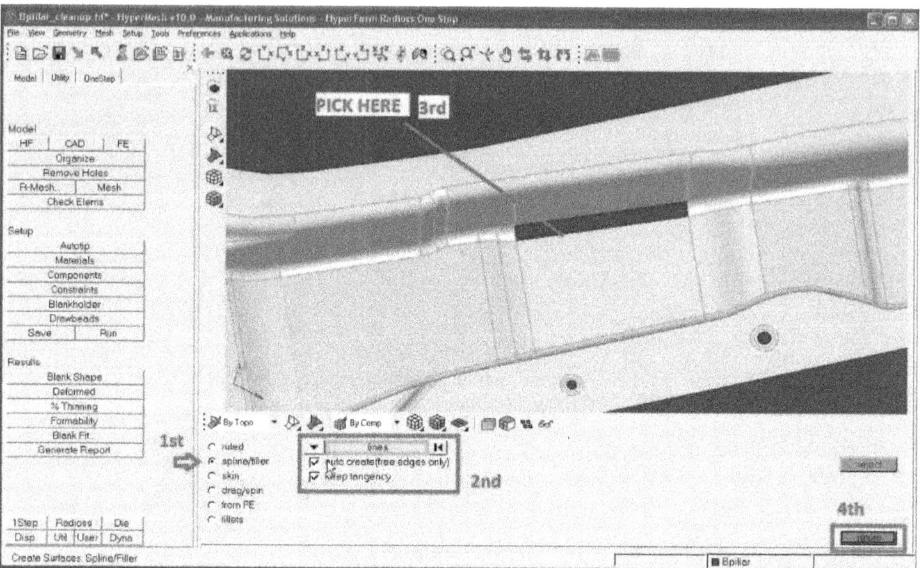

In the after picture of the geometry is shown hereby, the surface has been filled.

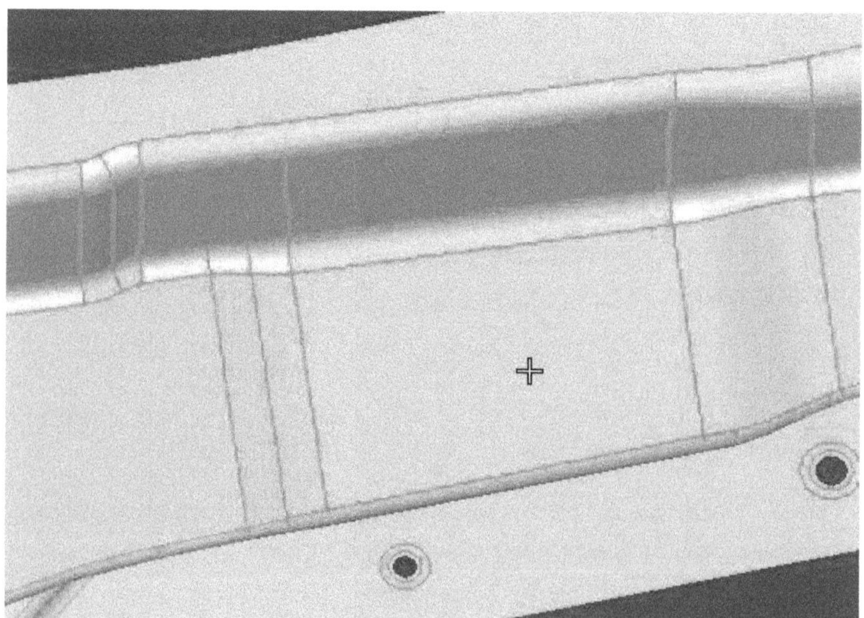

Similarly fill the 2nd hole and so on, in the same way as mentioned above. The image shown below clearly explains the process to fill any kind of hole.

4. Meshing Basics

What is a meshing?

In basic sense, meshing is simply a way to show a big body as the sum of smaller bodies. You take many small bodies (elements), and join them together to form a bigger one (hence creating a mesh).

Then you apply some loads (thermal, structural, etc.) on one (or more) of these elements, fix these bodies in certain ways (boundary conditions), settle on some predefined temperature/pre-stressing if necessary (initial conditions), and then see the results of these applied loads pass on from one body (element) to the next.

The problem was the mathematics of it all — understanding how the loads are passed on. A body in real life shows continuous behavior (at a macroscopic level), and needs the use of integration (continuum mechanics).

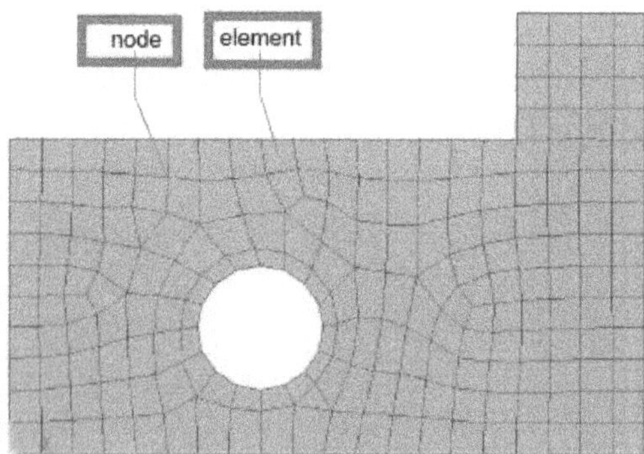

Geometry divided into finite number of elements

Finite element analysis is the process of dividing or discretizing our geometry into finite nodes and elements and solving it for stress and strains and the particular process of discretization is known as meshing. Meshing is the way of communicating our geometry to the FEA solver. In meshing we will divide our geometry into any one of the following shapes of elements like triangles, quadrilaterals, tetrahedron, quadrilateral pyramid, triangular prism, and hexahedron. and the selection of particular shape of the element depends on the type of analysis and the shape of the geometry.

Elements on the mesh of the geometry will only capture the structural response of the system so it is mandatory to understand the impact of element type and mesh quality before solving a problem. Even the density of the mesh can affect the output so it is best to have a more elements. If we want to analyze a circle, then the geometry of the circle has to be captured as much as possible the image below shows that how the mesh has to be done for circular geometry

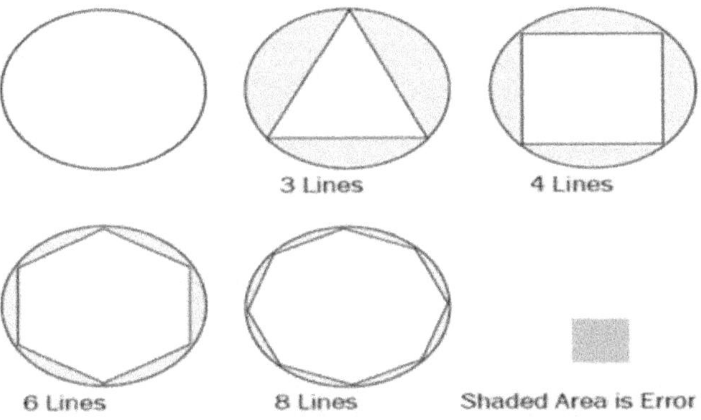

Also it is important to have fine structural mesh than coarse unstructured mesh, only at some critical points it is good to have coarse mesh to get accurate result. The image below shows the result variation for good structured mesh and unstructured mesh and also notes that the experimental result correlates more with the structural mesh.

Gravity analysis

Good Mesh

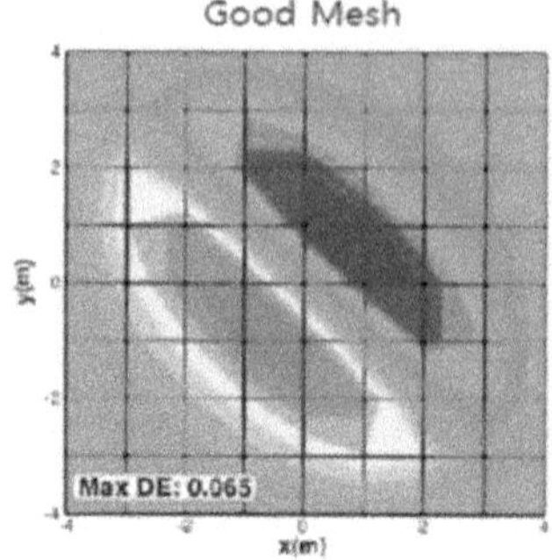

Bad Mesh

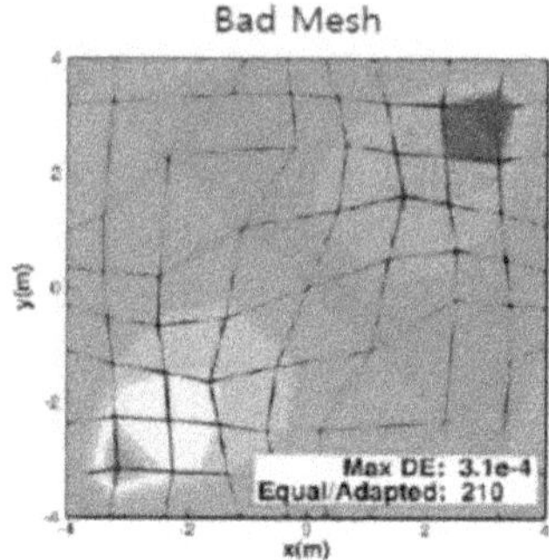

What all of FEM is — an approximation? An approximation used to get good enough results without having to wait weeks/months/decades (depending on the complexity of the question and the speed of the computer) for an exact answer to be found. An approximation where a weak form of an equation (the integral form) is changed into the strong form (the differential form) making the use of some boundary conditions.

Meshing is the essence of how that approximation is achieved.

Why Quad element preferred over the tri

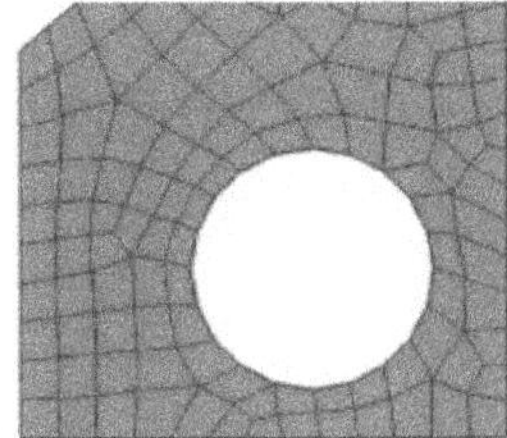
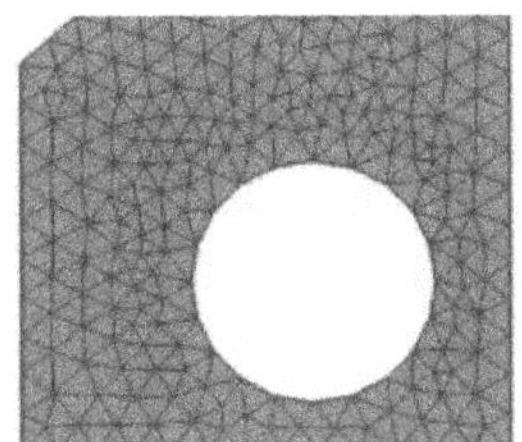

Quard mesh   **Tria mesh**

Quad will give better results than tri elements because tri elements have more stiffness than quad.

So when we going check break-in point or deforms of body tri elements shows its safe because of element stiffness. But quad elements show need to increase F. O. S or thickness of Materials.

Therefore, quad elements are preferred over the tri elements.

The triangular element is called as a constant strain triangle (CST) element. Value of the stress tensor in the whole element will be constant. This may not be true in the real situation. So this approximation may create a lot of error.

That is the reason we do not prefer triangular elements. But we will be forced to use this if the geometry is very complicated due to the difficulty in meshing with quad elements.

The CST nature of this element is coming from the nature of the shape function.

When to Use 2-D Elements

2- D elements are used when two of the dimensions are very large in comparison to the third dimension.

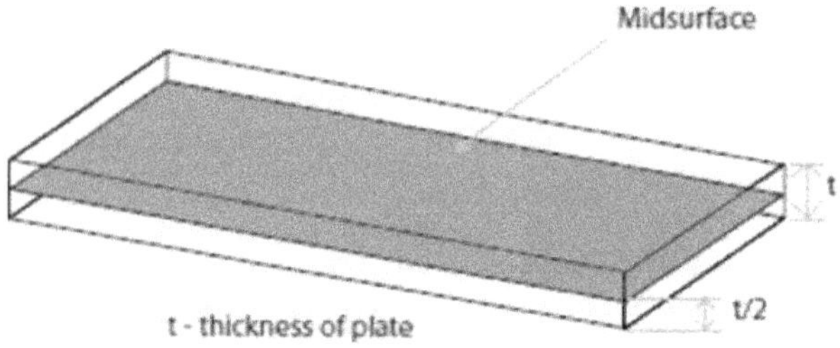

<u>Element shape</u> : Quad,tria

<u>Additional data from user</u> : Remaining dimension i.e. thickness

<u>Element type</u> : Thinshell, plate, membrane, plane stress, plane strain, axi-symmetric solid etc.

<u>Practical applications</u> : Sheet metal parts, plastic components like instrument panel etc.

Family of 2-D elements

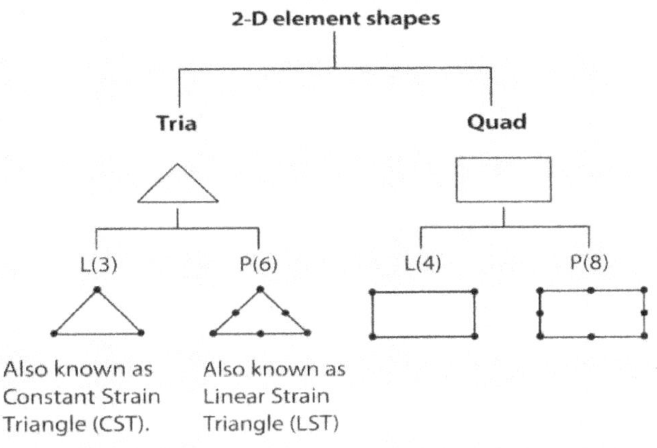

Best practices for Meshing

1) Back to back triangles should be avoided. Two tria elements should not be connected to each other directly.

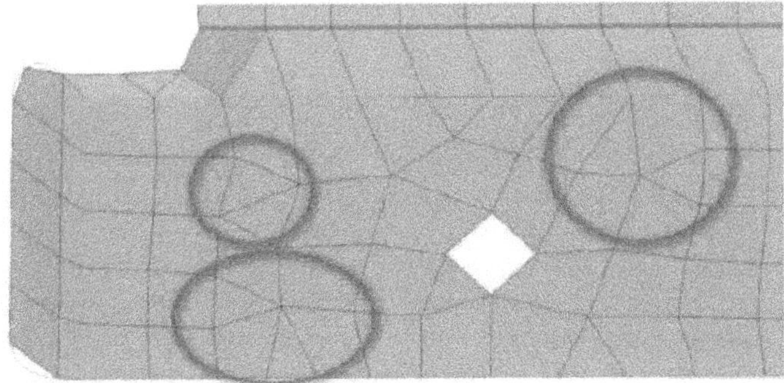

2)On plane surfaces triangular element should be avoided.

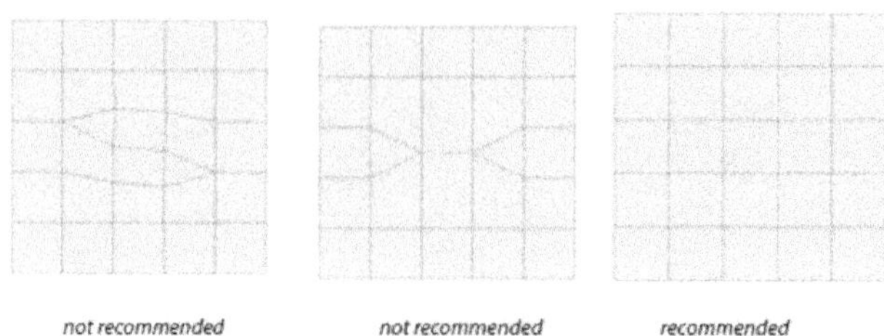

3)No mesh transition on constant radius fillets / curvatures, The mesh transition should be carried out on the planer surfaces

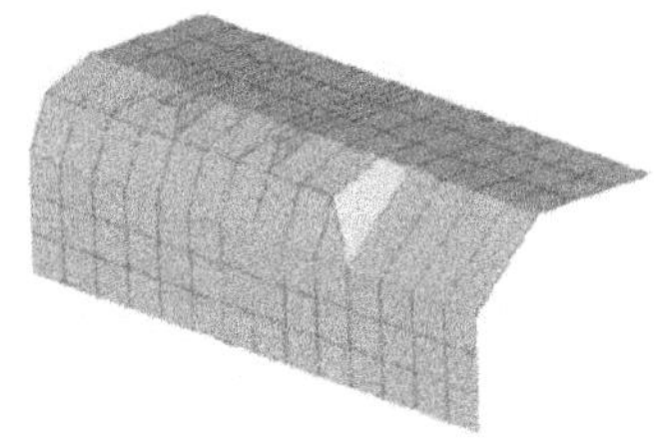

4)Circular holes should be modeled carefully with a washer (1.5 to 2 times diameter) and a minimum of two layers around the hole

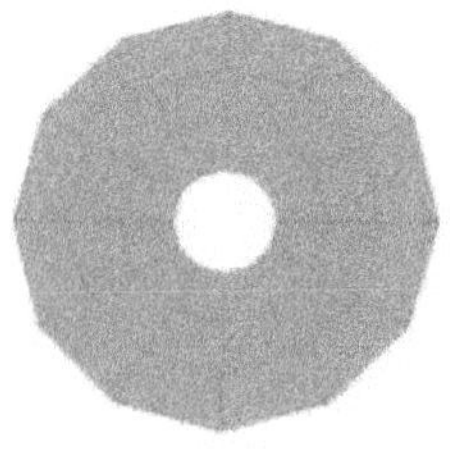

Instead of a zig-zag distribution, a structured or smooth mesh is recommended (nodes aligned in a straight line)

Not recommended   *Recommended*

5) Follow the feature lines (nodes should lie exactly on the edges)

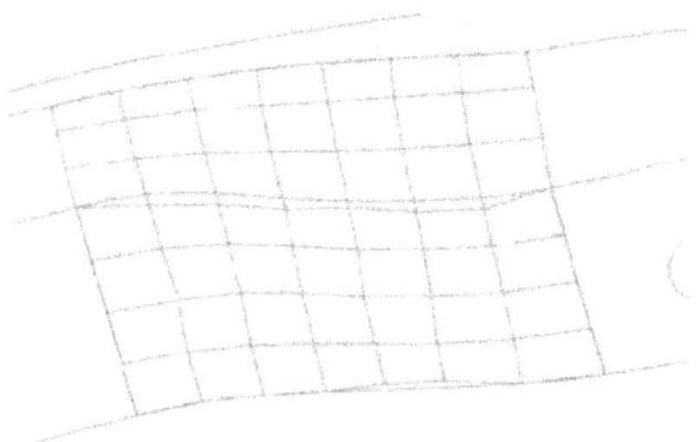

Quality checks of 2-D elements

1. Warpage

This is the amount by which an element (or in the case of solid elements, an element face) deviates from being planar. Since three points define a plane, this check only applies to quads. The quad is divided in to two trias along its diagonal and the angle between the tria's normals is measured. Warpage of up to five degrees is generally acceptable.

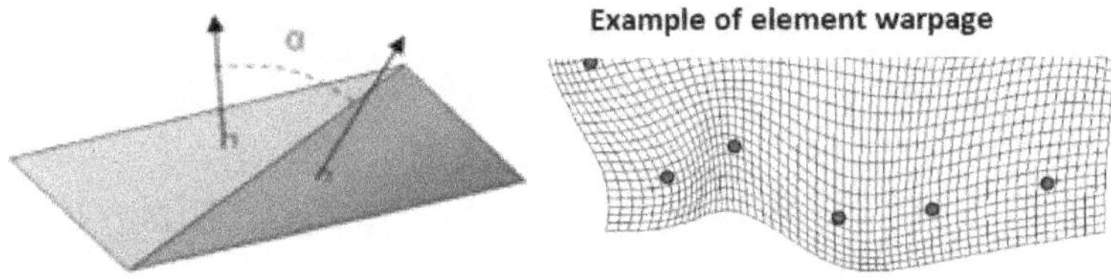

Ideal Value = 0° (Acceptable < 10)

Element warpage refers to the distortion or irregularity in the shape of a mesh element (like a triangle or quadrilateral) in 2D when it is stretched, bent, or skewed. Ideally, elements should be as close to perfect shapes (such as equilateral triangles or square quadrilaterals) as possible for accurate simulation results. When elements are warped, their angles and side lengths become uneven, which can lead to inaccurate results in finite element analysis. Warpage usually occurs when the mesh is generated too coarsely or if the geometry is complex, causing the elements to lose their ideal shape.

2. Aspect Ratio

This is the ratio of the longest edge of an element to either its shortest edge or the shortest distance from a corner node to the opposing edge. For 3-D elements, each face of the element is treated as a 2-D element and its aspect ratio determined. The largest aspect ratio among these faces is returned as the 3-D element's aspect ratio. Aspect ratios should rarely exceed 5:1.

Examples of Elemental aspect ratios during meshing

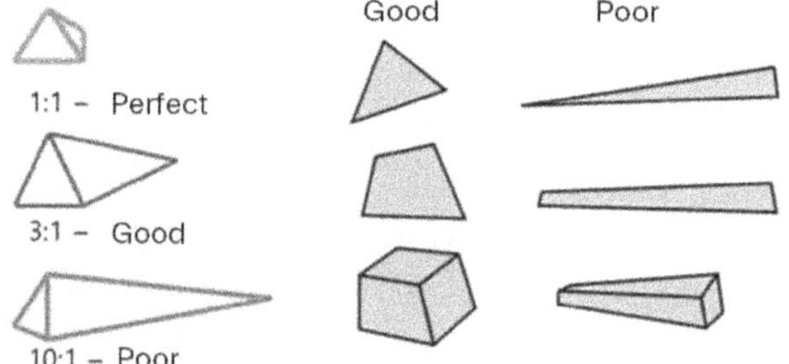

Ideal Value = 1 (Acceptable < 5)

A high aspect ratio (e.g., long and narrow elements) can lead to numerical inaccuracies and poor results, while a low aspect ratio (e.g., more uniformly shaped elements) typically ensures better accuracy and stability in the analysis.

3. Skew

Skew of triangular elements is calculated by finding the minimum angle between the vector from each node to the opposing mid-side, and the vector between the two adjacent mid-sides at each node of the element. The minimum angle found is subtracted from ninety degrees and reported as the element's skew.

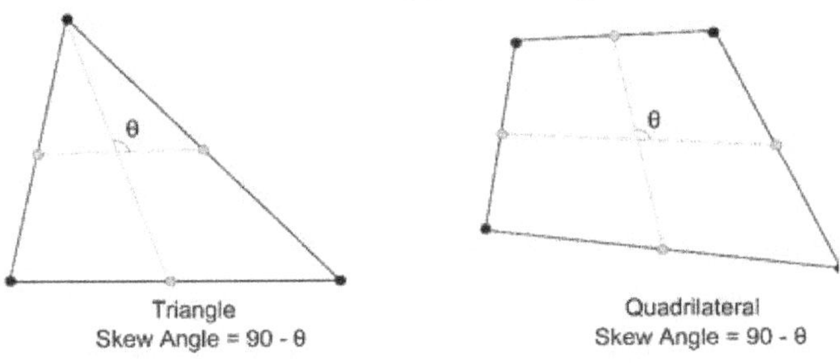

Ideal value = 0° (Acceptable < 45°)

Element skew in finite element analysis refers to the deviation of an element's shape from an ideal shape, such as a square or equilateral triangle. A high skewness means the element is distorted, which can lead to inaccurate results or poor convergence in the solution. Minimizing skewness helps improve the quality and reliability of the analysis.

4. **Chordal Deviation**
   Curved surfaces can be approximated by using many short lines instead of a true curve.

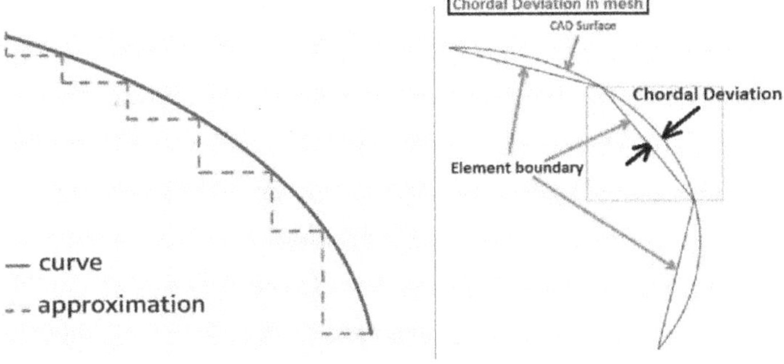

Chordal deviation is the perpendicular distance between the actual curve and the approximating line segments or Chordal deviation in finite element analysis refers to the maximum distance between the mid-point of an element's curved edge and the straight line (chord) connecting its endpoints. It measures how much an element deviates from a perfect straight line, and a smaller chordal deviation indicates better element quality and more accurate results in simulations.

5. Length (min.)

Minimum element lengths are calculated using one of two methods the shortest edge of the element. This method is used for non-tetrahedral 3-D elements. The shortest distance from a corner node to its opposing edge (or face, in the case of tetra elements); referred to as "minimal normalized height".

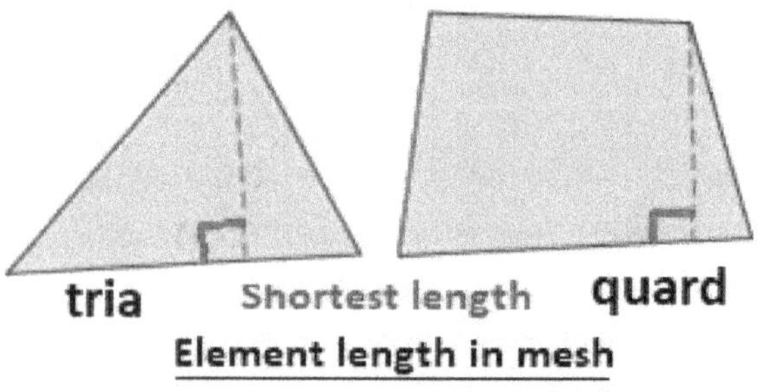

Element length in finite element analysis refers to the characteristic dimension of an element, typically the length of its edges or sides. It plays a crucial role in determining the resolution and accuracy of the analysis, with shorter elements generally providing more detailed results.

6. Jacobian

This measures the deviation of an element from its ideal or "perfect" shape, such as a triangle's deviation from equilateral. The Jacobian value ranges from 0.0 to 1.0, where 1.0 represents a perfectly shaped element. The determinant of the Jacobian relates the local stretching of the parametric space which is required to fit it onto the global coordinate space. HyperMesh evaluates the determinant of the Jacobian matrix at each of the element's integration points (also called Gauss points) or at the element's corner nodes and reports the ratio between the smallest and the largest.

In the case of Jacobian evaluation at the Gauss points values of 0.7 and above are generally acceptable.

7. Trias : min angle
The minimum allowable interior angle for a tria element. Any element for which any interior angle falls below the specified value is highlighted and remains highlighted until you exit the Check Elements panel or you select another check.

8. Trias : max angle
The maximum allowable interior angle for a tria element. Any element for which any interior angle is greater than the specified value is highlighted and remains highlighted until you exit the Check Elements panel or you select another check.

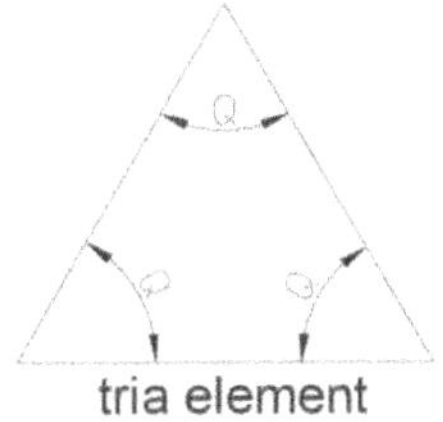

Tria: Ideal Value = $60°$ (Acceptable=$20°<\theta<120°$)

9. quads: min angle
The minimum allowable interior angle for a quad element. Any element for which any interior angle falls below the specified value is highlighted and remains highlighted until you exit the Check Elements panel or you

select another check.

10.quads: max angle

The maximum allowable interior angle for a quad element. Any element for which any interior angle is greater than the specified value is highlighted and remains highlighted until you exit the Check Elements panel or you select another check.

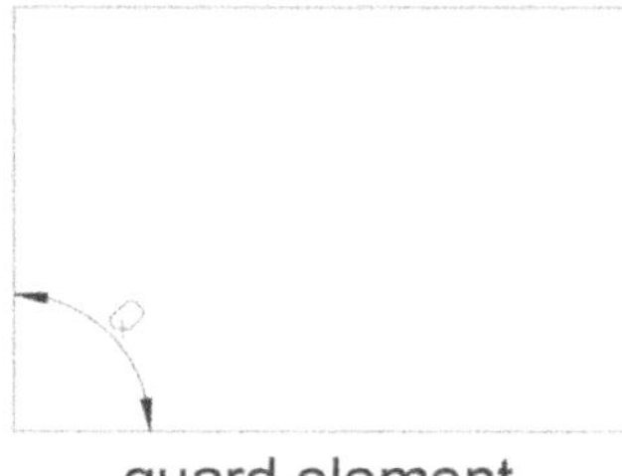

quard element

Quad : Ideal Value = $90°$ (Acceptable=$45°<\theta<135°$)

Practice Exercise

Get free video tutorials along with CAD files on Author's website

https://sharmarakesh.co.in/index.php/tutorials/

Password : Forming2025

Meshing Exercise

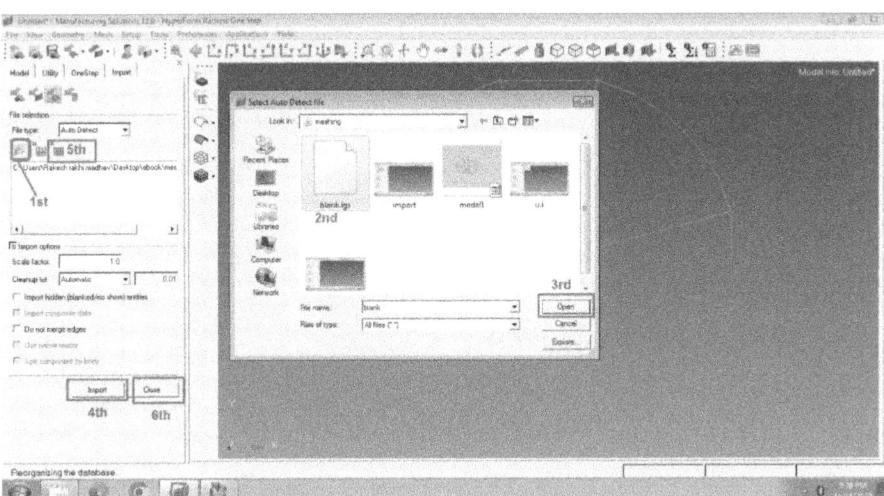

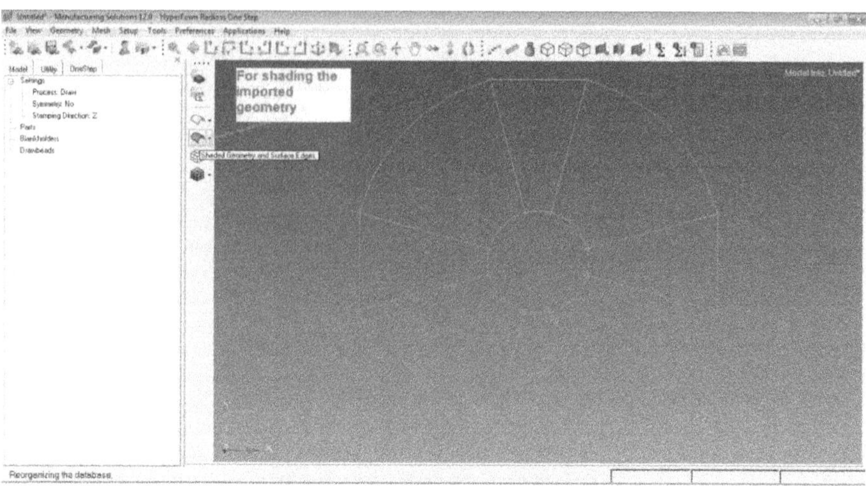
For shading the imported geometry
Shaded Geometry and Surface Edges

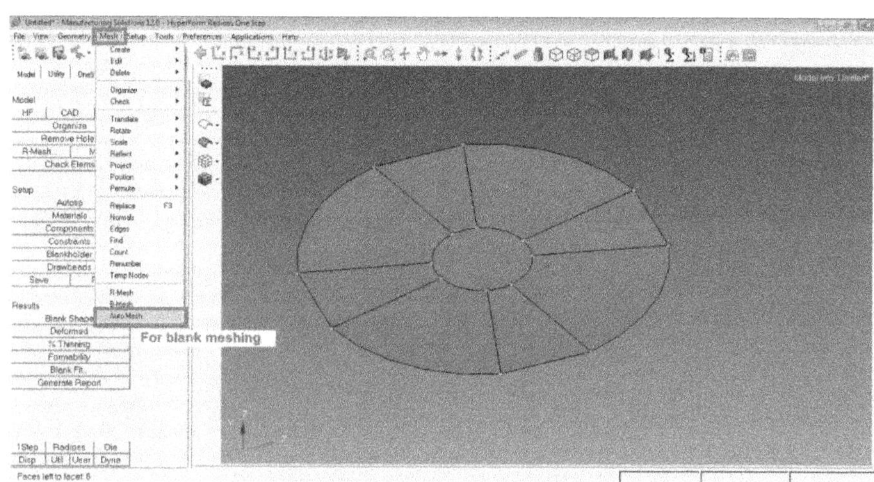
For blank meshing

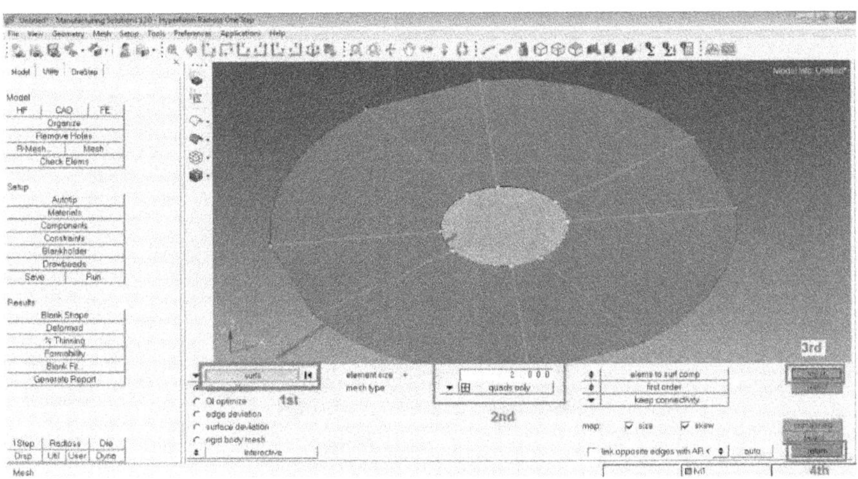

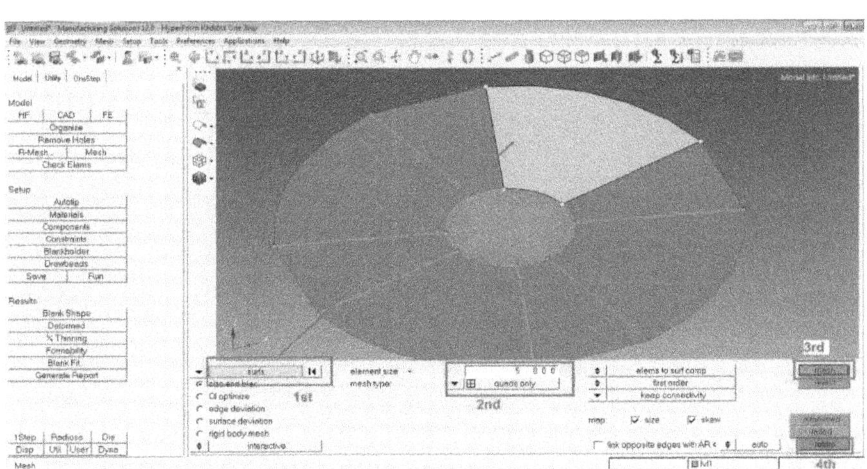

Meshing Basics

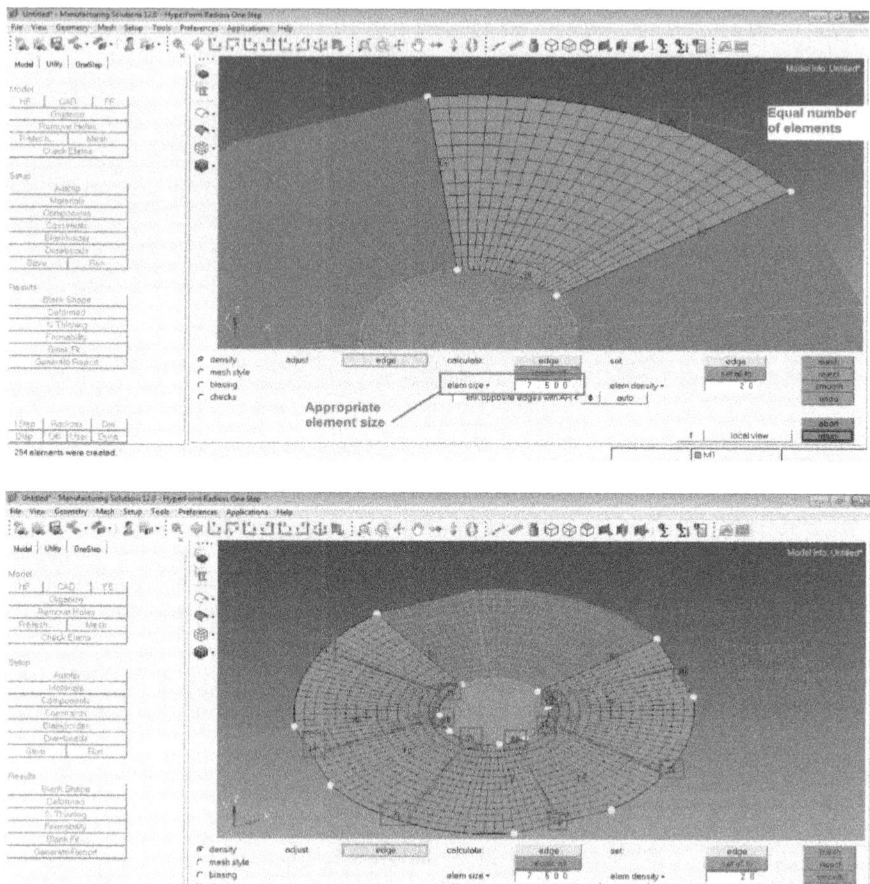

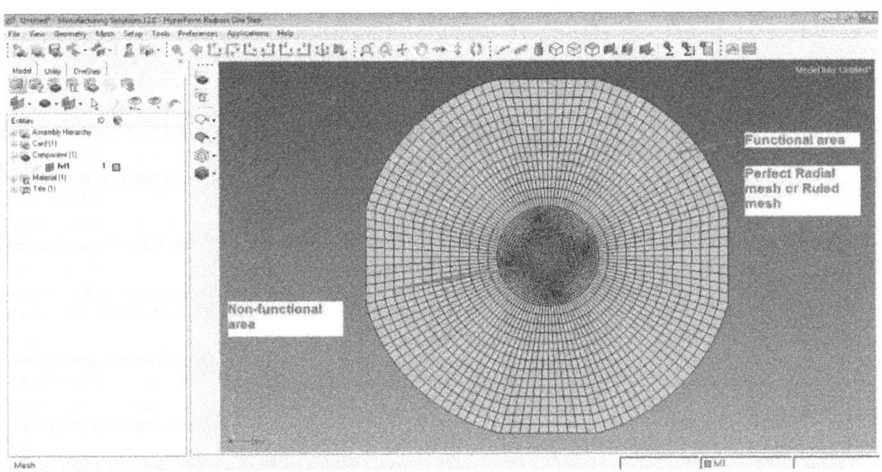

Functional area
Perfect Radial mesh or Ruled mesh
Non-functional area

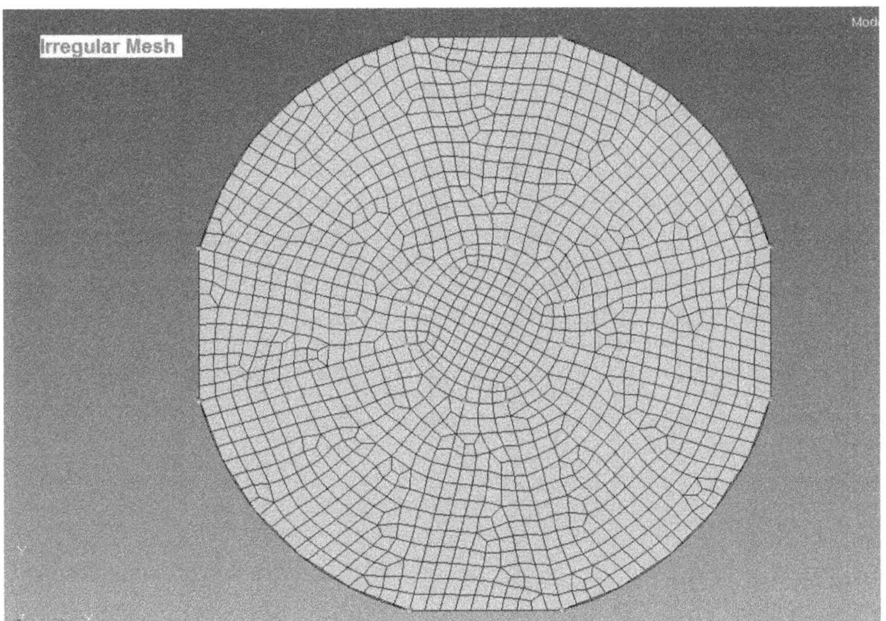

Irregular Mesh

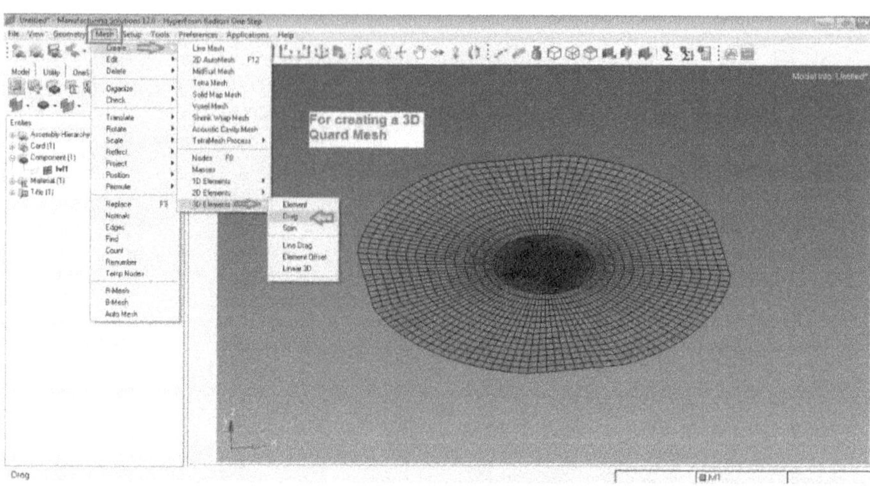
For creating a 3D
Quard Mesh

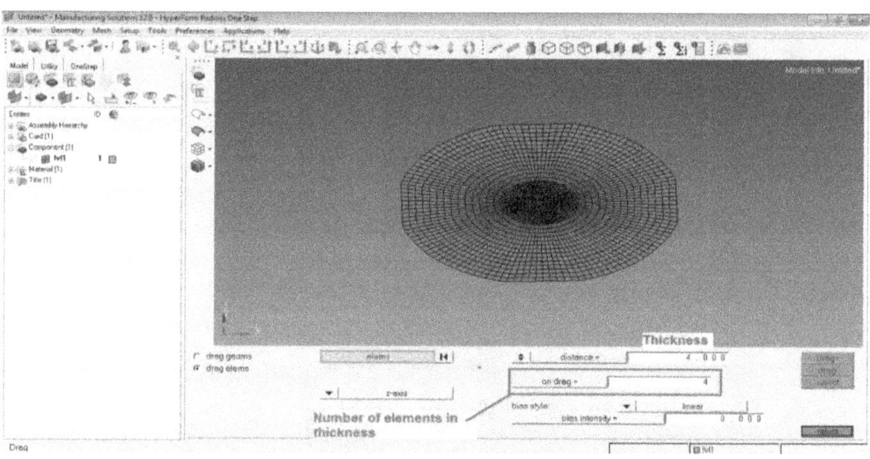
Thickness
drag geoms
drag elems
distance =
4 . 0 0 0
on drag =
4
bias style
linear
bias intensity =
0 . 0 0 0
Number of elements in
thickness

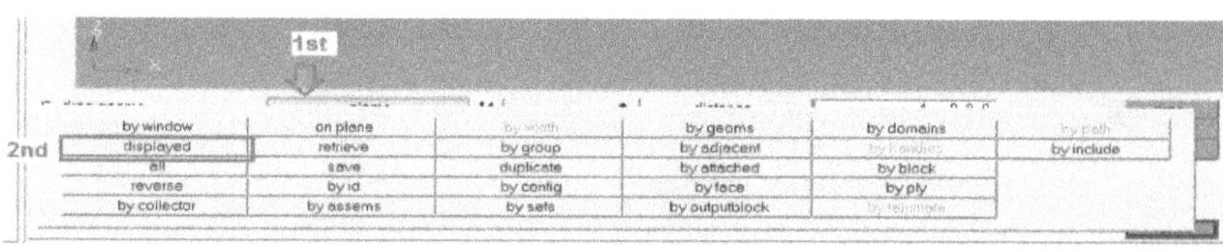
1st
2nd
by window   on plane   by width   by geoms   by domains   by path
displayed   retrieve   by group   by adjacent   by include
all   save   duplicate   by attached   by block
reverse   by id   by config   by face   by ply
by collector   by assems   by sets   by outputblock

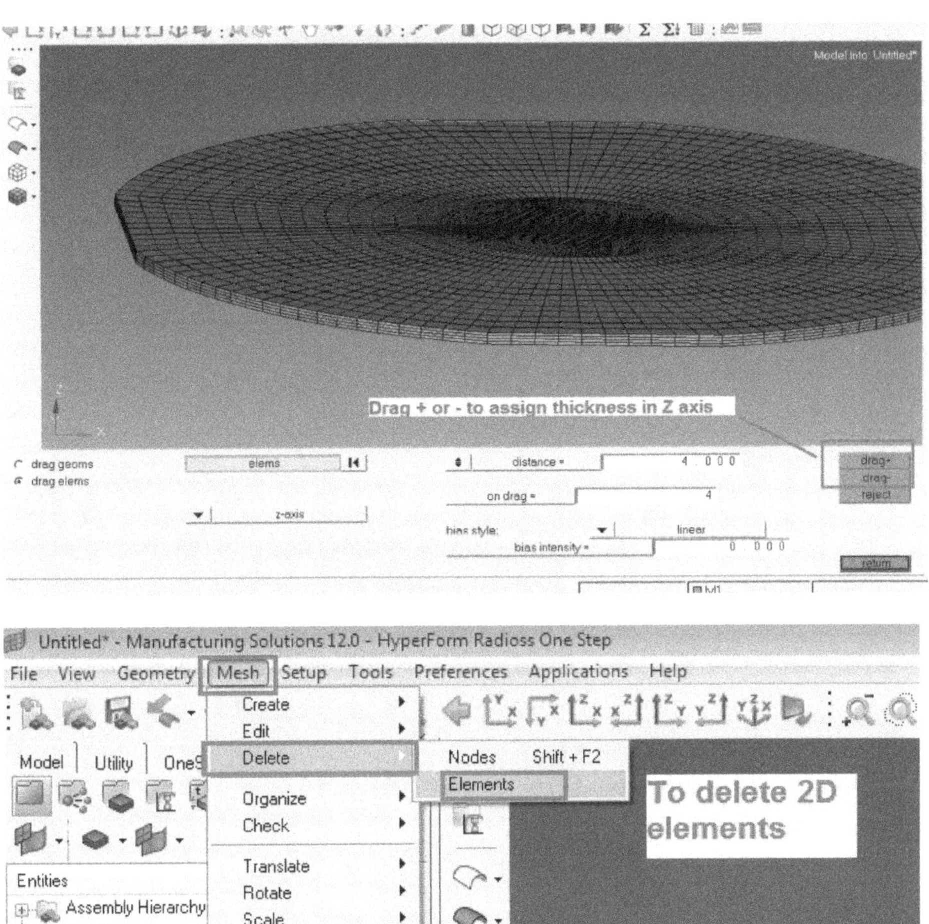
Model Info: Untitled*
Drag + or - to assign thickness in Z axis
drag geoms
drag elems
elems
distance =
4 . 0 0 0
on drag =
4
z-axis
bias style:
linear
bias intensity =
0   0 0 0
drag+
drag-
reject
return

Untitled* - Manufacturing Solutions 12.0 - HyperForm Radioss One Step
File   View   Geometry   Mesh   Setup   Tools   Preferences   Applications   Help
Create
Edit
Delete
Organize
Check
Translate
Rotate
Scale
Reflect
Project
Nodes   Shift + F2
Elements
To delete 2D elements
Model   Utility   One
Entities
Assembly Hierarchy
Card (1)
Component (1)

1st
2nd
by window   on plane   by surf   by geoms   by domains   by path
displayed   retrieve   by group   by adjacent   by handles   by include
all   save   duplicate   by attached   by block
reverse   by id   by config   by face   by ply
by collector   by assems   by sets   by outputblock by laminate

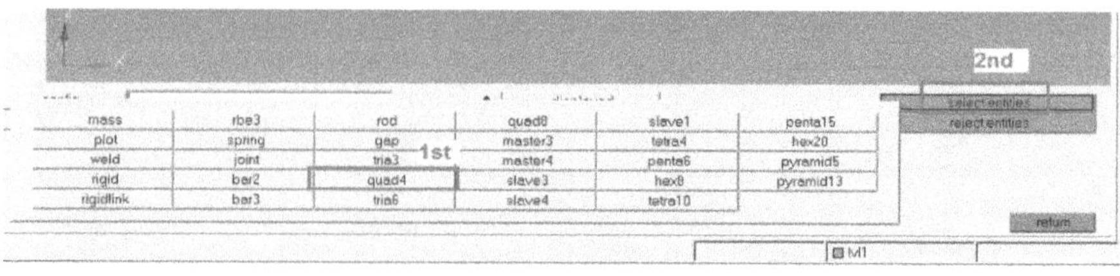
2nd
select entities
reject entities
config =
mass   rbe3   rod   quad8   slave1   penta15
plot   spring   gap   master3   tetra4   hex20
weld   joint   tria3 1st master4   penta6   pyramid5
rigid   bar2   quad4   slave3   hex8   pyramid13
rigidlink   bar3   tria6   slave4   tetra10
return
M1

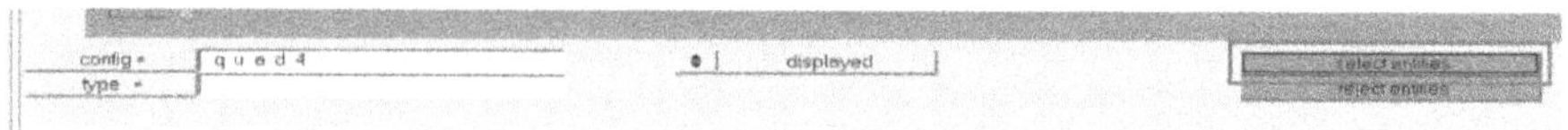
config =   q u a d 4   displayed   select entities
type =   reject entities

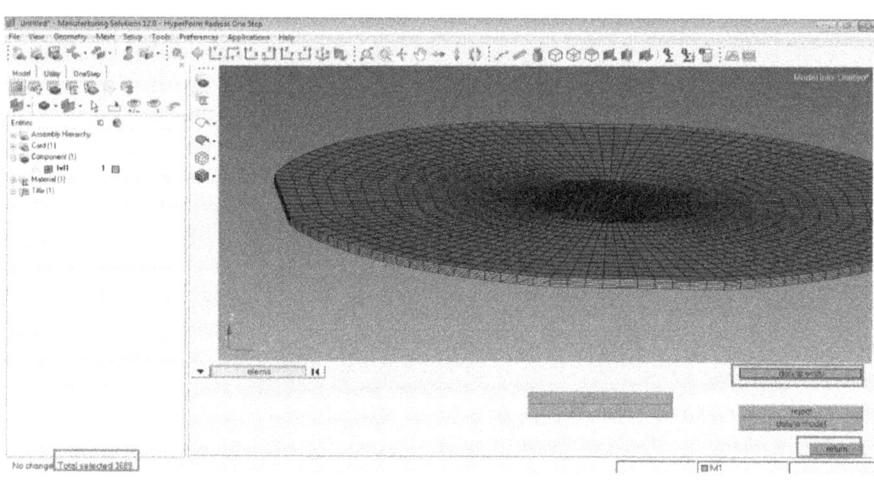
Untitled* - Manufacturing Solutions 12.0 - HyperForm Radioss One Step
File View Geometry Mesh Setup Tools Preferences Applications Help
Model Utility OneStep
Entities   ID
Assembly Hierarchy
Card (1)
Component (1)
lvl1   1
Material (1)
Title (1)
Model Info: Untitled*
elems
reject
delete model
return
No change Total selected 3689
M1

5.One step Forming analysis

What is One step forming analysis:

One step forming analysis is used to check the quick feasibility of any complex geometry, the critical areas which are prone to failures or defects such as thinning, thickening, wrinkles, cracks are easily identified prior to manufacturing.

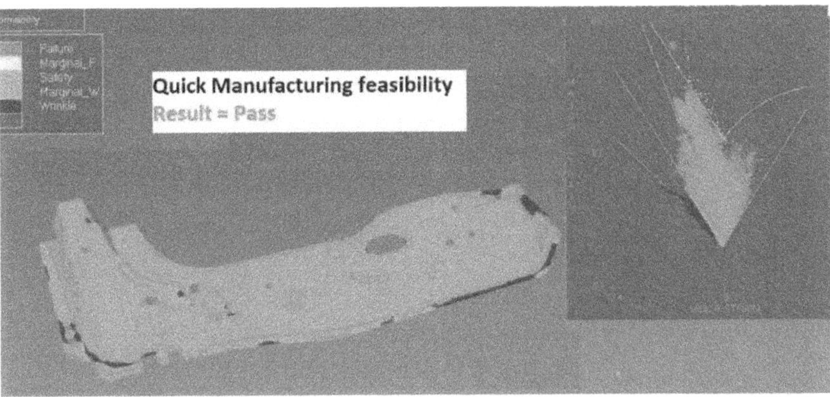

One-step forming analysis revolutionizes the manufacturing industry by condensing multiple steps into a single comprehensive simulation. Traditionally, engineers employed sequential analyses to predict and optimize material behaviour during shaping processes like forming or deep draw. Each step required individual modeling, data interpretation, and validation, leading to prolonged development cycles.

In contrast, one-step forming analysis integrates preforming, final forming, and post-forming processes into a unified simulation. Leveraging advanced finite element analysis (FEA) techniques and simulation software, engineers can accurately predict material deformation, stress distribution, and defect formation in a single computational run.

This holistic approach offers several benefits. Firstly, it significantly enhances efficiency by eliminating the need for iterations in modeling and data transfer between sequential analyses. Engineers can simulate the entire forming process in one go, enabling them to anticipate potential issues early in the design phase and make informed decisions promptly.

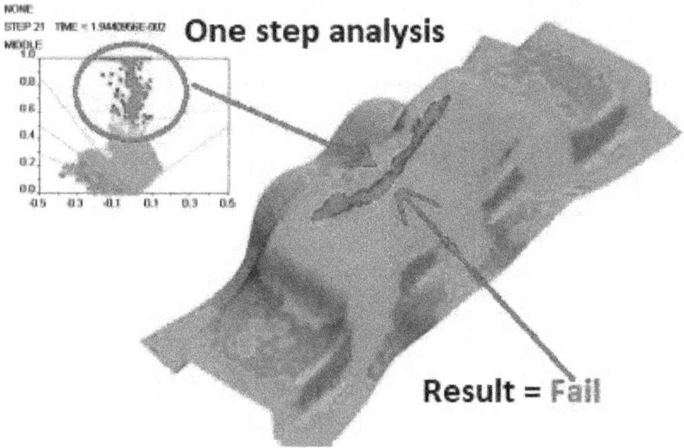

Moreover, one-step forming analysis ensures precision engineering by accurately modeling complex material behaviour and deformation processes. Engineers can simulate various factors such as material properties, tool geometry, and process parameters to identify potential defects and optimize tooling design accordingly.

One-step forming analysis also delivers substantial cost savings by reducing time, labour, associated with traditional forming analysis methods. By streamlining the simulation process and enabling proactive problem-solving, manufacturers can minimize the risk of costly rework or production delays.

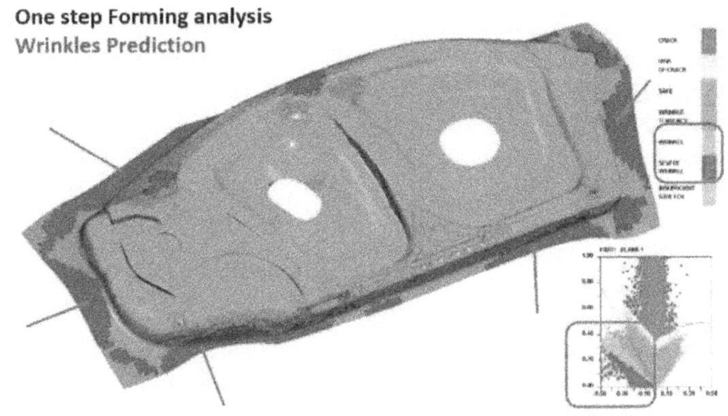

To sum up, one-step forming analysis represents a game-changer in the manufacturing industry, offering unparalleled efficiency, precision, and cost-effectiveness. As technology continues to evolve, leveraging advanced simulation techniques like one-step forming analysis will be crucial for staying competitive and driving innovation in an increasingly dynamic marketplace.

Benefits of one step forming simulation

- Introduces forming feasibility criteria early in the product development cycle where the most significant improvements are possible.

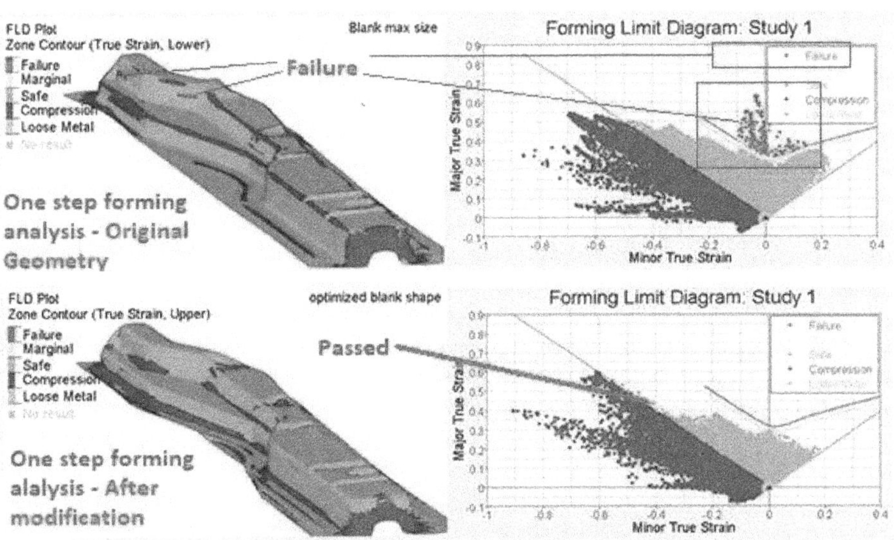

- Accurately predicts blank size for improved material utilization.

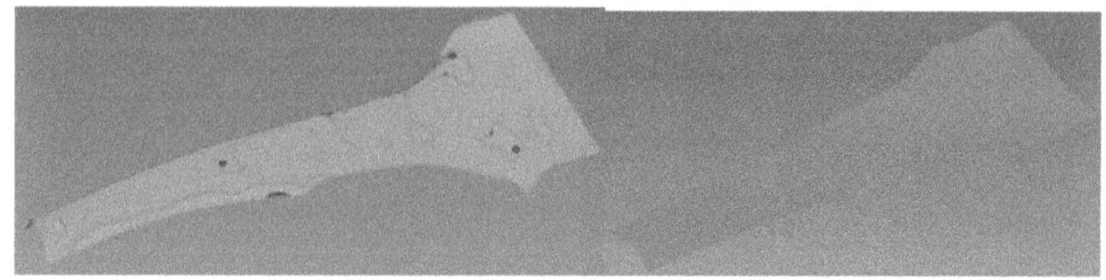

Geometry   **Blank shape**

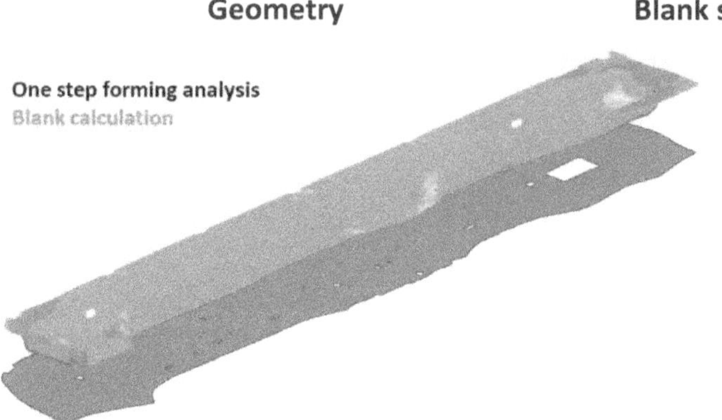

- Let's you modify and verify multiple process scenarios.

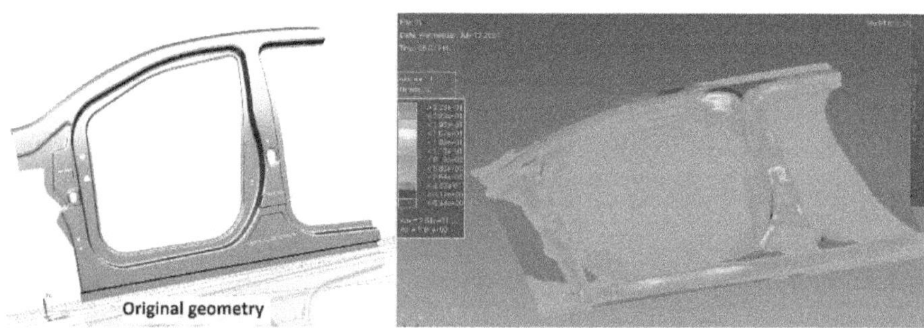

Original geometry   **Thinning analysis**

- Visually displays wrinkles and splits and lets you modify designs prior to the steel cutting process.

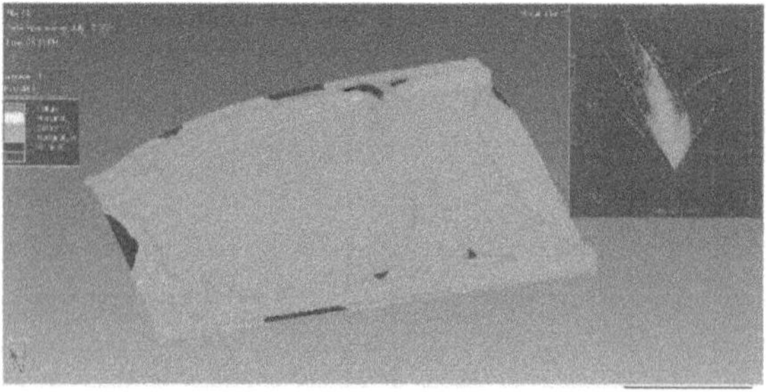

Forming analysis

- Provides powerful geometric tools for designing parametric addendum.
- Automates stamping optimization processes.
- Drastically reduces the product development cycle.

History of One step forming

Circle grid analysis for die makers (Old school method)

Before understanding the One step forming simulation or One step formability analysis, let's first understand the older method "Circle grid analysis", which was manual earlier in 1970's and nowadays bit electronic in terms of blank marking before forming try out. The main difference between the both is one is totally virtual and latter is pure manual or mechanical. The concept of virtual method one step forming analysis is the virtual version of the manual method, so called circle grid analysis.

In visits to numerous stamping and die building facilities, I've observed that most have circle grid analysis equipment on hand, usually confined to the metals laboratory. This is especially true for the stampers performing deep drawing or stretching.

Circle grid analysis (CGA) has long been used to help determine the forming severity of a stretched or draw product. Stampers and die builders use this technology to help decrease the probability of part failure such as splits and wrinkles.

No doubt, Circle Grid Analysis can be used to help solve for splits during the stages of die try out and production.

What Is Circle grid analysis or short form CGA?

During CGA, a blank is etched manually or electrochemically with a pattern of perfectly round circles or square, later deformed using the same variables used for high-volume production. The deformation of each circle then is measured using either a special camera system or a simple Mylar® scale, expressed as a percentage of change, and plotted on a forming limit diagram (FLD).

The FLD is a representation of the metal's deformation limits based on two primary values: the metal's thickness and its n value, or work hardening exponent.

By knowing how the metal has been deformed as well as its forming limits, you can adjust process variables to ensure that the process is robust. In simple terms, CGA is a way of measuring the forming severity of a formed part, refer below picture.

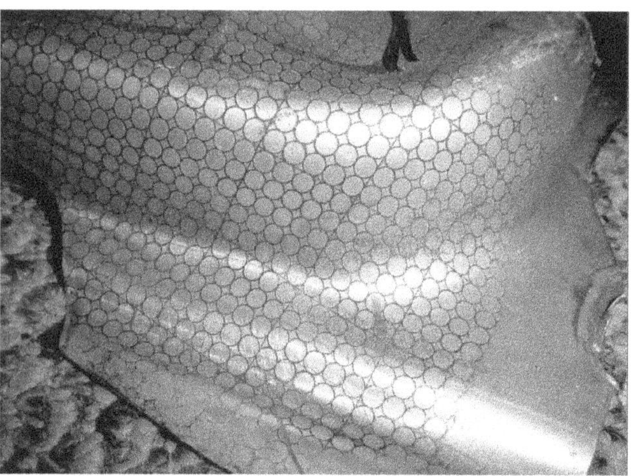

How CGA works

Circle Grid Analysis can be used to determine real flow patterns and how the metal is deforming, which can help you determine both the root cause of the failure and the solution. CGA is not just limited to the metal lab, but is also being used to help die engineers to make data-based decisions regarding corrective action.

To remain competitive, tooling professionals had to abandoned the trial-and-error method of solving problems and start using more databased processes. Die making and troubleshooting is not an art; it is a science. With the help of Circle grid analysis, they lose the die maker title and become a die engineers.

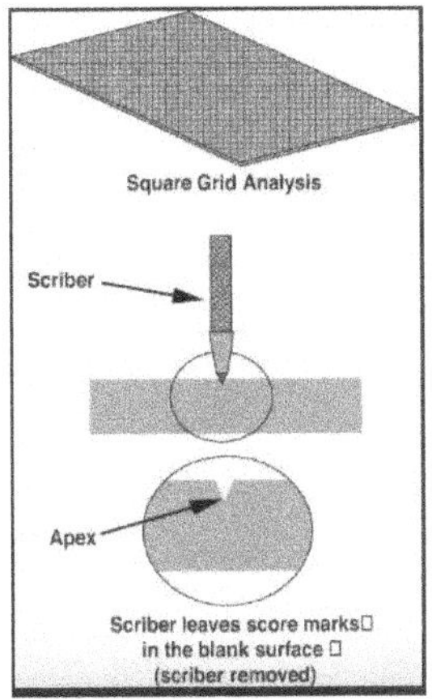

One-step forming simulation or One step formability analysis is the development of the circle grid analysis from manual to the computer aided virtual analysis. Since it automates meshing with the creation of high quality meshes based on best practices and eliminates the need to manually mesh the part. A fast and accurate state-of-the-art solver calculates the blank profile using industry proven formulas. Blank profile/outline generation and blank modelling with the very clear prediction of formability, thinning contour as shown in the below images.

The main basic steps to perform the one step forming simulation are:

1. Pre-processing
    a. Mid surface of the geometry
    b. Meshing of the geometry with optimum element size
    c. Assigning material properties (includes mechanical properties and thickness)
    d. Set stamping direction
    e. Orient the part to best suit for forming or Auto tipping
2. Processing
a. Save program and Run analysis, load results thereafter
3. Post processing
    a. Formability plot
    b. Thinning plot
    c. Blank creation

    d.   Blank layout or blank nesting

    e.   Create report

For example, let take an example of the following Engine oil sump. As a product designer I have to calculate the material size of that part. It's nearly impossible to calculate the material size by any means, however with the help of one step forming analysis, it's a blink of an eye.

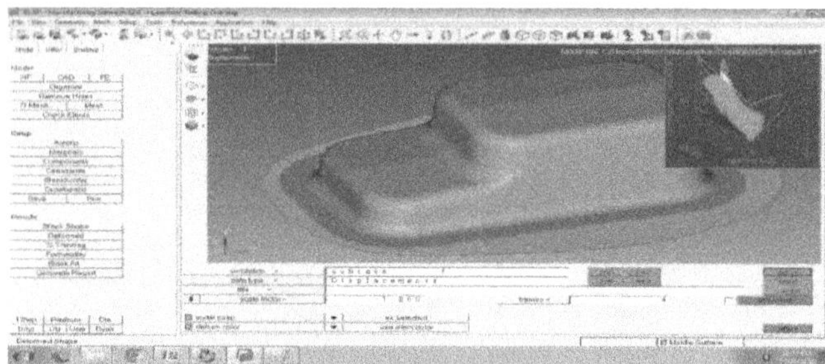

Apart from material size calculation, it also predicts formability and thinning.

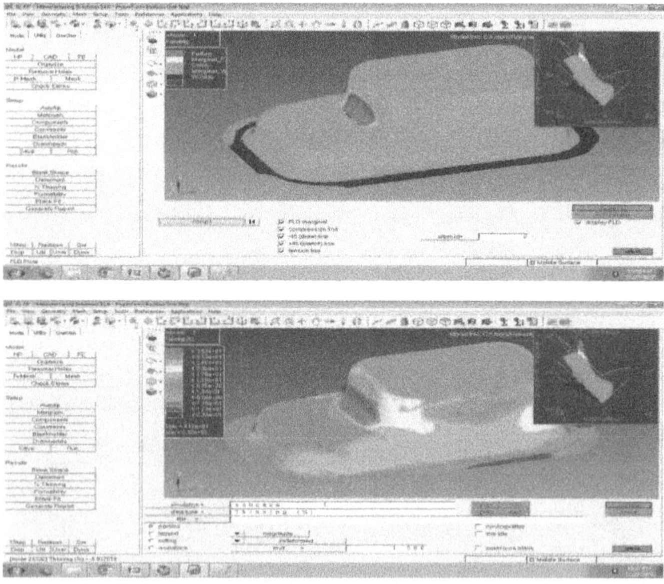

Few things need to be take care, while material size calculation.

Firstly, understand the manufacturing process: Since it's clear in the forming and thinning plots that it's not going to be formed in a single stage.

Secondly there should an extra trimming margin, to be added on the computer calculated material size.As a thumb rule, trimming margin usually is 15mm for higher thickness (6~12mm) and 10 for lower thickness (1~5mm). Since it has to absorb the forming variations and un-even stretching during forming.

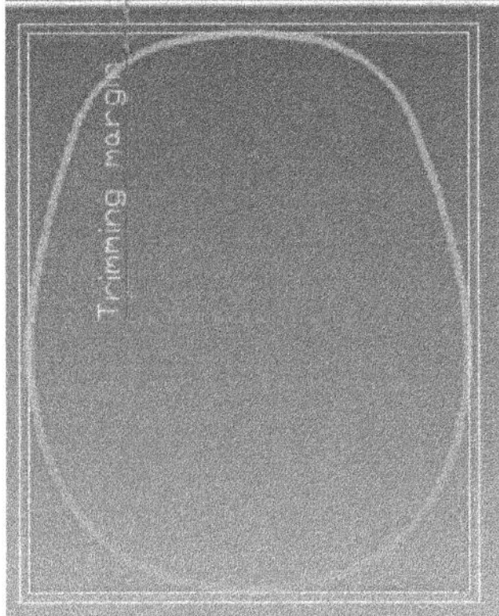

Practice Exercise
Get free video tutorials along with CAD files on Author's website

https://sharmarakesh.co.in/index.php/tutorials/

Password : Forming2025

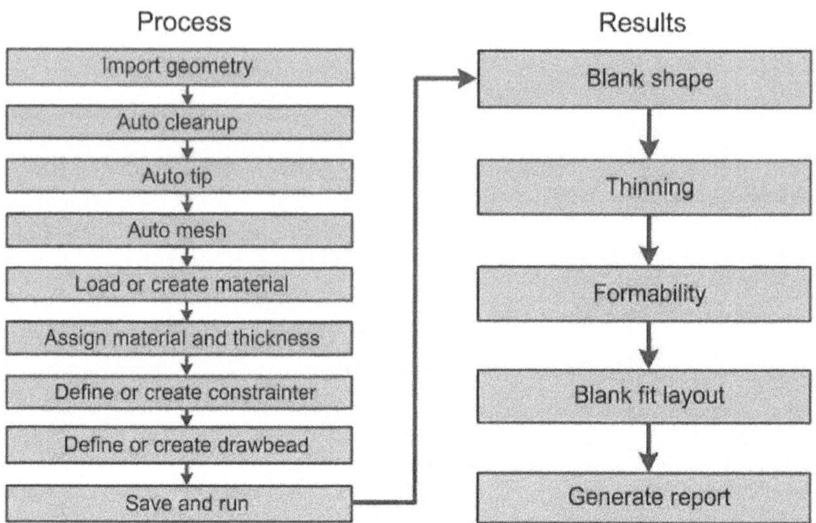

One Step User interface:

Important inputs:

3.1 Importing data: this option allows users to import geometry or mesh data inside hyperform irrespective of the formats, whether it is mesh data - HM, dat or Cad model data or assembly - iges, step etc or connectors-like welding, bolts etc. from other software's.

3.1A Import model: this option directly imports hypermesh binary files.

3.1B Import solver deck: this option import the data saved in the previous simulation, such as   the output of Draw-1 can be carried to draw-2 process. With the solver mesh data properties of the draw-1 will also be imported as well.

3.1C Import geometry: this option allows users to import cad geometry inside hyperform   irrespective of the common cad formats like iges, step etc.

3.1D Import BOM: Cad files in the form of assemblies of large parts can be carried out from catia, Nx or standard cad formats iges, step are also supported.

3.1E Import connections: Connection setup in other cad or FEA software can be directly   imported.

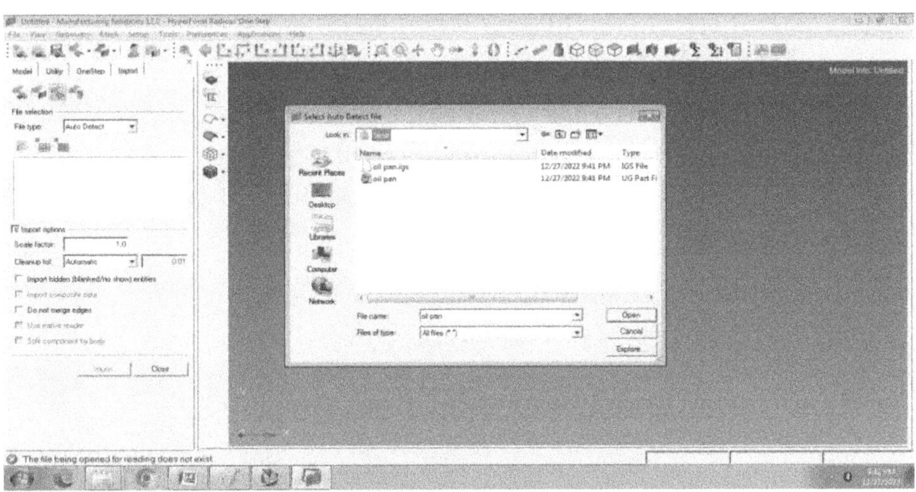

3.2 Create mid surface: After importing the cad model, it's time to extract it's midsurface, as you have to use 2D mesh which is less complex and easy to solve. In case you have already generated a midsurface in a cad file, you can directly import that.

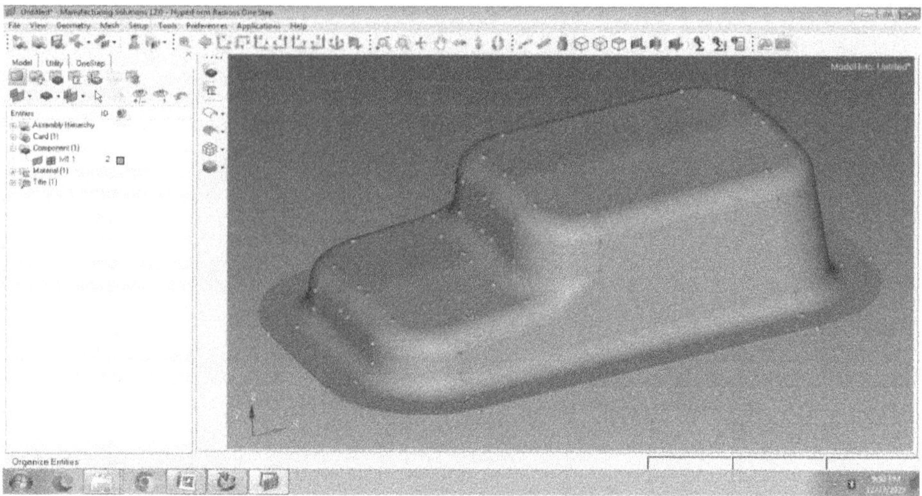

3.3 Meshing: Next step is to mesh the midsurface, out of all 2D mesh options, Quad mesh is most preferred due to its accuracy of the results. Element size is another key factor, which should be the optimum, since too large element size would distort the accuracy of the results and too short size increase the amount of data as well as processing times.

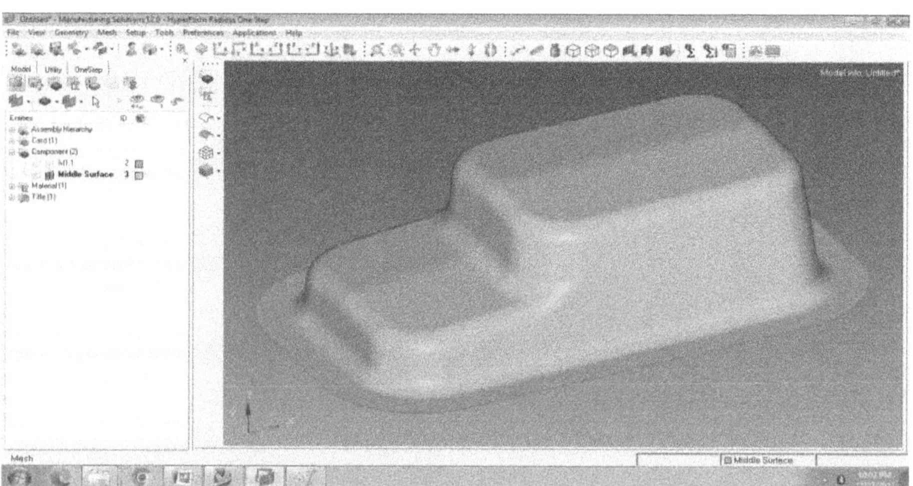

3.4 Material Selection: Material selection is another significant aspect, which can't be ignored. There are many materials are inbuilt, you have to choose the most identical in mechanical properties or you can create your own custom made, but make sure you have the relevant data to feed into the system, otherwise it would get complete.

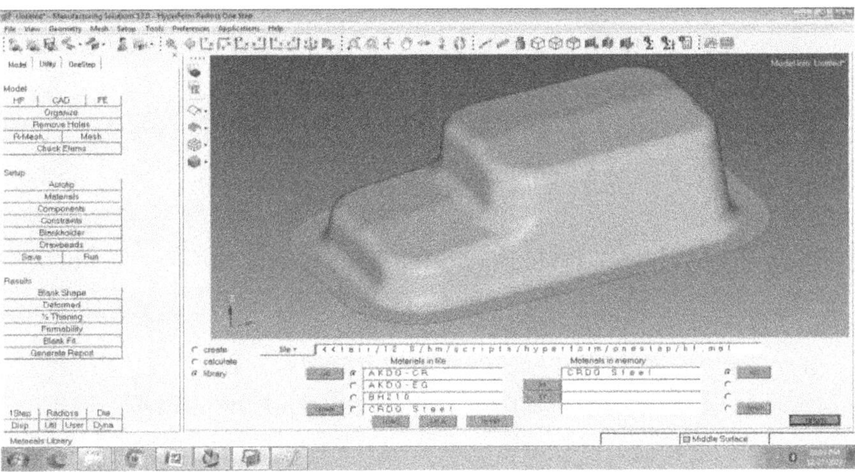

3.5 Assign material: Assign the already selected material grade and thickness to the target part.

3.6 Assign thickness: the importance of thickness is very well understandable, as the material behavior and results get changed with the change in thickness.

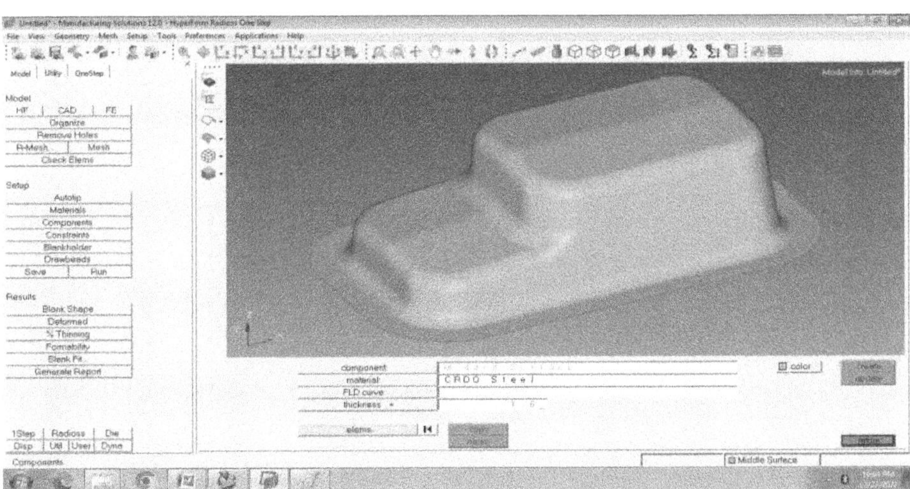

3.7 Autotip: The draw or forming direction by default is Z axis, unless you define it. In case, your direction is different from Z, then there is an autotip option, which orient the part automatically in the direction as supported by the software.

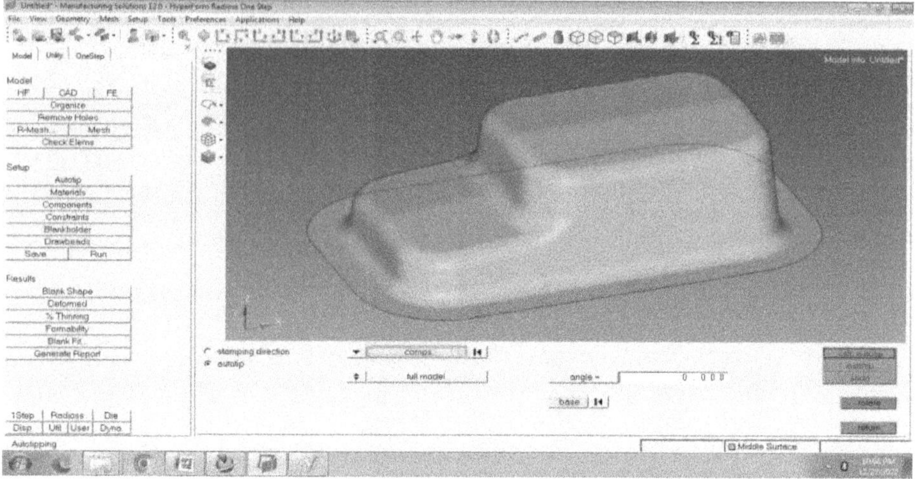

3.8 Constraints: used to lock/restrict some area of your part, which you don't want to move and keep or fixed.

3.9 Blank holder: The blank holder is the area, where you want to control the material movement.

3.10 Drawbeads: Some areas are prone to wrinkles during deep drawing at complex areas, where draw beads are used to restrain the material movement.

3.11 Save and run: Save your work done and run analysis, it will take few minutes to complete.

3.12 Load results: After post processing is completed, it's time to load the results from the same window.

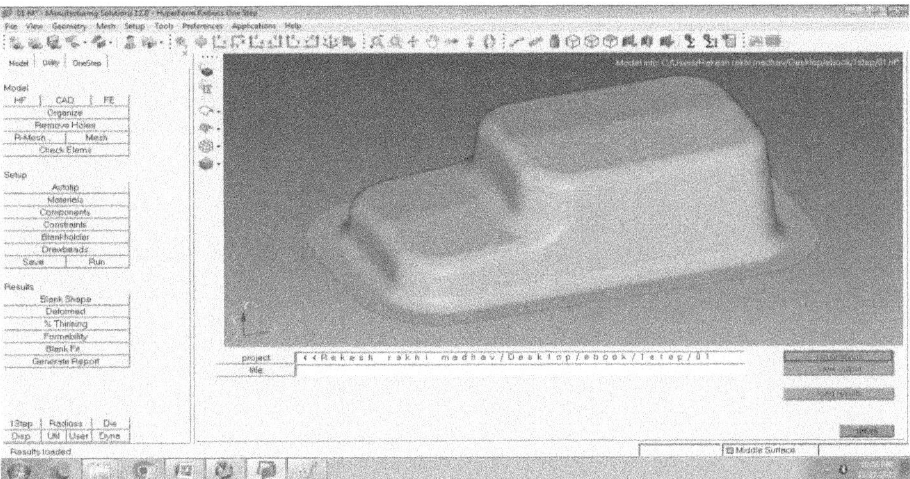

3.13 Formability: Under this window, you can see the forming limit curve and read the results for an abnormality. The colour coded result is showing area of the part with possible defects:

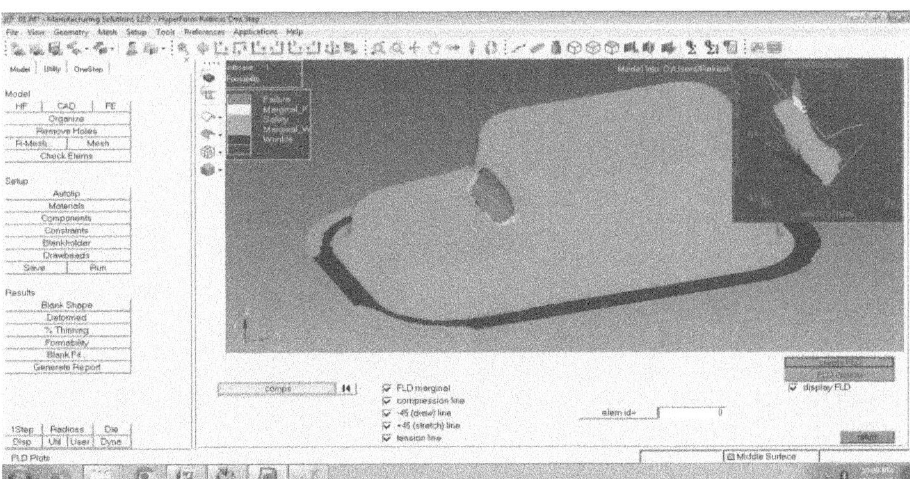

3.14 Thinning: The thinning is indicating the behavior, where it will prone to crack or tear due to excessive thinning. Normally, up to 20% thinning comes under safe zone, however it should be targeted near to 12~14%.

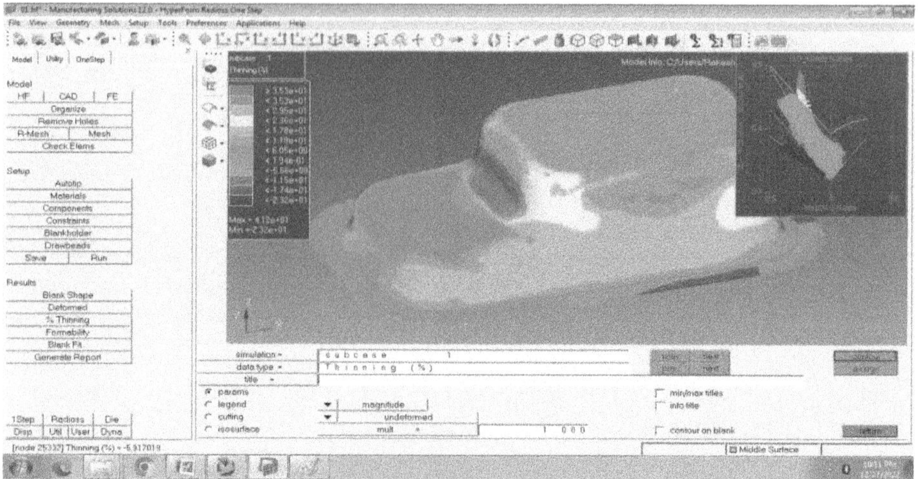

3.15 Blank shape: This feature unfolds the geometry and predict its blank shape, the accuracy is highly dependent on your meshing techniques, accuracy may vary up to 60~70%. Which can be further altered by using manual or CAD calculations, since it's generated from the midsuface or neutral fibre.

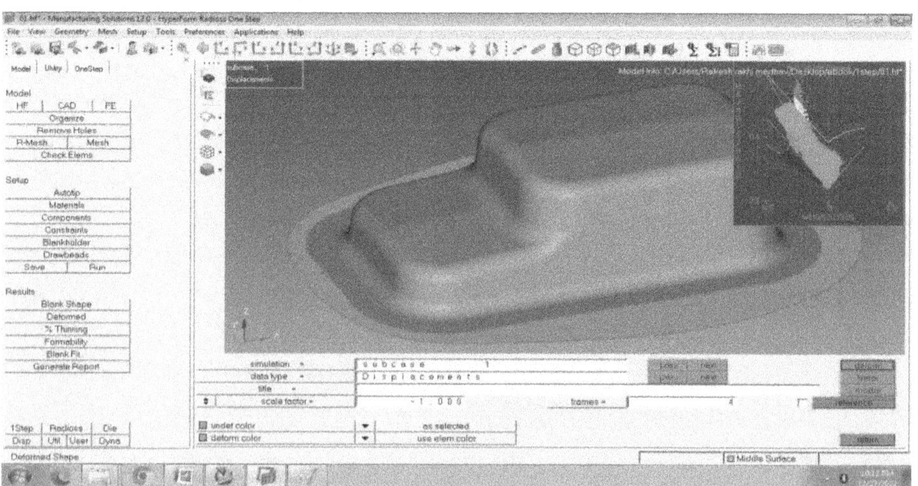

3.16 Blank fit: Allows you to create blank nesting with multiple layout options automatically, just with few clicks away. Max. material utilization is achieved in order to improve raw material yield.

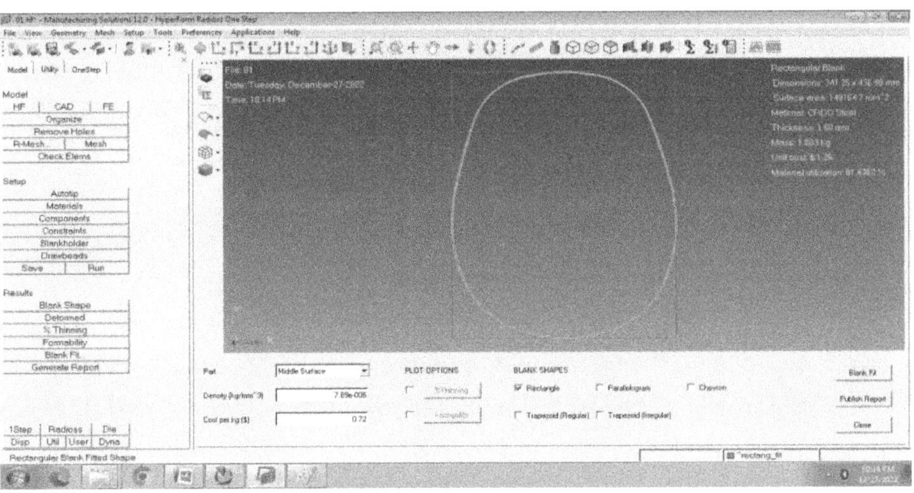

6. Die face development

What is a Die face or Draw face

Basically, when we are going to manufacture any sheet metal part, we need to think first, how it has to be made? In case, we have already some benchmark of similar shaped part, it is easy to decide the process. However, imagine the situation where you have to manufacture the part which is totally new to you. Thinking would be the critical process here and your team of engineers has to apply all of their know-how. After series of discussions and brainstorming sessions, you arrived at a conclusion to design the manufacturing sequence, about which you are not sure.

Here's how draw face development works in metal forming:

Initial Geometry Analysis: The process begins with analyzing the desired final geometry of the formed part. This includes determining features such as the outer contour, inner cavities, and any additional flanges or features that need to be incorporated into the final part.

Calculating Material Allowance: Once the final part geometry is established, engineers calculate the amount of material allowance required to account for the deformation and stretching that occurs during the forming process. This material allowance ensures that the final part achieves the desired dimensions and tolerances after forming.

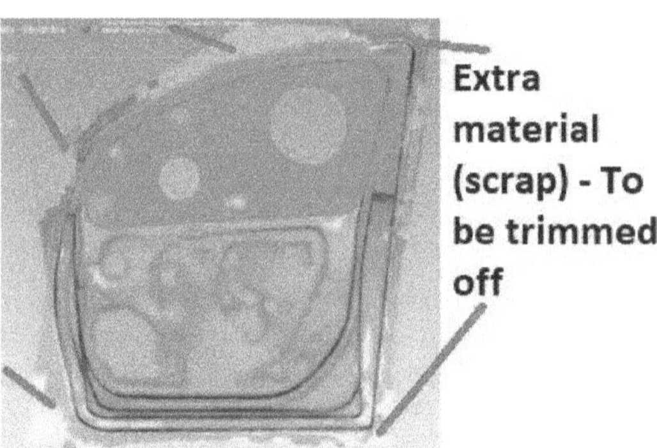

Developing the Draw Face: Using geometric principles and mathematical calculations, engineers develop the draw face, which represents the flat pattern or blank shape of the sheet metal required to produce the formed part. The draw face takes into account factors such as the material thickness, stretch ratios, and deformation characteristics during forming.

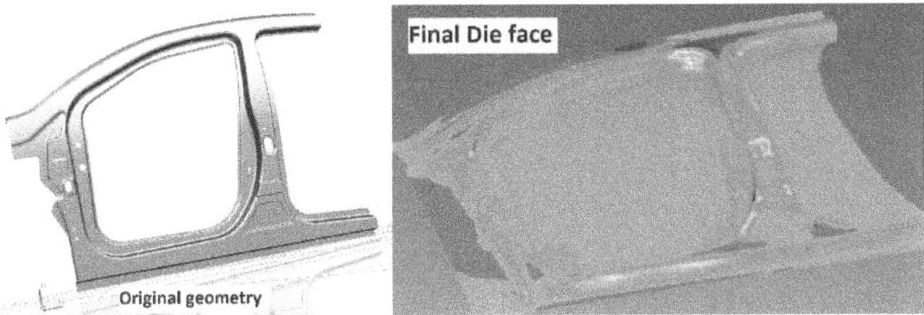

Consideration of Flange and Edge Conditions: In addition to the main draw face, engineers also consider the design of any flanges or edges that need to be formed as part of the final part geometry. Flanges are typically added to provide structural support or mating surfaces for assembly, and their design influences the overall shape of the draw face.

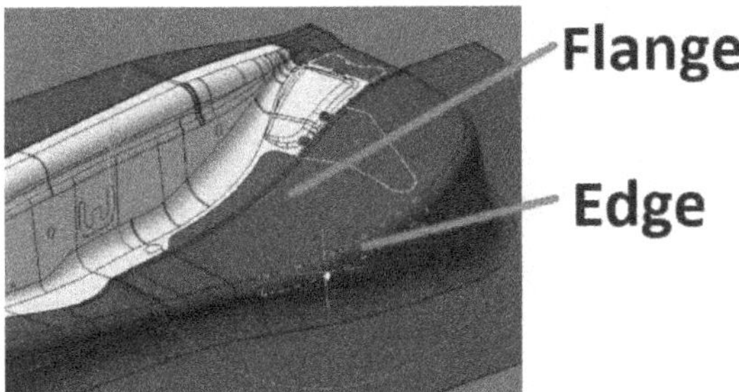

Validation and Iteration: Once the draw face is developed, it undergoes validation to ensure that it accurately represents the final part geometry and meets dimensional requirements. This may involve comparing the draw face to CAD models or physical prototypes and making iterative adjustments as needed to achieve the desired results.

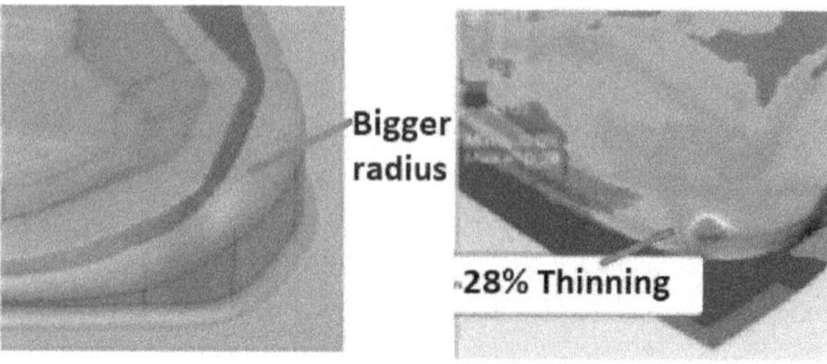

Geomerty modification based on the simulation results

Tooling Design and Implementation: Finally, the draw face is used as a blueprint for designing the forming tools and dies required to produce the formed part. The tooling design incorporates features such as punch profiles, die shapes, and blankholder configurations to ensure that the forming process accurately replicates the geometry of the draw face.

Overall, draw face development is a critical aspect of metal forming processes, allowing engineers to accurately predict and control the deformation of sheet metal to produce parts with complex geometries and tight dimensional tolerances. By carefully analyzing the final part geometry, calculating material allowances, and developing the draw face, engineers can optimize the forming process and ensure the production of high-quality formed components.

Benefits of accurate draw face development in metal forming

Accurate draw face development in metal forming processes offers numerous benefits that contribute to the efficiency, quality and cost-effectiveness of the manufacturing process. Here are several advantages of accurate draw face development:

Dimensional Accuracy: Accurate draw face development ensures that the formed parts meet precise dimensional tolerances and specifications. By accurately predicting the required flat pattern or blank shape, engineers can produce parts with minimal variation and achieve tight dimensional control.

Reduced Material Waste: With accurate draw face development, the amount of material used in the forming process can be optimized to minimize waste. By precisely calculating the material allowance needed for deformation, engineers can reduce scrap and material costs, leading to improved efficiency and cost-effectiveness.

Improved Forming Efficiency: Accurate draw face development facilitates efficient forming processes by providing clear guidelines for tooling design and setup. With the correct blank shape and material allowance, forming tools can be optimized to minimize setup time, reduce trial-and-error adjustments, and streamline the production process.

Enhanced Part Quality: Precise draw face development leads to higher-quality formed parts with consistent shapes, dimensions and surface finishes. By ensuring that the formed parts closely match the intended design, engineers can minimize defects, such as wrinkles, tears, or thinning, and produce parts with improved structural integrity and performance.

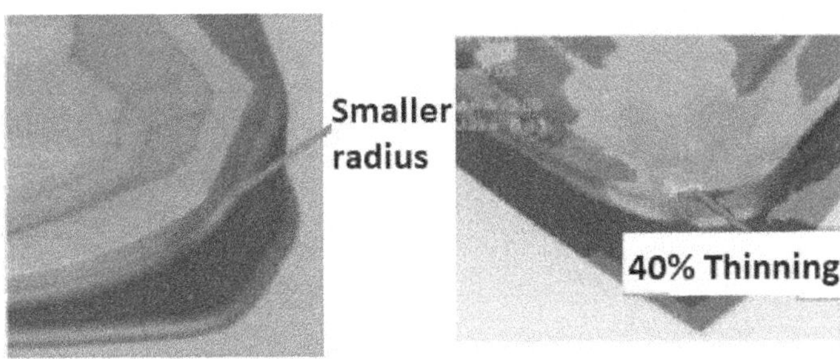

Original Design (before optimization)

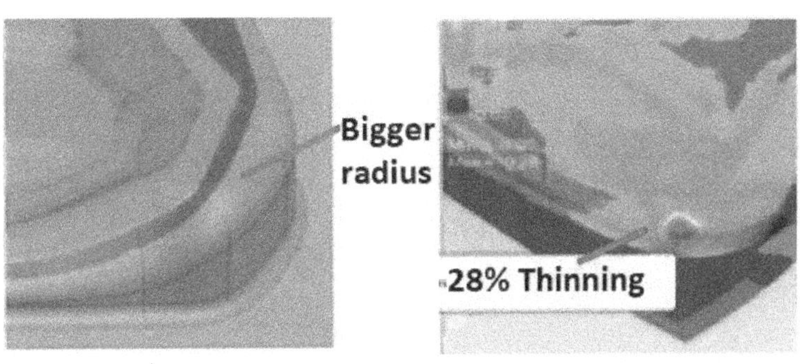

Optimized Tooling Design: Accurate draw face development serves as a blueprint for designing forming tools and dies. By providing clear guidance on punch profiles, die shapes, and blankholder configurations, engineers can optimize tooling designs to achieve the desired forming results efficiently and effectively.

Increased Production Efficiency: With accurate draw face development, production processes can be streamlined, leading to increased throughput and production rates. By minimizing setup time, reducing material waste, and improving part quality, manufacturers can enhance overall production efficiency and meet customer demand more effectively.

Cost Savings: Ultimately, accurate draw face development contributes to cost savings throughout the metal forming process. By minimizing material waste, reducing setup time, and improving part quality, manufacturers can lower production costs, improve profitability, and remain competitive in the marketplace.

To sum up, accurate draw face development in metal forming processes provides numerous benefits, including dimensional accuracy, reduced material waste, improved forming efficiency, enhanced part quality, optimized tooling design, increased production efficiency, and cost savings. By investing in accurate draw face development, manufacturers can achieve better outcomes, streamline production processes, and deliver high-quality formed components to customers.

How to design the manufacturing process sequence

There are few ways in which you can design the process of any steel metal part, the main challenge is to design its forming process. Since the probability of most common defects like thinning, cracking and wrinkles are more during forming, therefore it is considered to be the most critical out of entire cycle.

First of all, let's take example of small workshop, where the technician is the supreme authority to decide the process sequence. The simple geometries are easy to made, however where there is a critical one. The process can be turned out to be hectic due to increased number of hit and trials and increased timeline. Which customer doesn't allow and become annoyed. This is the biggest risk or threat to the whole business.

Secondly there is a case, where you have a team of engineers with proper CFT (cross functional teams). The brain storming or APQP (Advance product quality planning) are the most common. The potential risks are identified with the experience of the all members and the process sequences are decided after the mutual agreement of engineers.

After doing all the groundwork, the biggest question arises is that are they sure enough on their decisions?

The answer is no, even after diligent team work, the process of hit and trials are going on periodically. The final product is far different from the initial process design sequence. The cost is time, efforts and the loss of customer faith on your know how.

There is a third situation also exists, where you have a particular experts, who have a perfection in their respective domain and use CAE or computer simulation for process design. They also form CFT and work in line with the APQP procedures. The final results are totally opposite, they are confident enough before actual manufacturing takes place. They are also doing hit and trials, but with 80% accuracy. The process is matching almost 80~90% with their original designs and the lead time are too shortened, which means that their deadlines are met within 20% accuracy. That means if they have taken a target to deliver the part samples within 60 days, there is a max. Possible delay of 12 days, which is manageable.

Therefore, third approach is highly appreciated.

There are the various stages in the process sequence of any part, involves forming and cutting process. The process or stages of design of any component related to its forming are called Draw face design.

1. Original part geometry

This is the original gometry on which you have to work on. It may be simple or complex, the basi process remains the same. However it's not easy to handle the geometries with curvature at the bottom, many softwares failed to create features due to complexity of nature. High end CAD softwares like Catia or Siemenens NX are preffered.

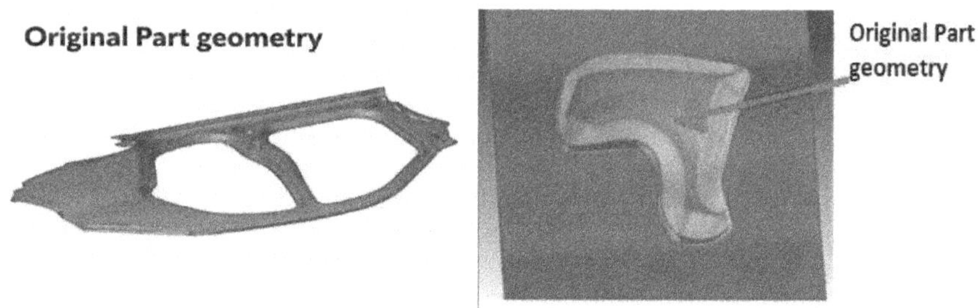

2. Flange Development

This stage defines the initial blank shape and flange geometry before forming. It considers material flow, strain distribution, and trimming allowances.The goal is to ensure proper material utilization while minimizing defects like wrinkling or thinning. Unfolding techniques or inverse FEA may be used to determine the optimal flange shape.

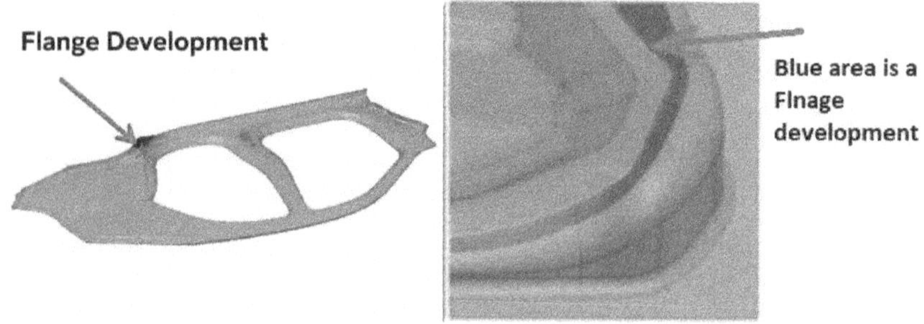

3. Fill holes or open areas

In this stage, small holes, cutouts, or open areas in the part design are surface filled. This ensures a more uniform material flow during forming, preventing stress concentrations, tearing, or excessive thinning. Closing these areas helps achieve better strain distribution and avoids distortions caused by uneven stretching. This step is particularly important for complex geometries where open features could cause instability in the forming process. After the major forming stages are completed, the holes and openings are reintroduced through secondary operations like trimming or piercing. Properly managing this stage improves formability and ensures better accuracy in the final part.

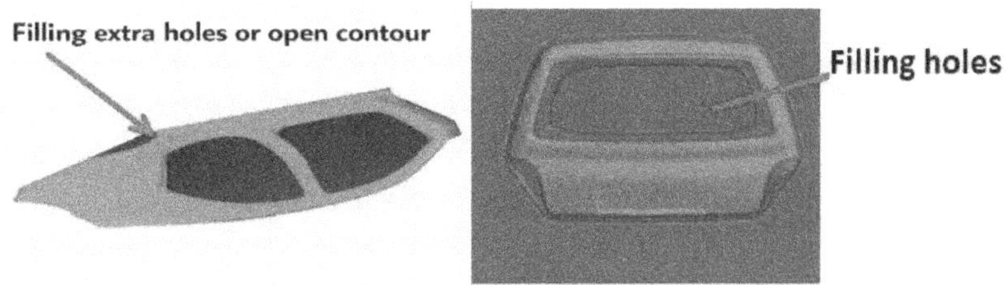

4. Creating a Parting line for Punch and die

Punch parting line (PPL) is the boundary where the sheet metal first contacts the punch before drawing begins. It defines material flow, affecting stretching and strain distribution. Proper PPL placement ensures controlled metal movement into the die cavity, reducing the risk of excessive thinning, tearing, or improper material flow during forming.

Die parting line (DPL) is the outermost edge of the die cavity where the sheet metal enters during forming. It controls material draw-in, influencing wrinkle formation and strain distribution. Proper DPL placement ensures uniform material flow, preventing defects like splits or excessive thinning while optimizing blank size and improving overall formability.

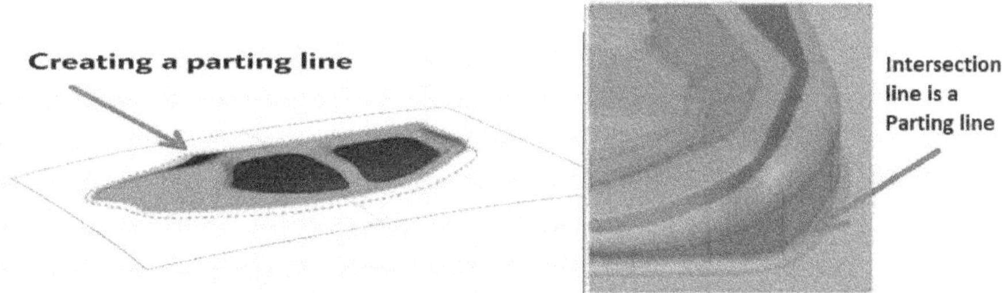

5. Addendum profile planning and CAD modelling

The addendum profile connects the part's functional shape to the binder, guiding material flow during forming. It helps control stretching, distribute strain, and prevent defects like wrinkles or splits. A well-designed addendum ensures smoother transitions, enhances formability, and minimizes thinning while optimizing material usage and die performance.

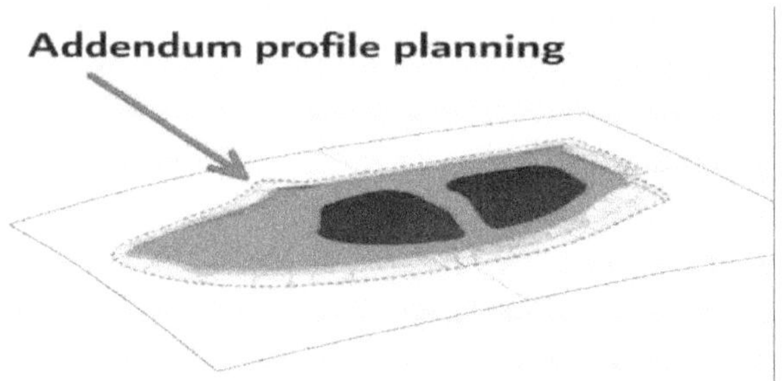

Generating an addendum involves defining smooth transitions between the part and binder, considering material flow and strain distribution. CAD tools and forming simulations help design and refine addendum geometry. Proper curvature, draw angles, and radii adjustments ensure controlled metal movement, reducing defects and improving the overall forming process.

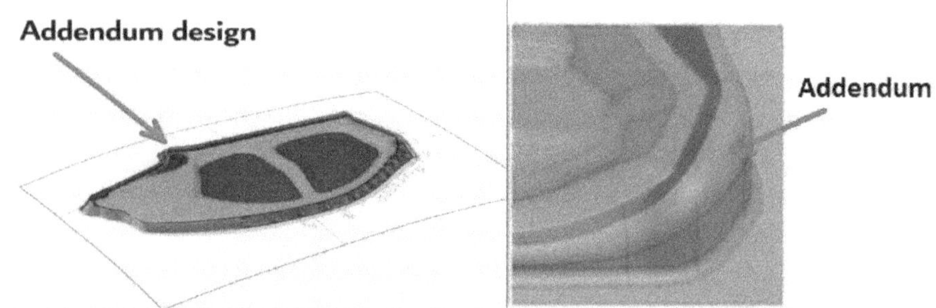

6. Create a Binder surface

The binder surface is a critical part of die face development, controlling material flow during forming. It is designed to hold and guide the sheet metal while ensuring uniform stretching and preventing defects like wrinkling or excessive thinning. The binder surface should provide proper pressure distribution, allowing controlled material draw-in. Its shape is influenced by the part geometry, material properties, and forming requirements. A well-designed binder helps optimize strain distribution, reducing the risk of splits or wrinkles. Advanced CAD tools and finite element simulations are used to refine the binder design for improved manufacturability and die performance.

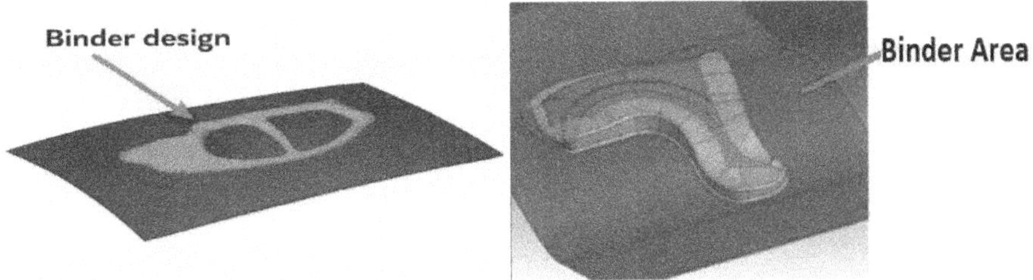

7. Finishing Die Face Design

Die face development finalizes the tooling surface, ensuring smooth material flow and defect-free forming. It includes optimizing punch, die, and addendum surfaces for proper strain distribution. Using CAD and FEA simulations, engineers refine clearances, radii, and draw angles to achieve precise part geometry, minimizing wrinkles, thinning, or splits.

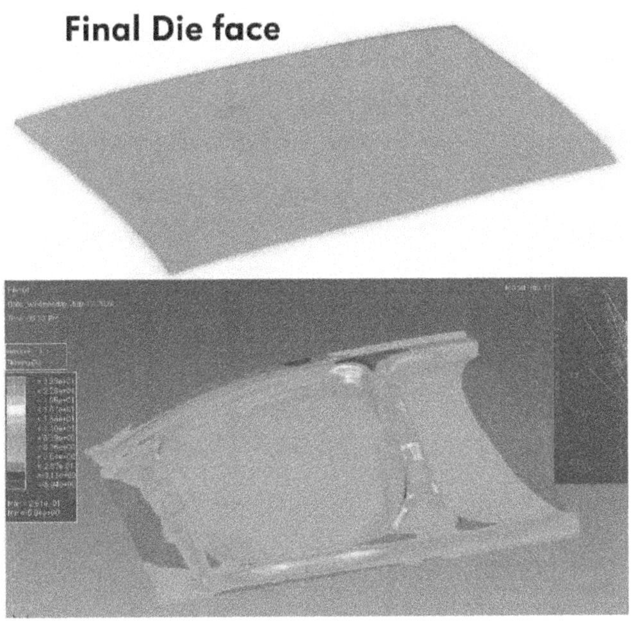

Images are the Examples of Final Die face

In metal forming processes, draw face development refers to the technique used to determine the flat pattern or blank shape required to produce a formed part with specific dimensions and geometry. This technique is commonly used in processes such as deep drawing, where a flat sheet of metal is transformed into a three-dimensional part with a cavity or recessed feature.

What is the cost to adopt simulation v/s its benefits?

Even though the computer simulation software's and the trained engineers add cost to the system. However, they will pay you exponentially in the long run due to the following key reasons.

- Improved product quality
- Lowers number of iterations
- Reduced development lead time
- Gain customer faith
- Be pioneers among competition
- Optimized product cost

Methods to develop the correct draw face or Die face

It's better to start from the scratch, since it will always leave the opportunity of an innovation. Here we are going to develop the draw face of some famous automotive sheet metal parts.

First of all let's take up with the Engine oil pan.

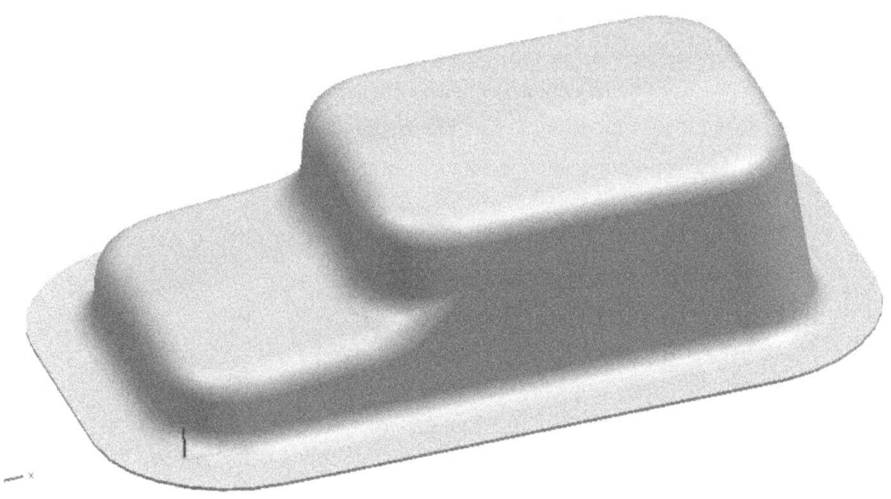

How blanks were calculated in the past?

I remember, when I was appointed as a GET in 2006, after completion of my graduating in Mechanical engineering, my r&d department usually receive the sample component. After tear down analysis, we usually take the help of tool room\manufacturing to flatten the sheet metal part via. Hammering, which takes a lot of time and cost you a loss of sample part. The flattened metal parts were scanned with the help of profile projector and then measured.

Later on, when technology evolved and 3d white line scanning came in to existence, it was much easier to scan the samples and convert those in to 3D cad parts. With the help of FEA software, you can easily process the child parts and calculate the blank size of any complicated parts.

How to check the forming feasibility?

To check the quick feasibility of any part, the first and foremost method is to check with the one step forming analysis. In this method you have to follow the generic procedure to quickly check the feasibility of any sheet metal part, irrespective of shape, size and thickness/material grade. The purpose is to check, whether the forming can be carried out in a single stage or it requires more than one stages. As a thumb rule, for cylindrical parts the following formula is generally used.

However, where the shape of the part is other than cylindrical, the forming simulation comes in to picture. The generic process flow is given herewith:

Essential steps to design a draw face or Die face

1. **Know your part:** the first and foremost is to know your component or sheet metal part. Note it's important or critical dimensions such as mating faces. Mating faces are that which has to join other parts and their matching is very important, whatever would be the joining media like spot welding (most commonly used) or taking with mig wire. The imperfection or distortions are due to spring back, especially in high strength material grades, where there is more carbon percentage and higher yield strength, thus resulting in more elastic recovery. Secondly there are free areas, which are relieved from the surrounding areas, however may contribute in the distortion of mating faces or mating areas.

   In conventional thinking, everything is vivid only after 1st try out. However, in engineering everything is calculated and FEA is here to solve such complex problems and to arrest the possible failures in virtual stages, therefore saving time and efforts.

2. **Symmetry:** the importance of symmetry is very practical to understand. Symmetry balances the forces exerted on to the part by machine and the counteraction or reaction force acting on to the Ram of the press machine. In the same way, the blank holding force also to be balanced for the safe operating practices and smooth running of the entire process. Let's take an example:

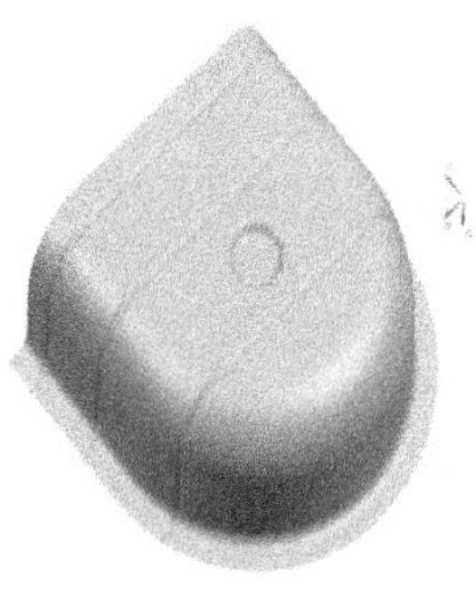

This component is non-symmetric, let's design its die or draw face.

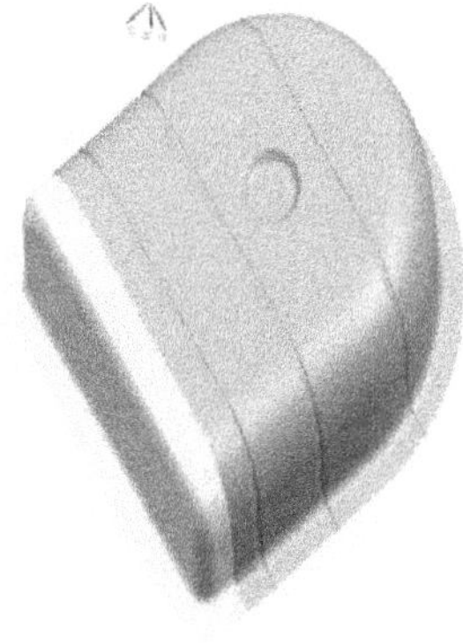

You can clearly see how un-balanced its die design would be.

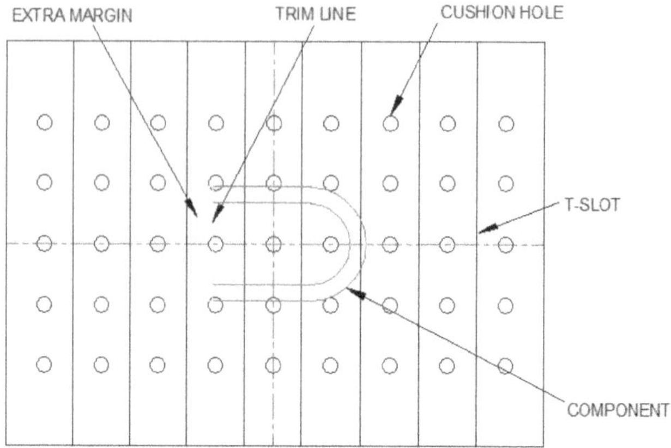

The imbalance of draw force and blank holding not only produce manufacturing defects the part, but also exerts unbalanced pressure on the Ram and cushion plate situated under the bolster.

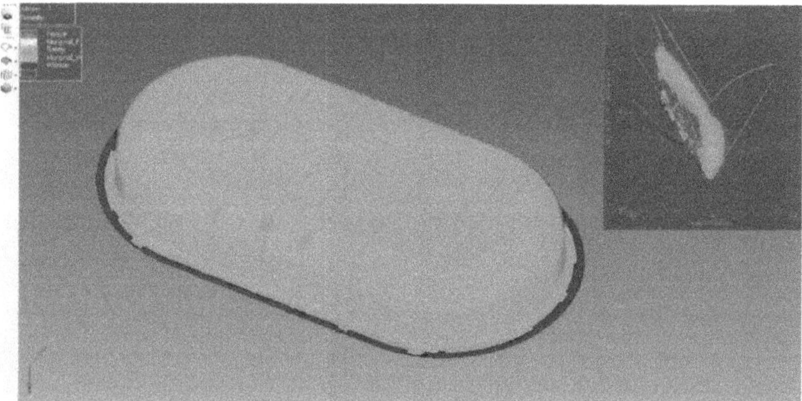

On the other hand, symmetric part covers the equal area on the press, therefore allow you to create balanced tool design, which often produce higher quality parts along with optimum machine life of both press Ram and cushion plate.

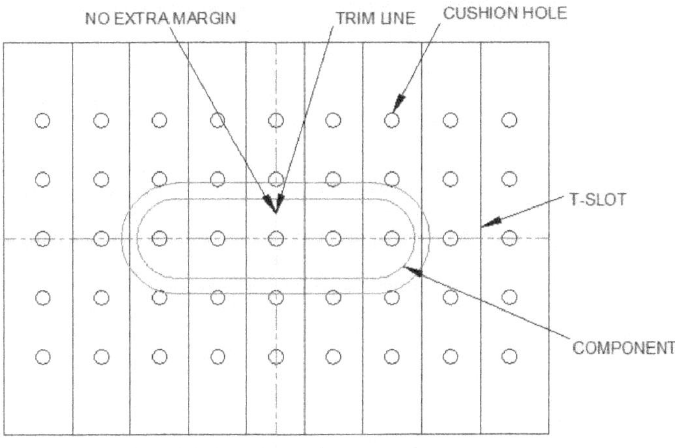

For bigger machines it is highly recommended to cover up the at least 70% of the bolster area for uniform load distribution and to prevent the distortion of bolster plate, since it is hollow from the inside.

3. **To avoid yield loss:** while doing the forming operations, there is certain amount of material required to be hold by blank holder, without which otherwise is not possible. As mentioned in the previous chapter "forming limit diagram" there are two axis of forming. 1st is major axis - direction of forming is vertical in major axis or forming is possible up to certain Limited depth beyond that excessive thing or cracks may take place, while try to form in single stage.

Second is minor axis - this axis is responsible for creating in sufficient stretch which often causes problem therefore morning limit diagram the form ability plot is the combination of both major and minor axis. Let us take an example of making draw face from single part. The input material size is more and the respective yield loss is more. While on the other hand, let's take an example of symmetrical blank, where we have saved the marked material and saved it to optimum level with yellow reduced to 50%.

4. **Draw bead:** Many times wrinkles are seen on certain areas, where there is an insufficient stretch or material holding or where the material movement is more towards the minor axis in FLD.

Wrinkles formed before Draw Bead

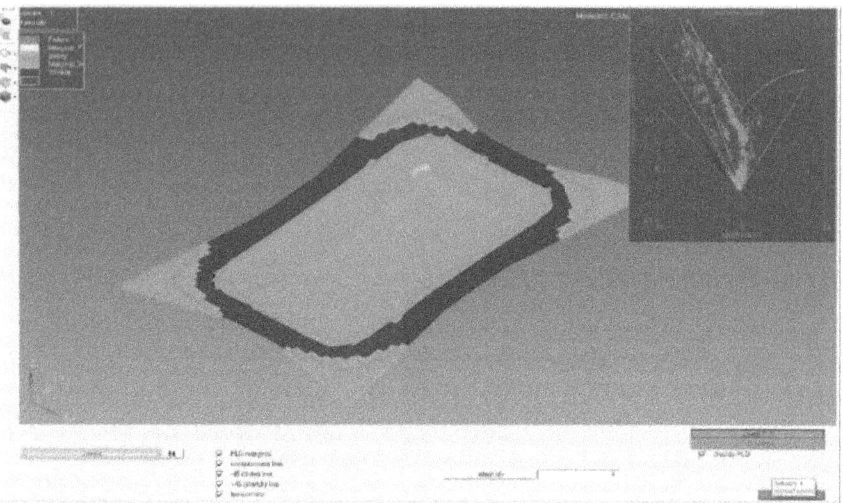

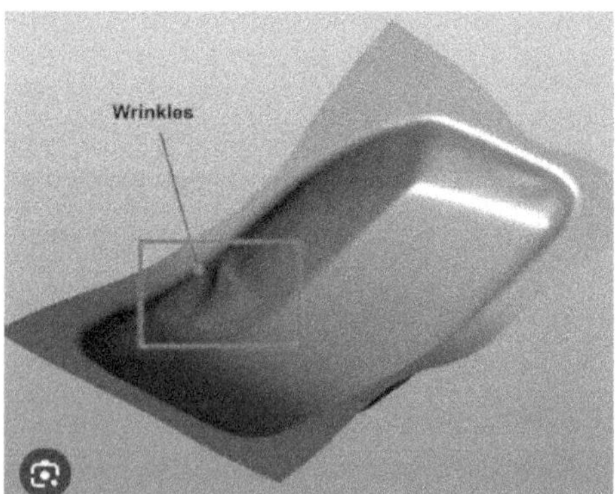

To prevent such situations, we put draw bead on the periphery, where there are wrinkles being shown in FLD plot during virtual simulation. Little bit material addition is there in draw face and addition in input material as well.

Wrinkles Disappear after Draw Bead
Remember one thing that the draw bead should be at sufficient gap from the trim line of the final part. Let's take an example of the part,

where there is wrinkle formed in FLD during one step analysis.

The design parameter of drawer should be ideally as per given diagram.

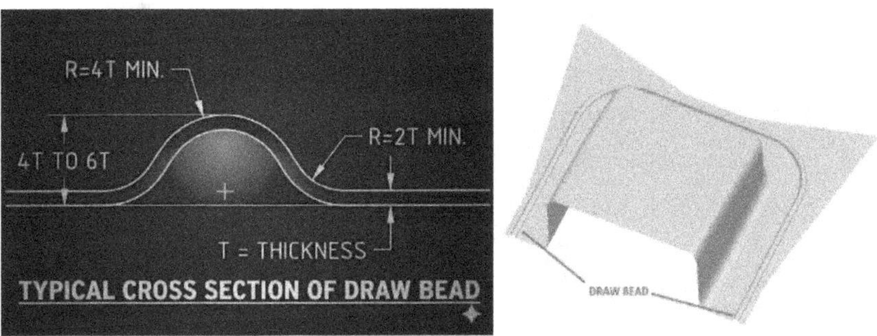

The location of the draw bead also to be chosen very carefully. Here in this case, I am going to measure it in FEA model.

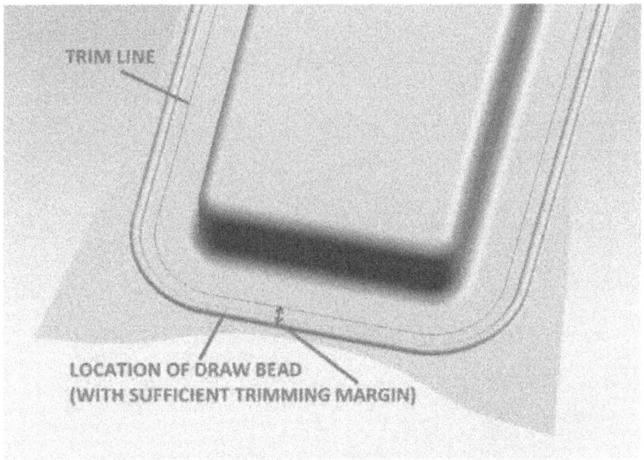

Draw bead restraint the flow of material and lock the additional material, thus prevent it to accumulate and form wrinkles. Since it is practically very effective and that is why widely used in metal bigger panels.

Let us see the FLD plot after addition of draw bead.

Get free video tutorials along with CAD files on Author's website sharmarakesh.co.in, with the purchase of this book

Examples of Draw bead on die and punch

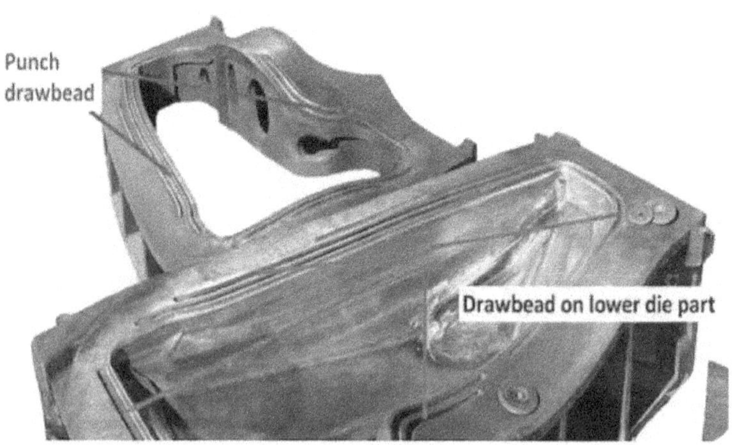

In the above picture you can see, the wrinkles disappeared totally from the affected area.

5. **Calculate the number of draw process:** For round/cylindrical parts, there is a generic method to calculate the number of draw stages. Check for Draw to Height ratio: The D/H ratio is the basic ratio to have a look at the feasibility to perform a round / cylindrical draw process in a one or more than one process.

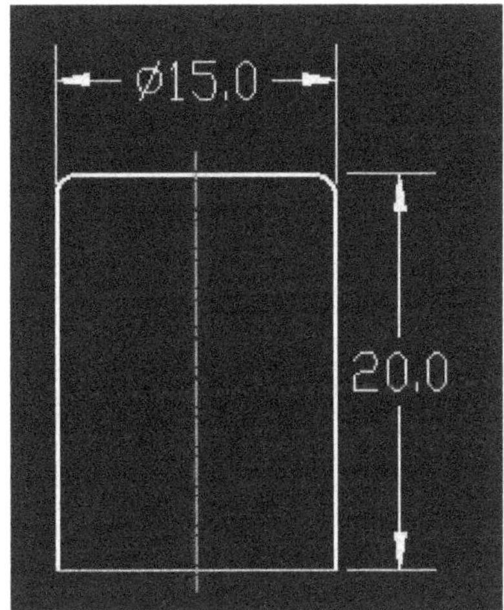

REFERENCE DEEP DRAWN PART

D = Outer dia. of the shell (15 inch, as shown in the sketch)

H = Height of the cylinder (20 inch, as shown in the sketch)

If D/H should be equal to or more than 1, there is a possibility to do it in a single draw.

In case, it is less than 1, then you have to go for a 2 or more draw operations.

For multiple draw process

In case D/H ratio is less than 1, then what is next. It is evident that it's more than one, but how much?

The answer is complicated, there is no thumb rule, however based on my experience and compilation of years of experimental data, the following rules has been established.

For 1st draw, there should be the 60-70% reduction in diameter.

For 2nd draw, there should be the 40-45% reduction in diameter.

For 3rd draw, there should be the 20-25% reduction in diameter.

The base / original diameter with respect to whom, the reduction is applicable, that is the blank diameter.

Calculate the blank diameter

To calculate the blank dia. of the cylindrical part, the volume method to be used.

Volume of a cylinder is = $\P r^2 h$

The volume of a blank, is also calculated by the same formula.

Volume of cylinder = volume of the calculated blank size

Let's say, the volume of cylinder is 108.6640 cubic inch.

Now for blank :

D = to be calculated

Thickness = 0.1 inch (same as thickness of the part)

108.6640 = 3.14 x R x R x 0.1

R = 18.6 and D = 37.2 inch

Decide the No. of Draw

Fore multiple draw process, there formula is same as mentioned earlier.

For First draw, the Final dia. of the part after draw is = (37.2 x 65%) = 24.18 inch

For Second draw, the possible reduction is = (24.18 x 40%) = 9.7 inch

Since our Target diameter is 15 inch, that means it's possible to draw the part in 2 draw stages.

Limitation of this basic method

This is a basic method, highly successful in the calculation of cylindrical deep drawn geometry.

Sometimes, other shapes such as square, pentagon and hexagon can be calculated. However, their blank size calculation is quite hard, since this is a volume based calculation best suited for round parts.

However, where there is a complexity in geometry, you need to go for a different method. Only learning FEA method is not the key, but you have to learn the effective ways to logically solve the problems with creativity.

Let's take an example of a Rear Floor of Famous Indian Sedan.

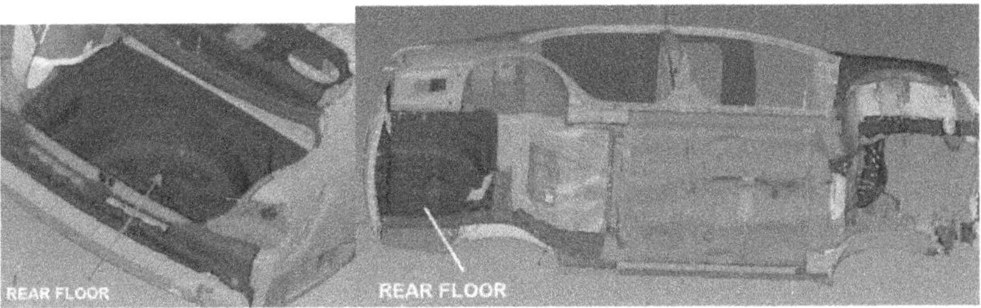

The first method of feasibility checking is with one step forming simulation, which means whether the part can be made in single step or not. Apart from that you can easily calculate the finish blank/material shape/size, based on that you can choose the most closed match. Since it has to be trimmed off, therefore don't forget to add trimming margin.

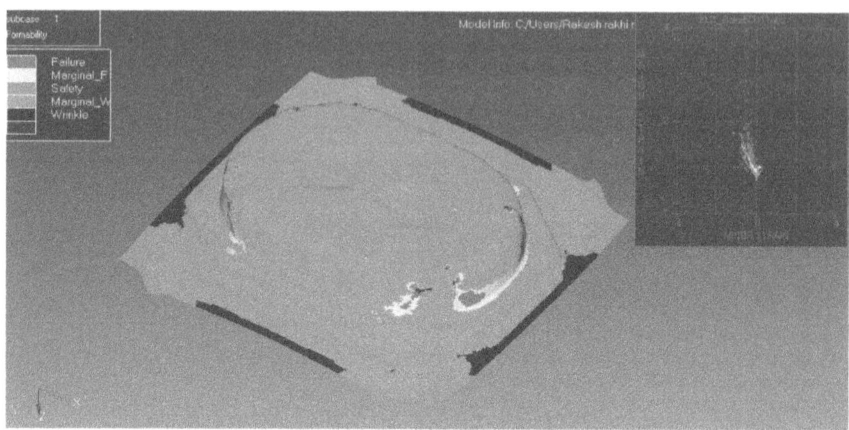

<u>One step Forming Simulation</u>

For example, once you make it clear that part is not feasible to made in single stage, but need to be made in more than one stage. Next challenge is, how much stages are required to make this part?

To calculate the number of stages, there is no automatic solution to tell you that in how many stages, part has to be made. However, there are certain techniques, which are surely helpful. The first technique is called "bench marking" and it is the best way to find out whether your idea will work or not. What I mean to say that you should study the similar shaped product from your organization. Suppose it is being made in two stages and what are the practical problems being faced by shop floor people during its manufacturing. Talk to people face to face and know in details, as it would generate the seeds of Ideas in your brain, in parallel to that you will create alert of potential risk or defects in your brain mapping. Replicate the same in your design and further simulation. Some fine tuning maybe required and may take couple of days, however experience gained will nurture your thought process.

Second method is to use of experience, that means use your previous relevant experience.

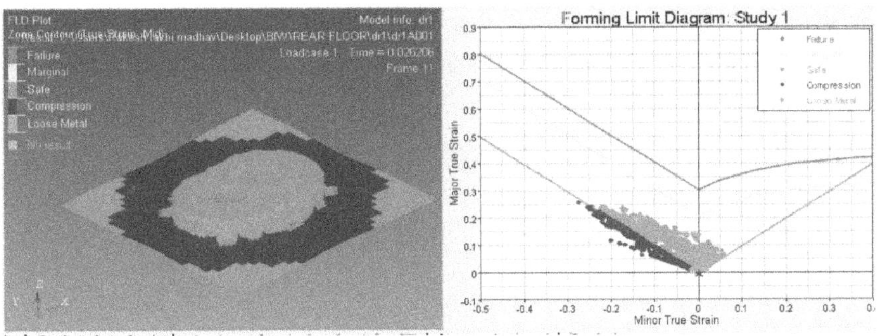

Draw -1 Simulation

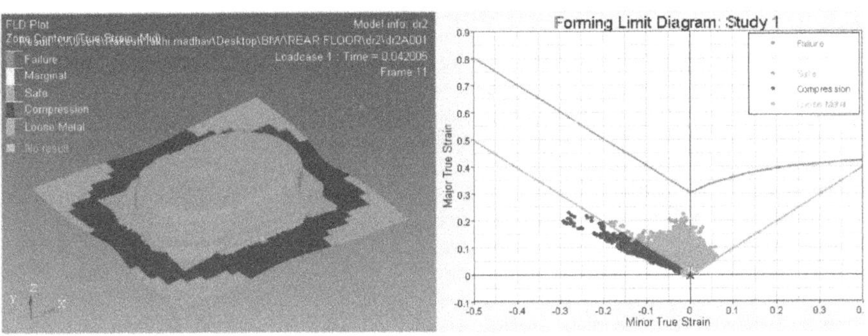

Draw -2 Simulation

Practice Exercise

Get free video tutorials along with CAD files on Author's website

https://sharmarakesh.co.in/index.php/tutorials/

Password : Forming2025

It will help you to give direction to your thought and design. Lots of time and effort will be saved and guaranteed to achieve satisfactory results with in limited time. In case you did not have relevant experience with yourself take the help of any senior or known person, even don't have hesitate to get advice from unknown people. Advice is for free and don't Cost you anything, but add to your experience

In case, method one and two are not applicable to you, which mean this is a totally new product to the market and to you also. Then critical thinking is the key, look it from different angles and different thought process. Make multiple models or design with multiple alterations. Compare all and choose the best. The process consumes time but add some value to you know how.

7. Incremental analysis for multistage Metal forming

Understanding Incremental Forming Analysis:

At its core, incremental forming analysis utilizes computer simulations and mathematical models to predict and optimize the deformation process. Through finite element analysis (FEA), engineers can simulate the complex interactions between the tool, blank sheet, and forming forces, enabling precise control over the manufacturing process. By iteratively refining these simulations, manufacturers can minimize material waste, reduce production time, and enhance the quality of the final product.

One of the key advantages of incremental forming analysis lies in its versatility and adaptability to a wide range of materials, including ordinary, deep drawn and extra deep drawn materials. Apart from that forming of ultra-high strength materials, usually hot formed is still a big problem for simulation engineers. Unlike traditional forming techniques that often require specific tooling for each part, Incremental Forming Analysis can accommodate various geometries and material properties with minimal setup changes. This flexibility not only streamlines production workflows but also opens up new possibilities for designing innovative and lightweight structures.

Moreover, incremental forming analysis offers unparalleled geometric freedom, allowing manufacturers to produce highly customized components with intricate shapes and complex geometries. By controlling the trajectory of the forming tool, engineers can achieve precise material distribution and optimize structural integrity, leading to superior performance and functionality in the final product.

The adoption of incremental forming analysis has significant implications across diverse industries, from aerospace and automotive to biomedical and consumer electronics. By leveraging advanced simulation techniques, manufacturers can push the boundaries of design innovation while simultaneously improving efficiency and reducing costs.

To summarize, incremental forming analysis represents a groundbreaking approach to modern manufacturing, empowering engineers to create highly customized, lightweight, and structurally optimized components with unparalleled precision and efficiency. As technology continues to evolve, Incremental Forming Analysis is poised to revolutionize the way we conceptualize and fabricate complex geometries, driving innovation and progress across a myriad of industries.

Benefits of Incremental forming analysis

In this type of forming simulation, the actual processes decided by you, number of stages are simulated virtually for any possible defects before actual die try out. The detailed analysis is being used by Stamping die designers, to do virtual try in design stage, that means before actual tool try out, you can predict the output of your process design. Mainly to arrest the defects like thinning, cracks, wrinkles and sprigback.

Nevertheless, it saves your time and cost involved, thereby is referred as virtual try out. With the help of forming simulations, the successful process flow is designed before there is an actual process exists.

The HyperForm Incremental (Incr) interface provides a customized interface to set up incremental metal forming analysis using Radioss solver.

The Incremental interface allows you to accurately model forming processes. Instead of modeling just the final part shape, as in One Step analysis, the Incremental interface uses amore rigorous modeling approach. As the name implies, small solution steps or'increments' are taken to solve the problem. In this way, the incremental method allows you to accurately model important metal forming processes (such as binder wrap, single or multi-stage forming, trimming, and springback). Solving a problem incrementally thinning or tears)occurs in the blank. You can then take corrective action to eliminate these defects by modifying the process in various ways (changing tool loads, tool motion, or tool shape,for example,). The Incremental method allows you to represent all tool surfaces, prescribe the tool motions, apply tool loads, define material properties of the blank, and model the contact interaction between the tools and the blank.

For example, in the previous chapter, we have concluded that the forming of Engine oil pan is not feasible in single process, which however is an indication that we have to opt for more than one stage. It's utmost important to think practically, how to decide the shape of 1st forming process. Apart from the theory, It's merely practice and experience, which is furthermore validated through the process of simulation. In the chapter of Draw face design, it's given in more elaborated form.

Practice Exercise
Get free video tutorials along with CAD files on Author's website

https://sharmarakesh.co.in/index.php/tutorials/

Password : Forming2025

PROCESS FLOW :

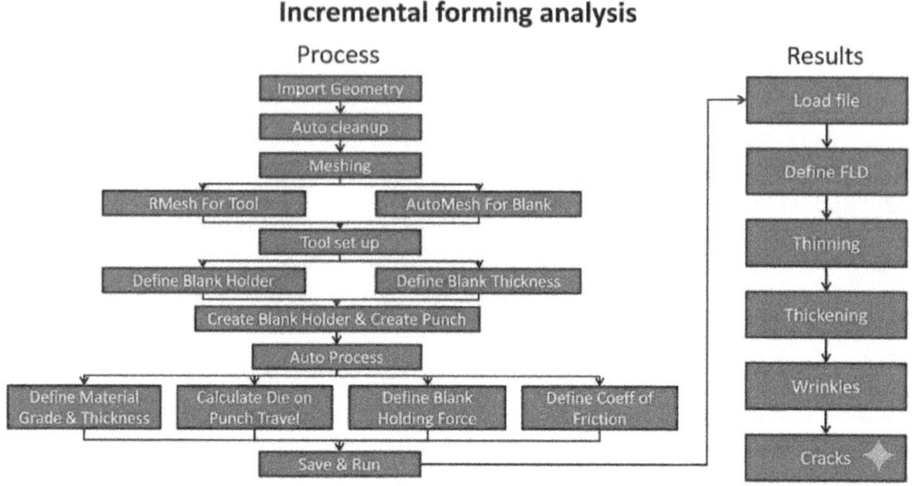

Incremental User interface:

This section introduces the HyperForm Incremental Interface using process-specific examples to illustrate the ease with which it is possible to set up an incremental metal forming analysis.

Important inputs:

4.1Importing data: this option allows users to import geometry or mesh data inside hyperform irrespective of the formats, whether it is mesh data - HM, dat or Cad model data or assembly - iges, step etc or connectors-like welding, bolts etc. from other software's.

4.1AImport model: this option directly imports hypermesh binary files.

4.1B Import solver deck: this option import the data saved in the previous simulation, such as the output of Draw-1 can be carried to draw-2 process. With the solver mesh data properties of the draw-1 will also be imported as well.

4.1C Import geometry:this option allows users to import cad geometry inside hyperform irrespective of the common cad formats like iges, step etc.

4.1D Import BOM: Cad files in the form of assemblies of large parts can be carried out from catia, Nx or standard cad formats iges, step are also supported.

4.1E Import connections: Connection setup in other cad or FEA software can be directly imported.

4.2 Remove holes:

4.2A Pin holes: these are the small holes which can be easily removed from the surface to prevent meshing errors.

4.2B Surface fillets: surface fillets are the small surface errors, producing defective mesh as well defective results and can be removed with this command.

4.2C Edge fillets: These are the same kind of defects present on the edges of geometry and can be recovered with this command.

4.2D Duplicate surface: with this command, you can clean up your geometry for any duplicate surfaces and replace with new ones.

4.2E Symmetry: Delete any additional surface beyond the plane, where your body tend to be symmetrical.

4.3 R-Mesh: R-Mesh (Rigid tool surface mesh) allows you to quickly mesh a rigid tool surface by specifying the max length of element, minimum length of element, chordal deviation, and fillet angle.

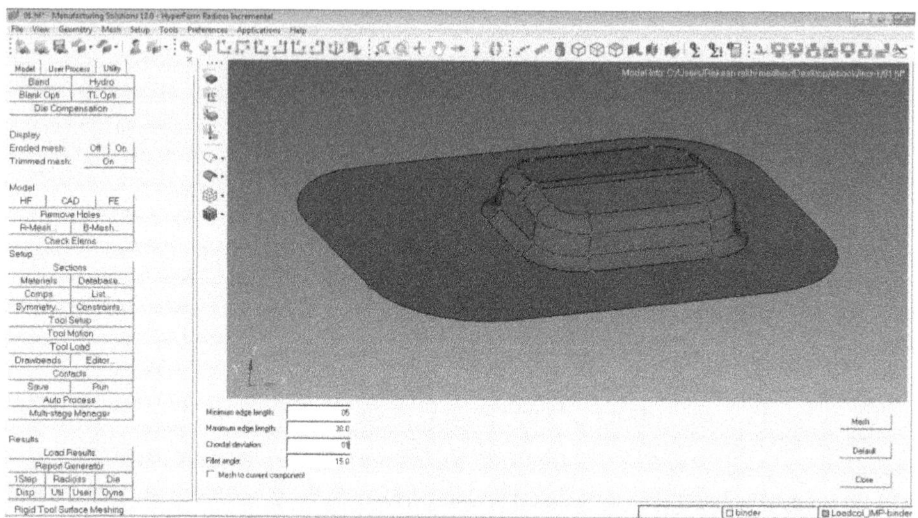

4.4 B-Mesh: -Mesh (Blank surface mesh) allows you to quickly mesh a blank component. You can specify an average edge length and mesh selected surfaces. B-mesh is discussed in incremental analysis tutorials.

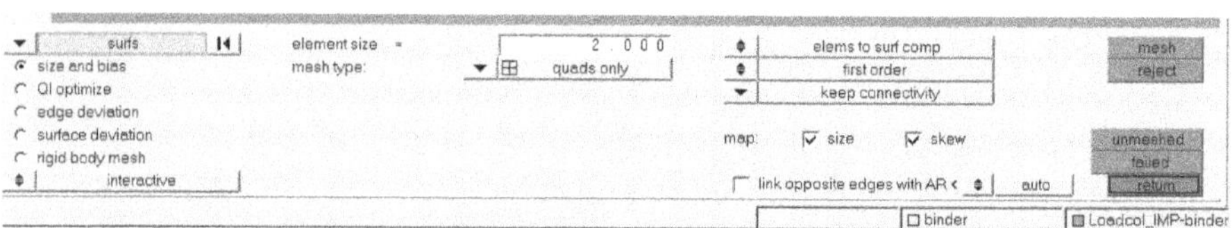

4.5 Assign materials: Material selection is another significant aspect, which can't be ignored. There are many materials are inbuilt, you have to choose the most identical in mechanical properties or you can create your own custom made, but make sure you have the relevant data to feed into the system, otherwise it would get complete.

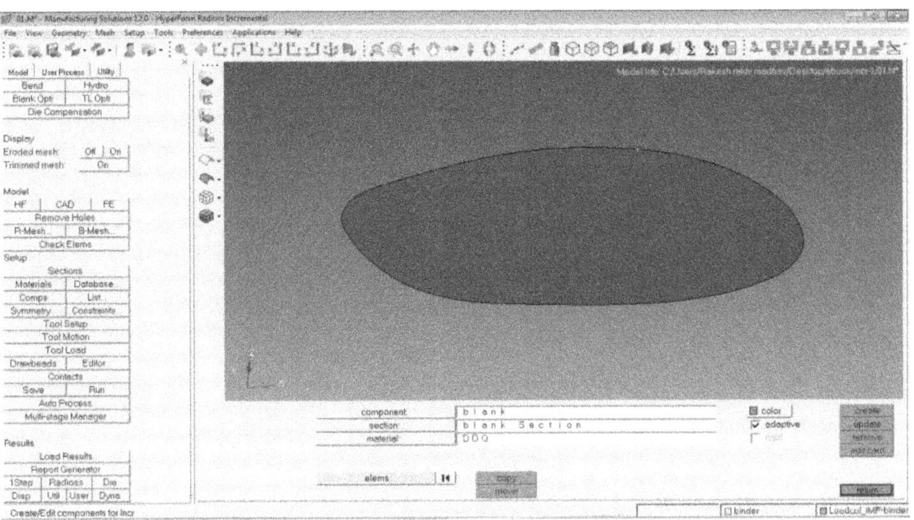

The Materials panel is used to define the materials for the forming simulation. For Incremental_RADIOSS, Hill Orthotropic Tabulated is recommended for steel. For aluminum, 3-parameter Barlat Orthotropic materials is recommended. The same material model must be used for forming and springback. All tools are modeled as elastic.

For LS-DYNA, Transversely Isotropic Elastic Plastic material is recommended for steel. For aluminum, 3-parameter Barlat material is recommended. The same material model must be used for forming and springback. All tools are modeled as rigid.

User defined materials can be saved to the database by clicking the Add to Database button.

4.6 Symmetry: Symmetry planes can be useful for limiting the analysis area of a part that is symmetrical, therefore reducing complexity and computation time.

You can specify symmetry planes on XZ, YZ, or XY planes. You can also define multiple symmetry planes to achieve the desired effect, e.g. XZ + YZ planes to create a quarter-sized model.

4.7 Constraints: The Constraints panel allows you to specify boundary conditions. From the Setup menu, select Constraints to display this panel.

You can use the Constraints panel to reduce run time by analysing only half of a symmetrical model, with material flow, across the plane of symmetry locked.

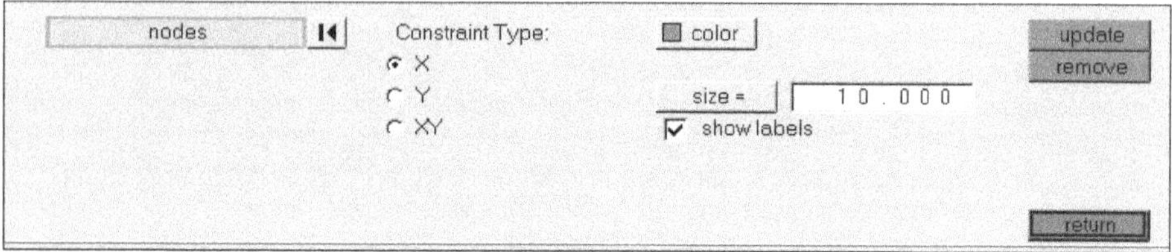

4.8 Tool setup: Automatically creates and positions the tools for stamping analysis. Creating the Punch and binder surface from the die surface, another inputs are sheet thickness and press type- single or double action.Consists of several tool creation and positioning options. Typically, you will be starting with a mesh for the blank and the face of the die. The auto build/setup function automatically creates additional tools by offsetting, creates material definitions, creates contact definitions and auto positions the tools. The tool offset function creates a new mesh component by offsetting elements of another.

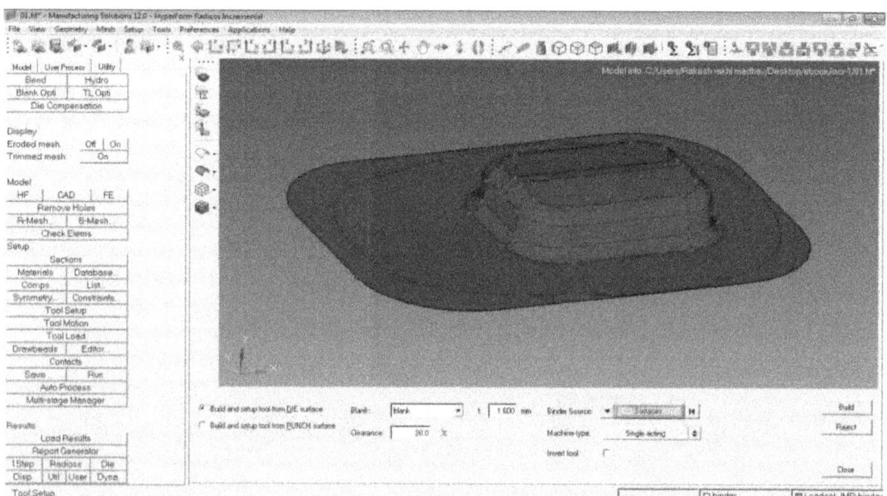

4.9 Tool Motion: Lets you define the tool motion parameters, as well as the solution control and output history parameters. Allows you to prescribe the motion of the tools. It automatically calculates the velocity curve and termination time for a moving tool based on its expected travel and maximum velocity. The history function automatically calculates a time step for a stable and accurate solution and also allows you to prescribe the intervals at which the results are output.

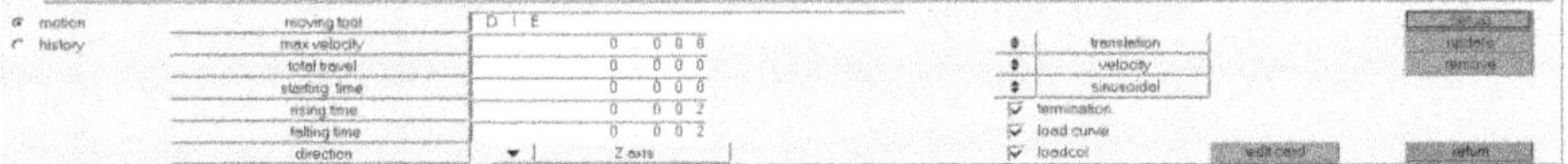

4.10 Tool load: Lets you define the force on a blankholder or pad, and activates a rigid body stopper. Allows you to prescribe a force to a specified rigid tool. It allows you to choose rigid body stoppers to limit the displacement and velocity in order to minimize the inertial effects for the rigid tool under a specified force.

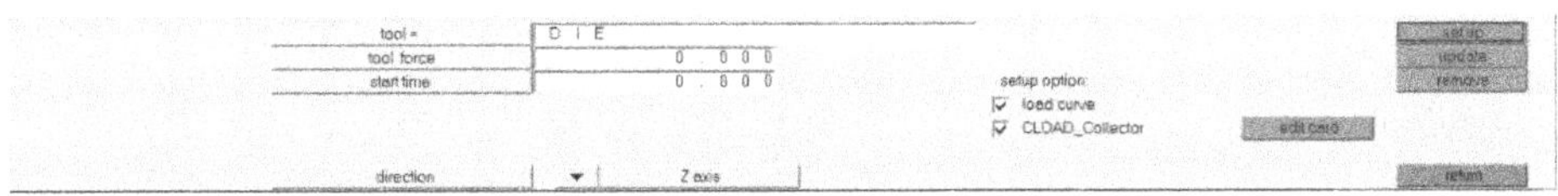

4.11 Drawbeads: Lets you define the drawbeads and the corresponding restraining forces. Either a line or a set of nodes may be used to describe the drawbead location. Option to turn On and Off the Drawbead editor from the Auto Process. Let's you specify two values: 1: Enabled; 0: Disabled. Default value: 1. Allows you to set up analytical drawbeads that create restraining condition during stamping. The inputs for the drawbead forces can either be numbers corresponding to the restraining and closure force or you can just prescribe it as a percent of the locking force. The calculate function computes analytically, the restraining, closure and locking force as well as the geometry that causes locking based on a prescribed drawbead geometry, material properties and friction conditions for the deforming blank.

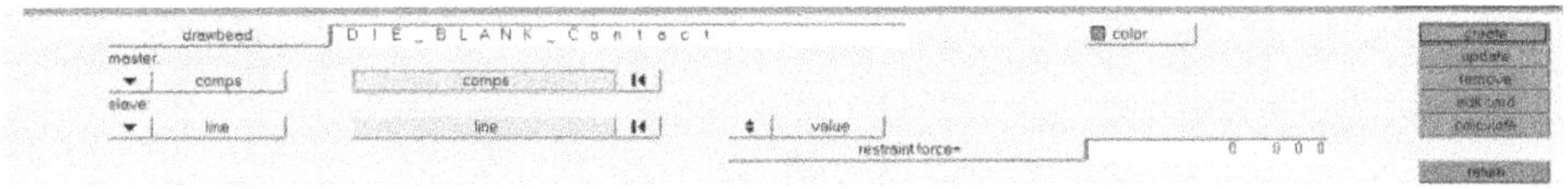

4.12 Contacts:Lets you set up either single or multiple contact definitions between the blank and tools. Applies a contact type between the tool and blank for the RADIOSS solver. Options include Type 21 or Type 7. Default: Type 21. Allows you to set up contact condition between a single pair of components or multiplesets of components.

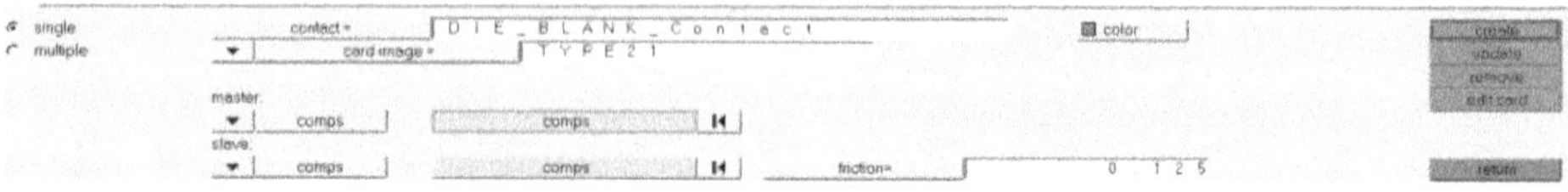

4.13 Save: Saves your file.

4.14 Autoprocess:Provides an easy-to-use setup for various process types. The Auto Process macro prompts you for all necessary parameters for a given analysis type.

The Auto Process option provides an intuitive graphical interface for setting up processes such as single/double action draw, springback, and gravity analyses. The interface includes two tabs: Setup and Details. You can access Auto Process via the Utility menu or Tools > Auto Process.

Auto Process shortcuts are available in the following toolbar:

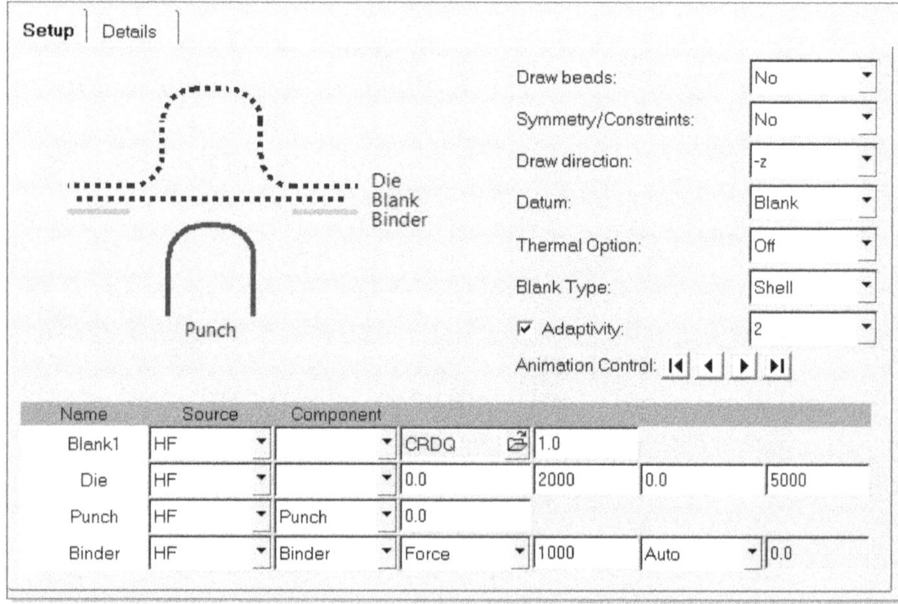

Name	Source		Component					
Blank1	HF			CRDQ	1.0			
Die	HF			0.0	2000	0.0	5000	
Punch	HF		Punch	0.0				
Binder	HF		Binder	Force	1000	Auto	0.0	

Auto Process showing a single action draw setup

Setup Tab

The first step of using the **Auto Process** macro is to select the type of analysis you want to perform from the **Process** field at the top of the dialog. The dialog is customized for the type of process you have selected.

Once an analysis type is selected, you specify the essential input parameters for the analysis in the fields that are available in the dialog. (Details about the specific fields for each analysis type are described in the **How Do I** topics listed below.) Each component of the process is listed in a row consisting of options you can specify. The type of option differs by component type. When you click a component in the table, the labels for the columns change to indicate what type of data you are specifying for that component.

A visual representation of the process setup is shown in the left side of the **Setup** tab. Note that when you have specified a HyperForm component for a process component, the visual representation changes from a dashed-line to a solid color for that component.

Once you have provided the required data, you can click the *Autoposition* button to automatically adjust the position of the assembly parts to achieve an efficient process. You can override some of the settings from the Autoposition feature via the fields on the dialog, such as the clearance value for a punch. Note that every tool is auto positioned with respect to the blank and a positive clearance value corresponds to movement away from the blank.

The default values for the velocities and binder force that appear under **Setup** can by changed by editing the process_defaults.dat file. This file also enables you to vary several other process parameters such as element formulations, number of output states, friction coefficient, etc.

The **Animation Control** buttons makes it possible to visually step through the process to verify that the process motion is correct. Click the arrow buttons to move forward or back through the process.

Finally, click the *Apply* button to save your changes and generate all the settings for your analysis.

The settings.dat file enables you to customize the environment for the **Auto Process** macro. For example, you can set the default process to something you commonly use.

Details Tab

From the **Details** tab of the **Auto Process** macro (shown in the image below), you can review the settings for the complete analysis, and in some cases, make modifications to the values.

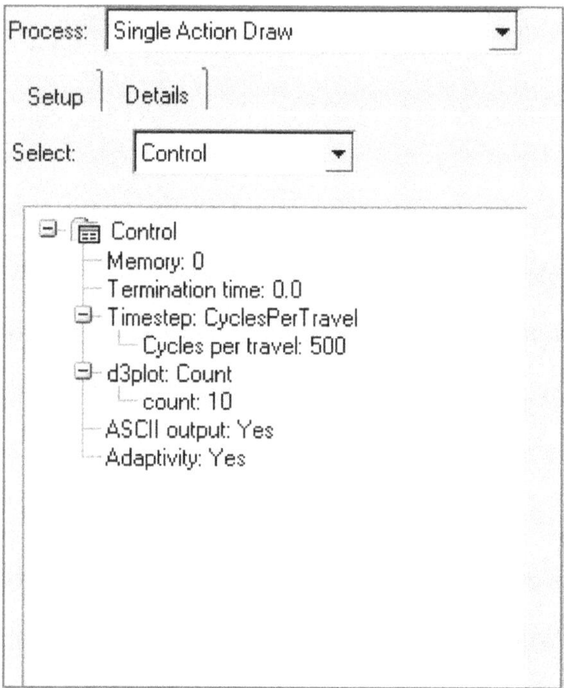

Details tab of the Auto Process macro

In the **Select** field, select a component whose data you want to review or select **All** to see all details at once. The details about various categories of data appear in a tree view in the box below the **Select** field. Information is provided for the following categories: control, summary, blank1, die, punch, binder, tooling, and trim. You can change the amount of displayed information by changing the corresponding parameter in the settings.dat file.

4.15 Multi-stage Manager: Provides a convenient graphical setup for process sequences that include multiple stages of processing. The Multi-Stage Manager also enables you to define the parameters for each process stage.

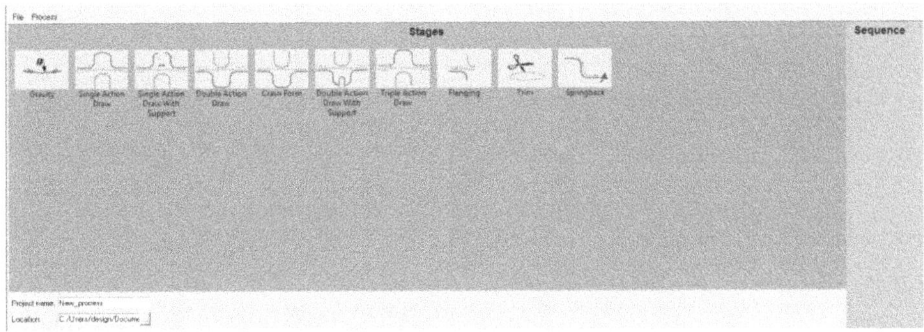

4.16 Run: Launches a Radioss analysis and lets you select the component for which a Radioss output is required during subsequent analysis. From here, you can also get a summary of your model and a preview of the tool motion before launching the analysis. After you have set up the process using the Auto Process macro, you are ready to run the analysis. However, before running the analysis, ensure that you have specified the path to your Radioss executable. Click Run to save the Radioss keyword file and the analysis begins.

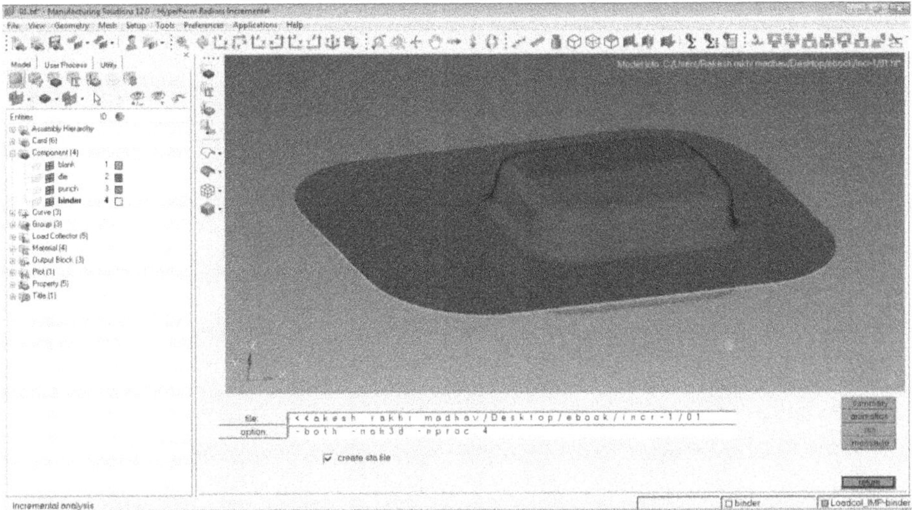

4.17 Load results: Lets you directly launch the post processor

(HyperView) with the results for the current model. Allows you to automatically invoke HyperView for visualizing the results corresponding to the current model. HyperView is a high performance visualization tool with a multitude of features to help review metal forming analysis results.

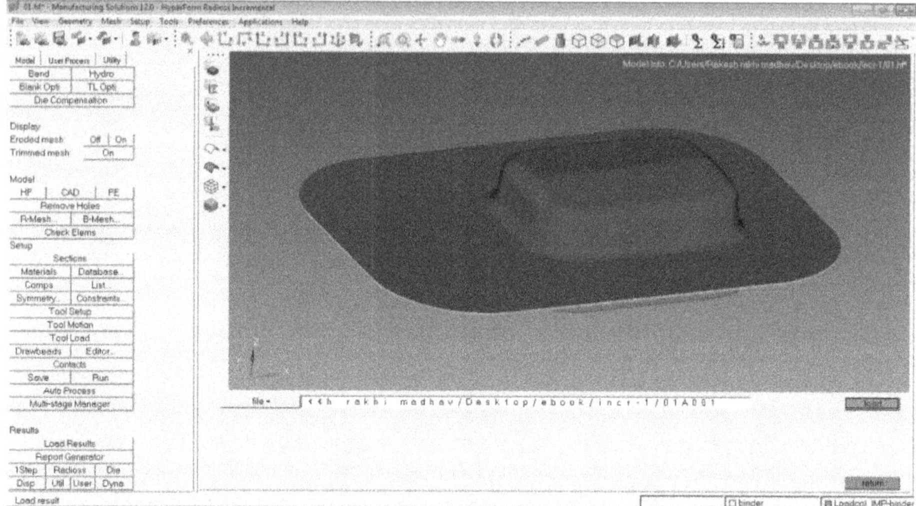

4.18 Report Generator: Creates an HTML-based or PowerPoint presentation containing results from the forming analysis. Choose from among five result types and export as H3D, JPEG, or AVI files.

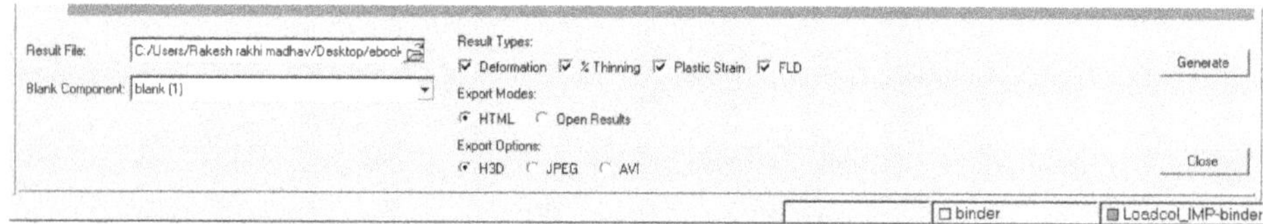

Practice Exercise
Get free video tutorials along with CAD files on Author's website

https://sharmarakesh.co.in/index.php/tutorials/

Password : Forming2025

Practice Exercise :

Incremental Setup procedure for 1st Draw

6.1 Import geometry:

Pick the "1st option" as marked in the below image.

Pick the "2nd option – Import geometry" as marked in the below image.

Pick the "3rd option – iges or step or any supported cad format" as marked in the below image.

Open folder location, marked as "4th" and select ".igs files marked as 5th" followed by open option marked as 6th.

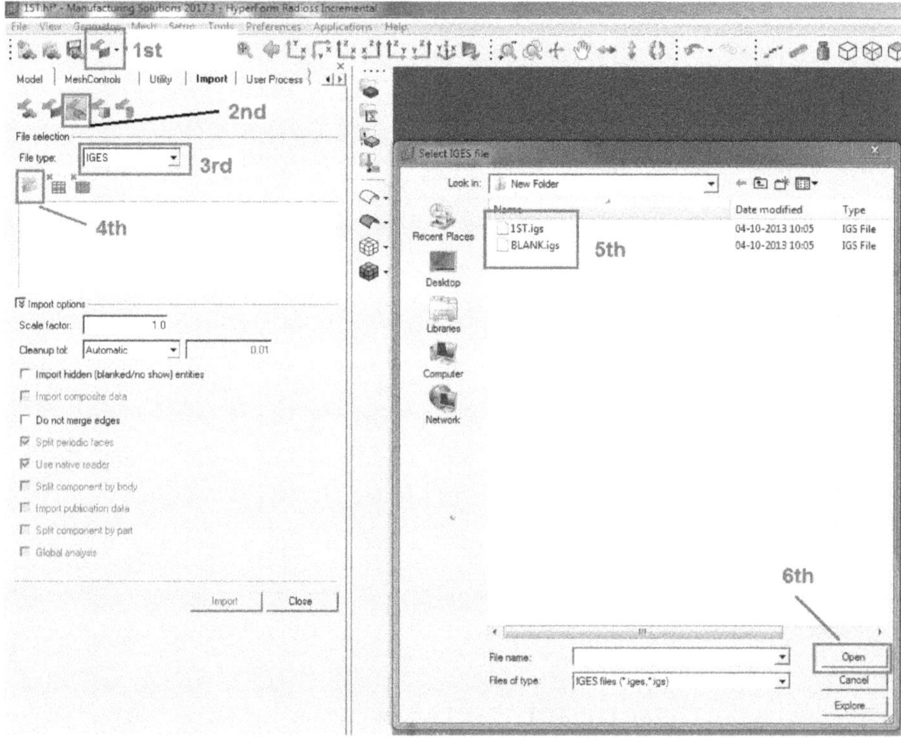

6.2 Blank meshing:

Rename the imported part to "blank as marked 1st" in the below image.

Pick the "1st option – Automesh from the mesh drop down menu" as marked in thebelow image.

Pick the "3rd – surface command"

Pick the blank face – 4th marking

In the 5th marking select the mesh type – Quad only and element size – 12mm. The optimum element size selection is important, as too bigger size may spoil your results and too small may take extremely high solving/running time. As a thumb rule, the max. element size must be equal to min. radius present on the final/die geometry.

By pressing the 6th-mesh option, you are done.

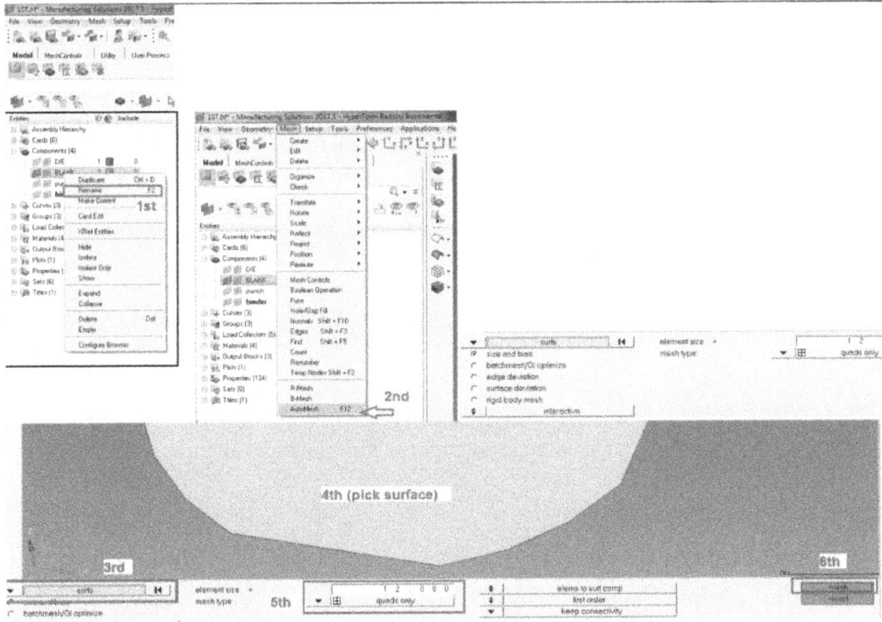

6.3 R mesh:

Rename the imported part as Die – marked as 1st, in the below image.

Select R mesh – 2nd marking and change the value of red marked as shown-3rd marking.

Select mesh-4th marking and the pop up command "Surface-5th marking" will appear followed by selection pick option as "displayed part-6th marking". Part colour will turn white after selection, pick proceed-7th marking.

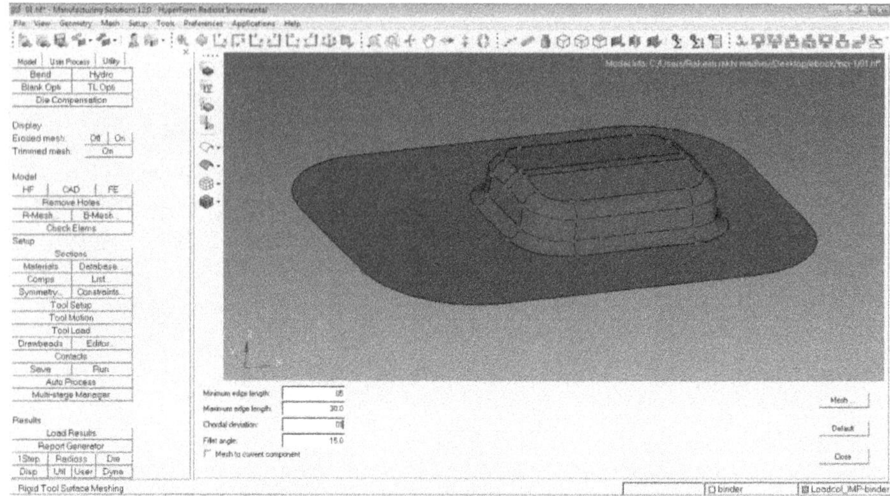

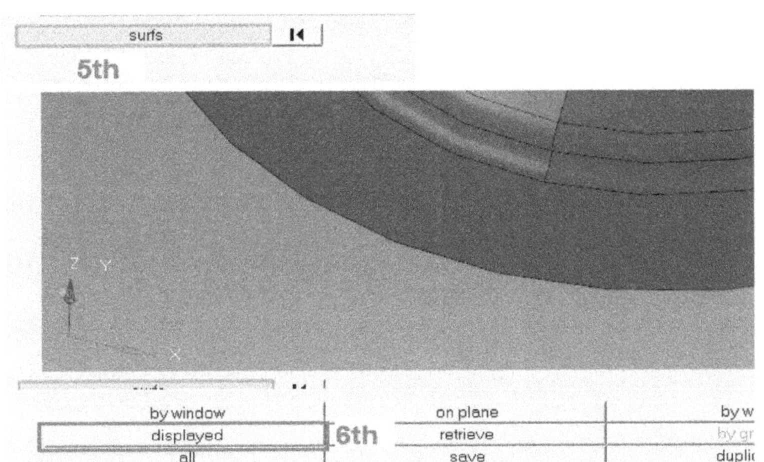

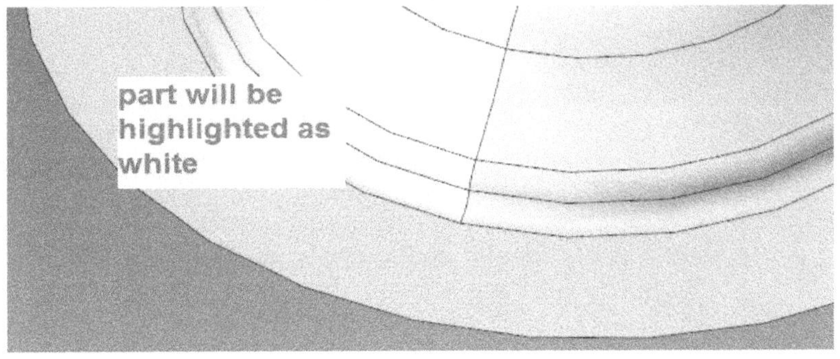

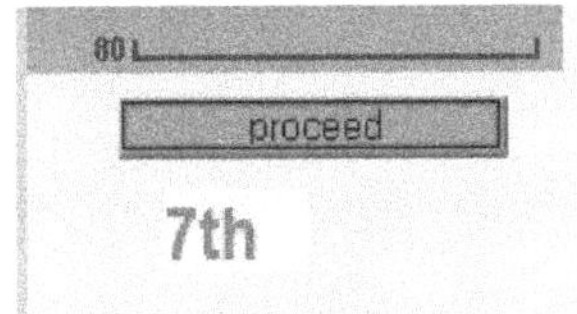

6.4 Tool setup:

Select Tool setup – 1st marking

Pick blank thickness – 2nd marking

In the 3rd marking – select press type-single or double acting (the geometry or die working will change with change in press type) and select the surface.

After picking the surface option, the "element-4th" window will appear, after picking it, next step is selection of "geometry option-5th marking".

Pick the surface option-6th marking and pick the marked face-7th. Then pick the 8th- Add to selection and press proceed-9th marking.

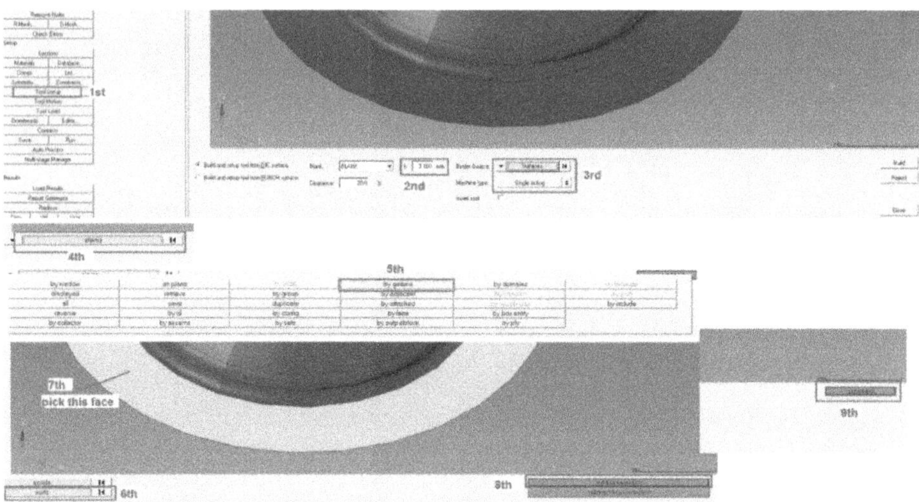

6.5 Material database: Pick the database command and select the appropriate equivalent grade from inbuilt library.

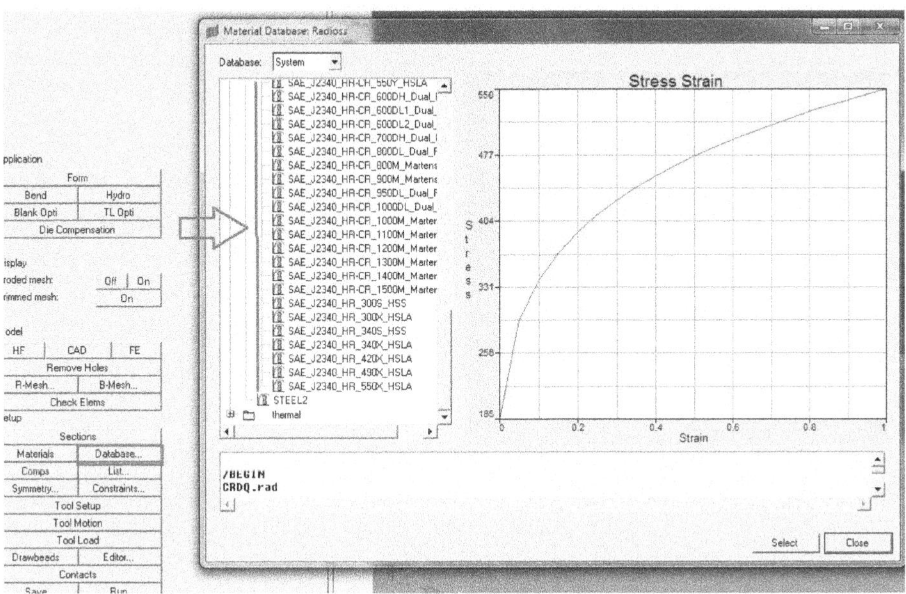

6.6 Autoprocess:

Pick the autoprocess-1st marking.

Pick the ''gap-2nd'' option under binder part.

Press autoposition-3rd and apply-4th marking, then close the tab.

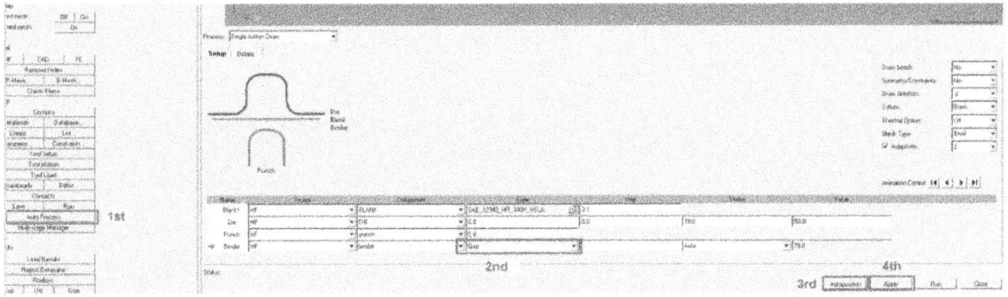

6.7 Save file: Saving the data at desired location with the proper name.
Leave no gap in the name, it may create some errors.

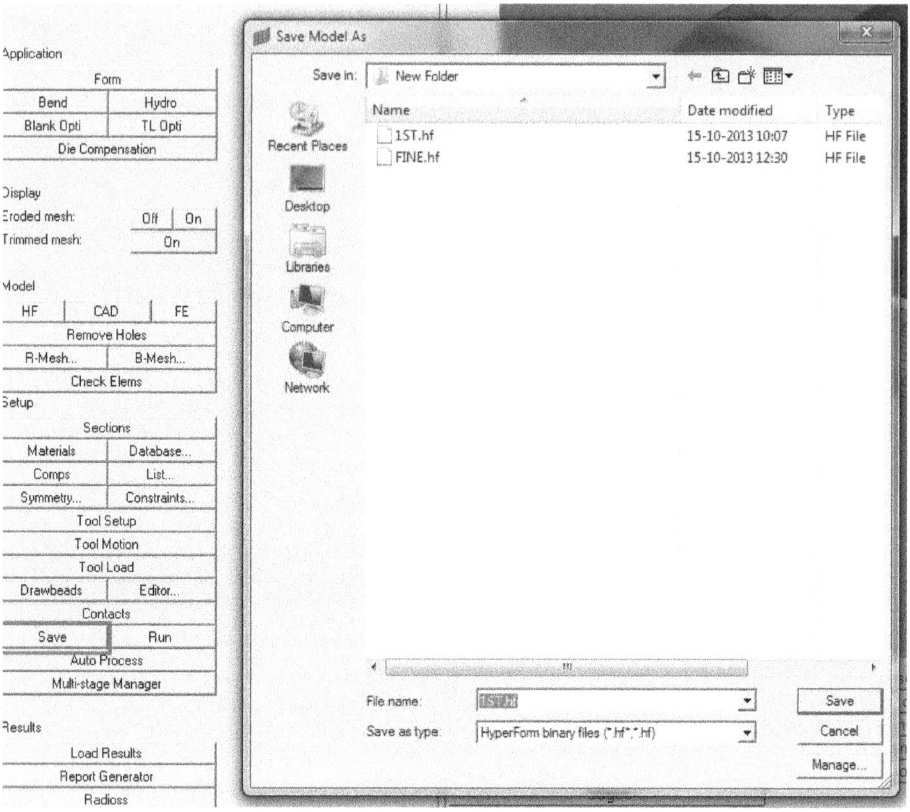

6.8 Run file: Select the shown option with the same settings to run the project.

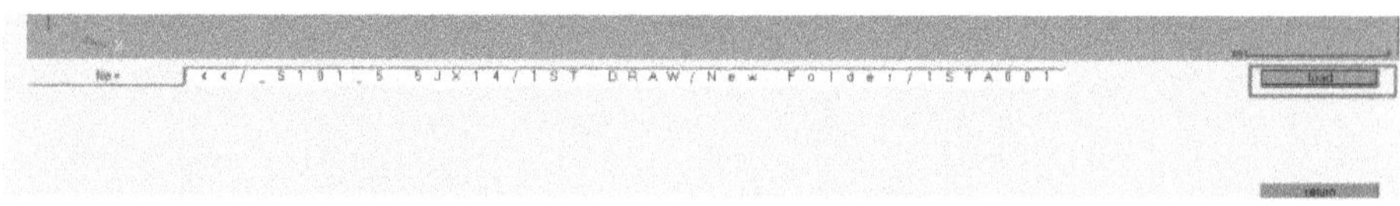

6.9 Load results: Pick below option with automatically taken path, press load will direct you to the other window in hyper view.

6.10 Prepare for results:

Hide all the parts, except blank- 1st marking.

Select the FLD option and put the n value (from material supplier or material database) and blank thickness – 2nd marking under FLC.

Under FLD select the mid surface-3rd marking.

Under component, select displayed option-4th marking.

Click apply- 5th marking.

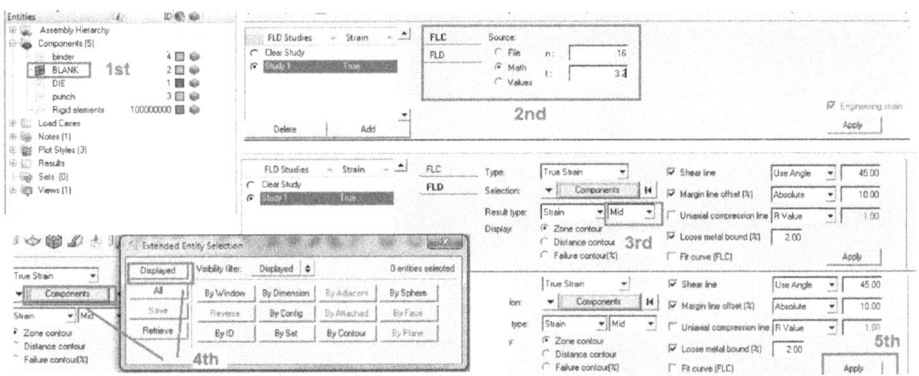

6.11 Animation control: Select the marked tab for animation control, as shown in the below image.

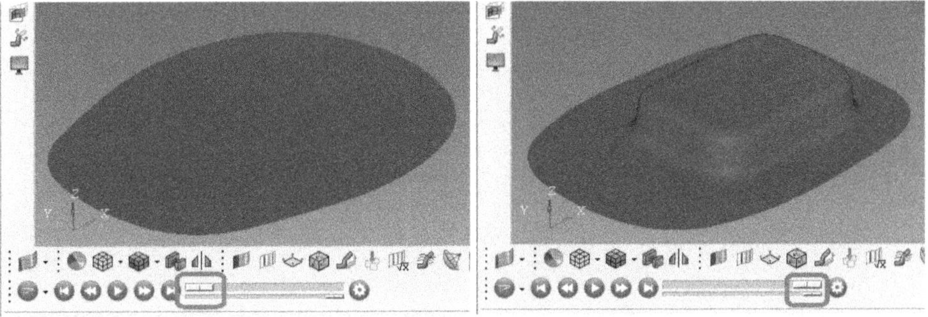

6.12 Thinning contour plot:

Select the contour option-1st and select thinning-2nd marking, from the drop down menu.

Under component selection-3rd marking, select displayed option-4th marking and then apply-5th marking.

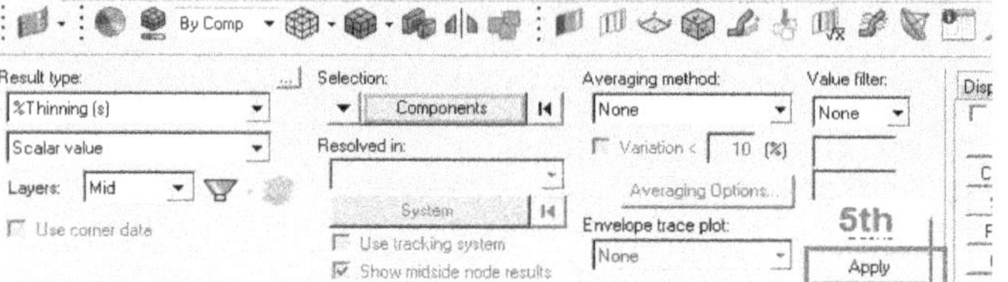

6.13 To edit the precision:

Select edit ''legend-1st marking''

Pick the shown settings – 2nd marking and click apply-3rd marking.

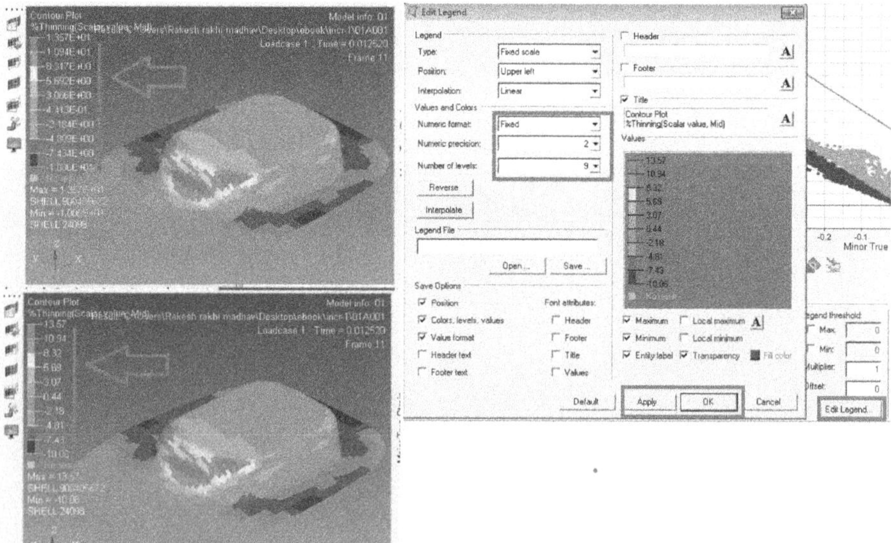

Practice Exercise

Get free video tutorials along with CAD files on Author's website

https://sharmarakesh.co.in/index.php/tutorials/

Password : Forming2025

Incremental Setup procedure for 2ND Draw

7.1 Importing and renaming the die: The importing and renaming the die is same as we did in the earlier stage of Draw-1. The R-mesh is also same as mentioned in the in earlier stage.

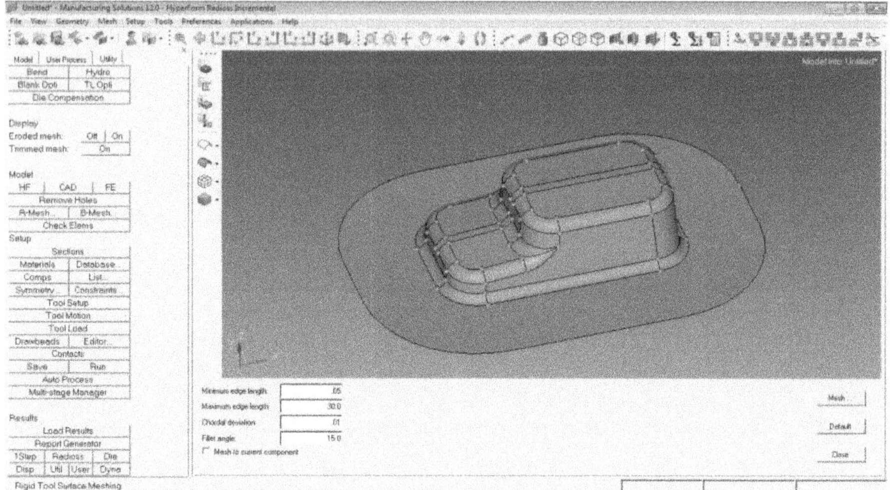

7.2 Importing blank data: The blank in this case is the solver deck data, as we did in the draw1 stage.

Import solver deck data-1st marking.

Open the file from the selected folder- 2nd and 3rd marking, the ''.sta'' file is supported here.

Pick import option-4th marking.

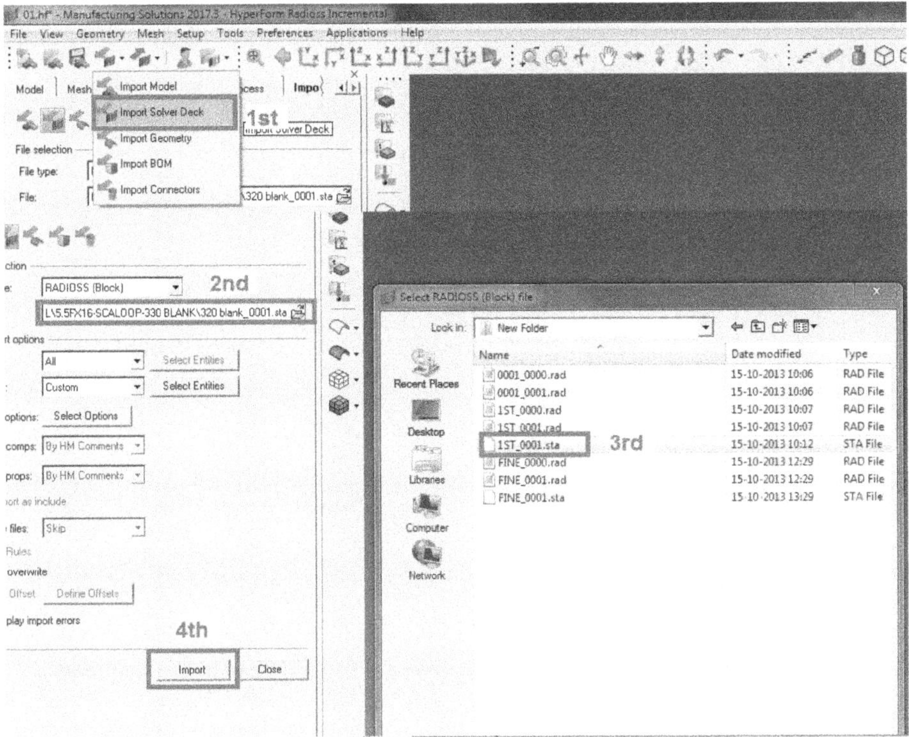

7.3 Tool setup:

Select Tool setup – 1st marking

Pick blank thickness – 2nd marking

In the 3rd marking – select press type-single or double acting (the geometry or die working will change with change in press type) and select the surface.

After picking the surface option, the "element-4th" window will appear, after picking it, next step is selection of "geometry option-5th marking".

Pick the surface option-6th marking and pick the marked face-7th. Then pick the 8th- Add to selection and press proceed-9th marking.

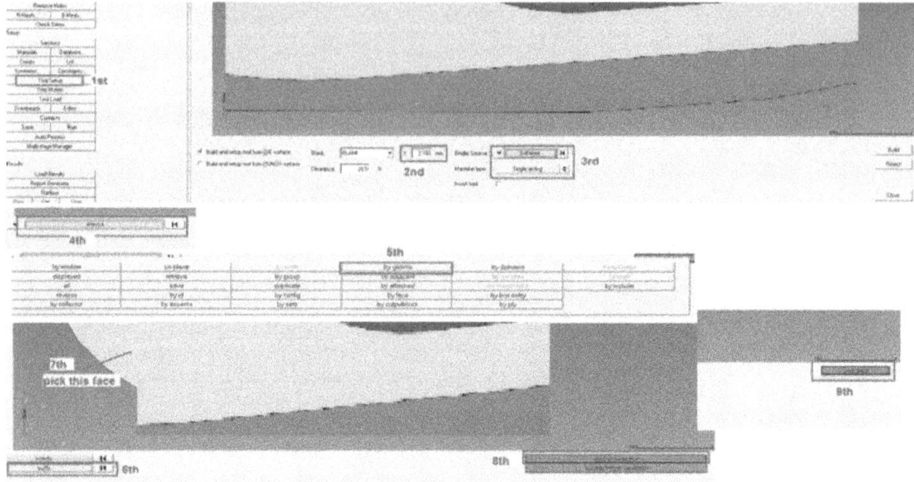

7.4 Material database: Pick the database command and select the appropriate equivalent grade from inbuilt library.

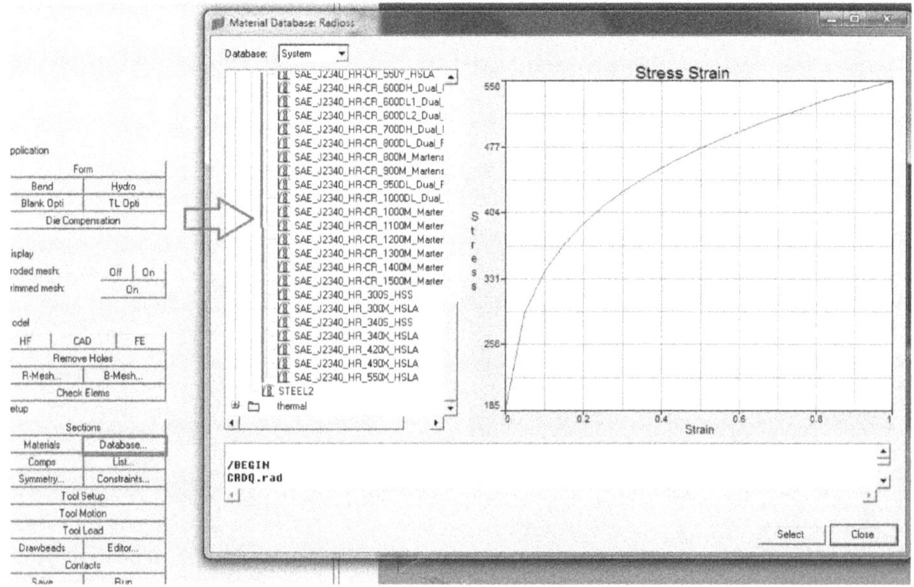

7.5 Autoprocess:

Pick the autoprocess-1st marking.

Pick the ''gap-2nd'' option under binder part.

Press autoposition-3rd and apply-4th marking, then close the tab.

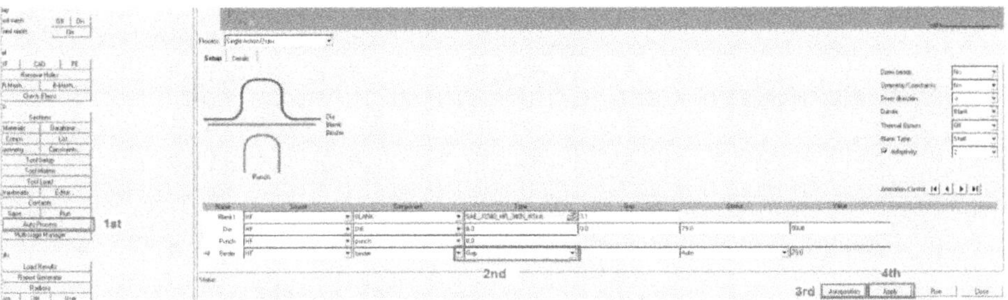

7.6 Save file: Saving the data at desired location with the proper name. Leave no gap in the name, it may create some errors.

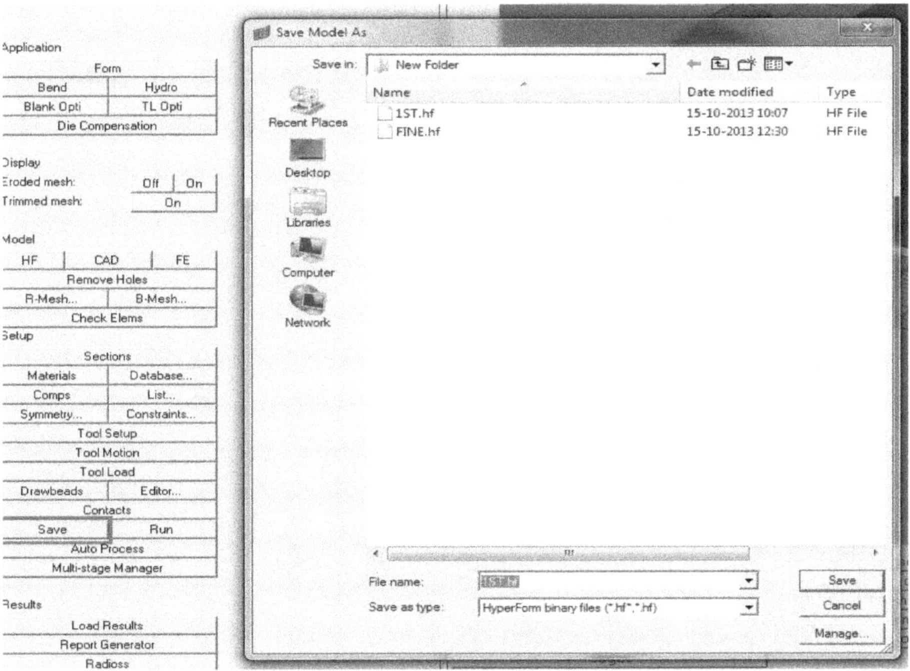

7.7 Run file: Select the shown option with the same settings to run the project.

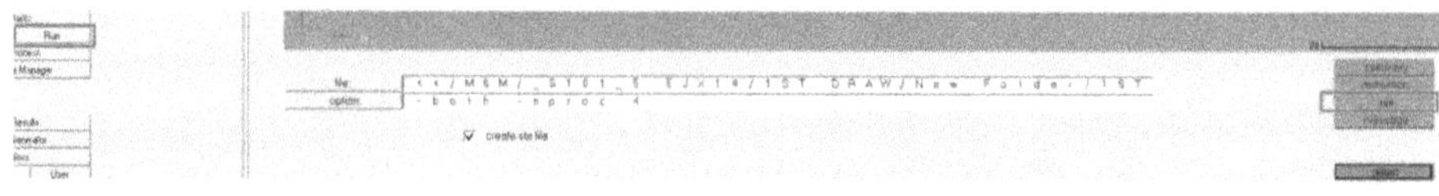

Load results: Pick below option with automatically taken path, press load will direct you to the other window in hyper view.

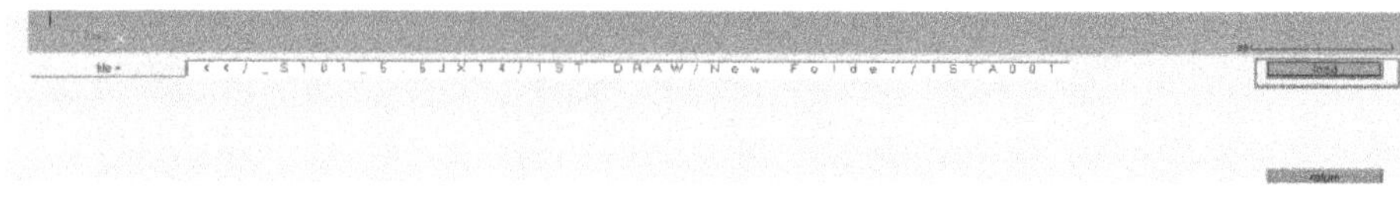

7.8 Prepare for results:

Hide all the parts, except blank- 1st marking.

Select the FLD option and put the n value (from material supplier or material database) and blank thickness – 2nd marking under FLC.

Under FLD select the mid surface-3rd marking.

Under component, select displayed option-4th marking.

Click apply- 5th marking.

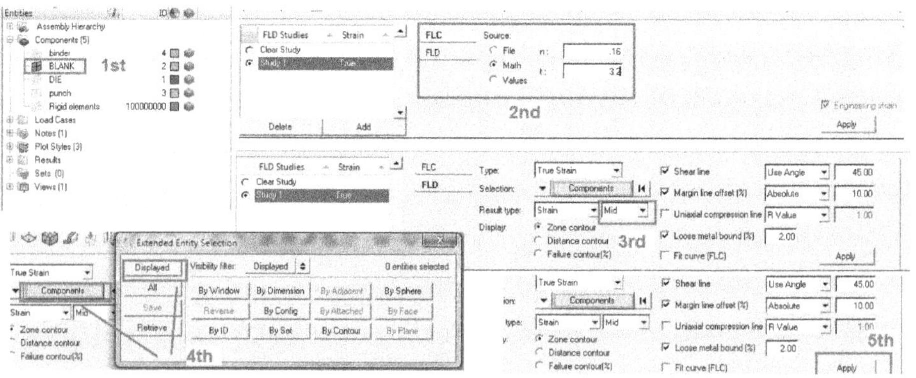

7.9 Animation control: Select the marked tab for animation control, as shown in the below image.

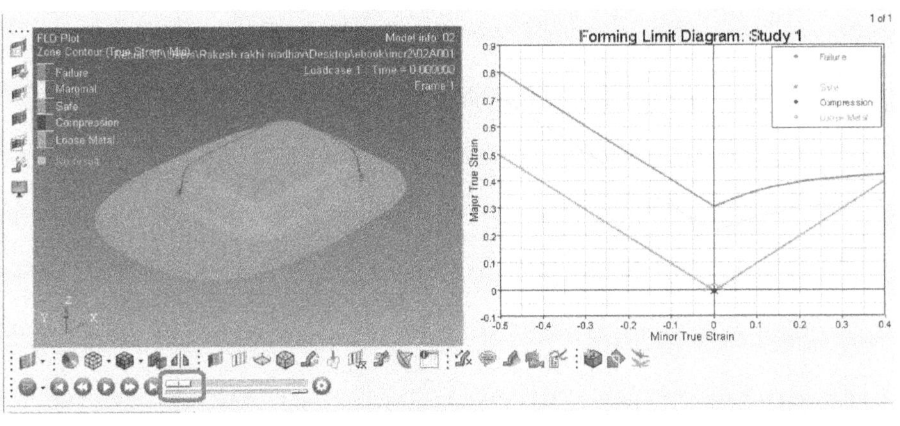

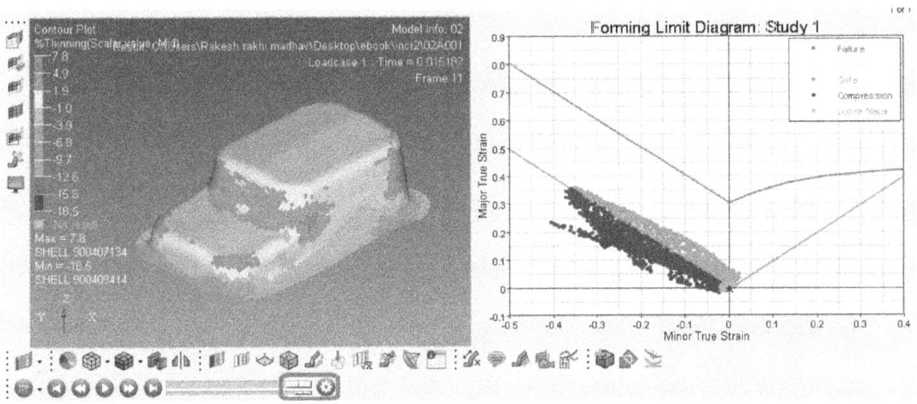

7.10 Thinning contour plot:

Select the contour option-1st and select thinning-2nd marking, from the drop down menu.

Under component selection-3rd marking, select displayed option-4th marking and then apply-5th marking.

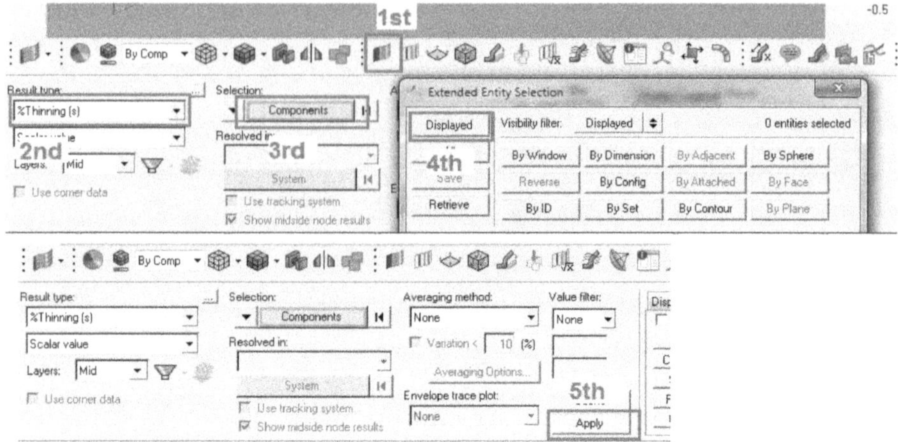

7.11 To edit the precision:

Select edit "legend-1st marking"

Pick the shown settings – 2nd marking and click apply-3rd marking.

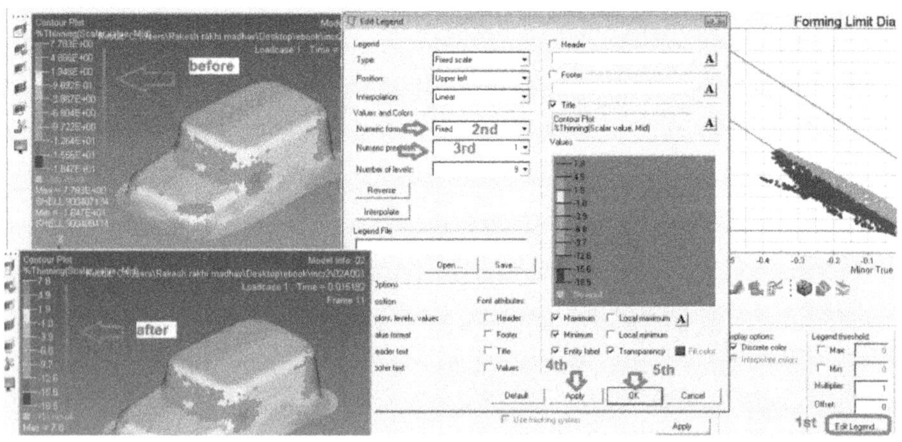

8. Post Processing

What is post processing in incremental forming analysis

In incremental forming analysis, post-processing refers to the phase of analysis that occurs after the incremental forming process has been completed. Incremental forming is a manufacturing technique used to shape sheet metal into complex geometries through a series of small, localized deformations. This process is often simulated using computational methods such as finite element analysis (FEA) to predict the behavior of the material during forming.

Post-processing in incremental forming analysis involves analyzing the results obtained from the simulation to extract meaningful insights and evaluate the quality of the formed part. This phase is crucial for understanding the performance of the manufactured component and optimizing the forming process for future iterations. Here are some key aspects of post-processing in incremental forming analysis:

1. **Deformation Analysis**: One of the primary objectives of post-processing is to analyze the deformation patterns in the formed part. This includes examining factors such as thinning, wrinkling, and material flow to assess the quality of the formed geometry. Visualization tools and techniques are often used to identify regions of interest and understand the distribution of deformation across the part.

2. **Stress and Strain Evaluation**: Post-processing involves analyzing the stress and strain distributions within the material during forming. This helps identify areas of high stress concentration or potential failure, allowing designers to optimize the forming parameters to minimize these issues. Understanding the material behavior under different loading conditions is essential for ensuring the structural integrity of the formed part.

3. **Springback Prediction**: Springback refers to the tendency of a formed part to return to its original shape after the forming process is complete. Post-processing techniques are used to predict the amount of springback expected in the formed component. This information is valuable for designing compensatory measures to achieve the desired final geometry accurately.

4. **Tool Path Optimization**: Post-processing analysis can also be used to optimize the tool path strategy for incremental forming. By analyzing the material flow and deformation characteristics, engineers can fine-tune the tool path parameters to minimize forming defects and improve the overall efficiency of the process.

5. **Validation and Iteration**: Post-processing serves as a validation step to compare the simulated results with experimental data obtained from physical forming tests. Discrepancies between the simulation and actual forming behavior are analyzed to refine the computational model and improve its accuracy for future simulations.

In conclusion, post-processing in incremental forming analysis plays a vital role in evaluating the quality of formed parts, predicting material behavior, and optimizing the forming process. By leveraging computational tools and techniques, engineers can gain valuable insights into the forming process and make informed decisions to enhance manufacturing efficiency and product quality.

Use of post processing in Incremental forming analysis

Post-processing in incremental forming analysis serves as a critical step in extracting valuable insights and optimizing the manufacturing process. This phase encompasses various techniques and methodologies aimed at enhancing the understanding of the formed part's behavior and improving the efficiency of the forming process.

Firstly, post-processing is instrumental in analyzing the deformation characteristics of the formed component. By examining factors such as thinning, wrinkling, and material flow patterns, engineers can gain valuable insights into the quality of the formed geometry. Visualization tools allow for the identification of potential defects or areas of concern, enabling engineers to make informed decisions to optimize the forming parameters.

Moreover, post-processing involves evaluating the stress and strain distributions within the material during forming. Understanding the mechanical behavior of the material under different loading conditions is crucial for ensuring the structural integrity of the formed part. By analyzing stress concentrations and potential failure points, engineers can optimize the forming parameters to minimize the risk of defects and ensure the reliability of the final product.

Additionally, post-processing techniques are used to predict springback, which is essential for achieving the desired final geometry accurately. By simulating the relaxation of stresses after forming, engineers can anticipate the amount of springback expected and implement compensatory measures to achieve the desired dimensional accuracy.

Furthermore, post-processing plays a pivotal role in optimizing the tool path strategy for incremental forming. Analyzing material flow and deformation characteristics allows engineers to fine-tune the tool path parameters to minimize forming defects and improve process efficiency. By optimizing the tool path, manufacturers can reduce production time and costs while enhancing the overall quality of the formed parts.

Finally, post-processing serves as a validation step by comparing simulated results with experimental data obtained from physical forming tests. Discrepancies between simulation and actual forming behavior are analyzed to refine the computational model and improve its accuracy for future simulations.

In essence, post-processing in incremental forming analysis is essential for evaluating the quality of formed parts, predicting material behavior, optimizing the forming process, and validating computational models. By leveraging post-processing techniques, engineers can enhance manufacturing efficiency, minimize defects, and ensure the production of high-quality components.

Practice Exercise

Get free video tutorials along with CAD files on Author's website

https://sharmarakesh.co.in/index.php/tutorials/

Password : Forming2025

<u>View results in Hyperview:</u>

5.1 Loadresults: Lets you directly launch the post processor (HyperView) with the results for the current model. Allows you to automatically invoke HyperView for visualizing the results.

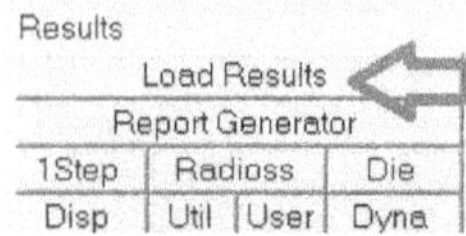

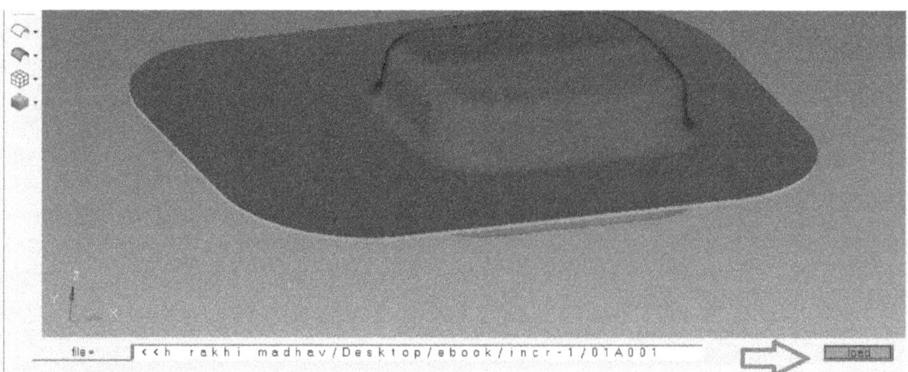

5.2 Show/hide parts: This option available on the left panel will allow you to show hide parts.

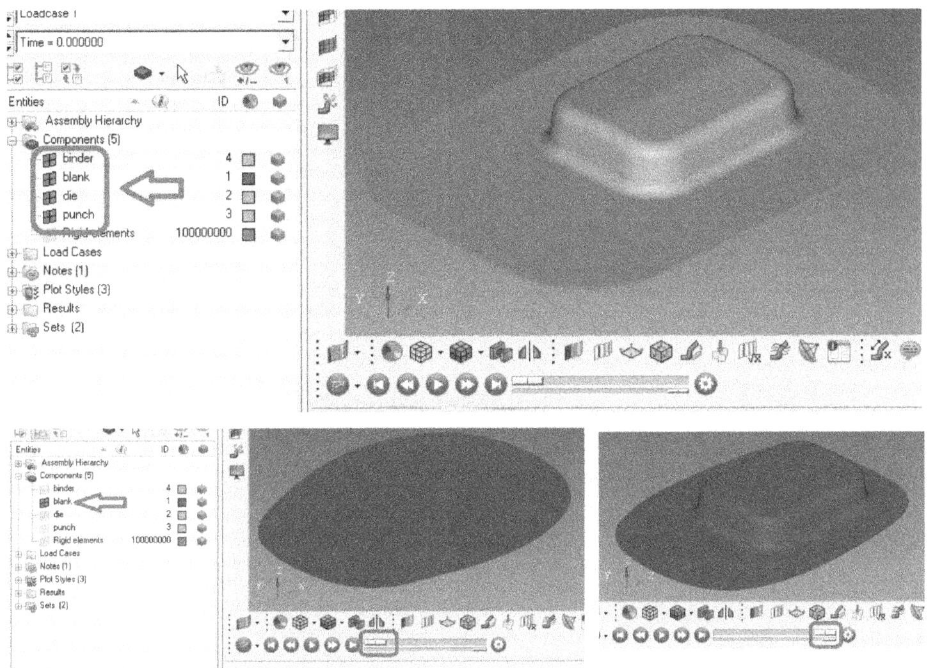

5.3 Adding FLD: The FLD panel allows you to a plot a Forming Limit Diagram (FLD) based on a material Forming Limit Curve (FLC) and the major and minor strain output results of a forming simulation. To access the panel, click the FLD icon on the Tools toolbar, or select FLD from the Tools menu.

An FLD study consists of the HyperView and HyperGraph windows related to an FLC, FLD, and contour plot. Studies belonging to the current session are listed in the FLD Studies box along with the study type (Engineering or True).

Enter n value (from material supplier or database) and t (thickness).

5.3A Type of FLD curve: Select Engineering or true strain to select a type of FLD curve. Allows you to define the metric for the FLD as True strain or Engineering Strain. By default, it is assigned the metric of the input FLC curve, however you can change the type at any instance by clicking Apply (the metric of FLD will then be updated along with data points and the FLC curve to the corresponding metric).

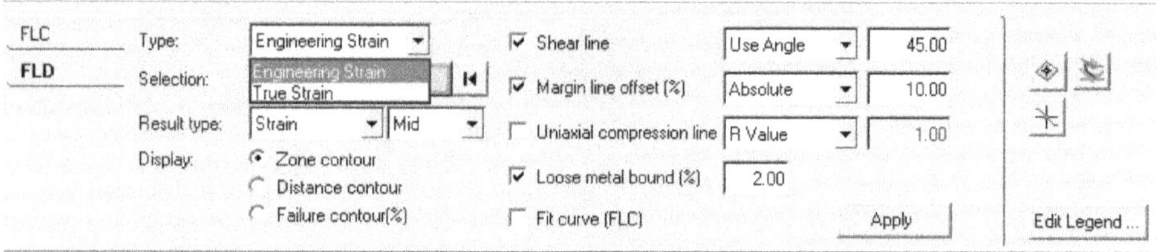

5.3B Selection: Before plotting an FLD, you must pick one or more components from the model. You can do this by picking entities directly from the screen, using the quick window selection.

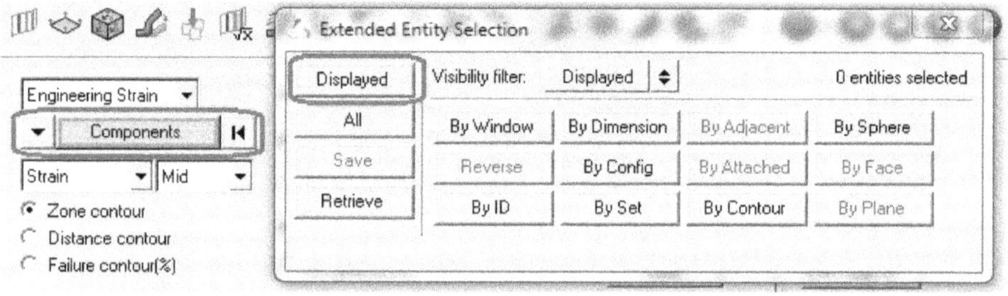

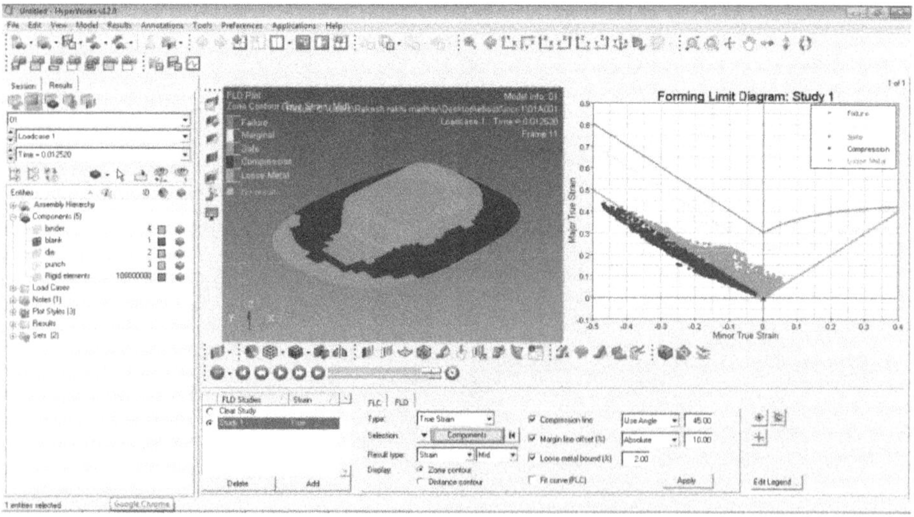

5.3C Result type: The Result type section selects Strain as the result data type that is used to plot the FLD. The second drop-down menu in the Result type section allows you to select the layer at which the FLD is being created. Here we will select, midsurface, as we are working on that. Wrong selection would project wrong results. Leave all other values like shear line, margin line offset, loose metal bound, as it is in the default position.

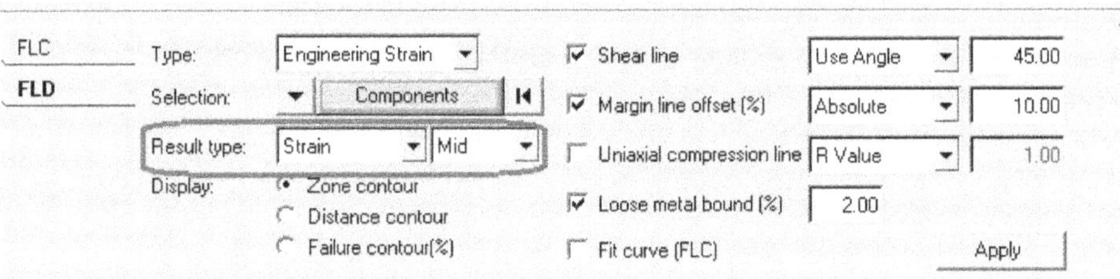

5.4 Thinning: Excessive Stretching in the vertical wall due to high tensile stresses cause thickness reduction specifically on the small radius in the metal parts. The image highlights the thinning portions, however up to 20% thinning is allowed due to process limitations.

5.4A Contour panel: The Contour panel allows you to create contour plots of a model and graphically visualize the analysis results.

To access the Contour panel, click on the Contour button on the Results toolbar, or select Plot > Contour from the Results menu.

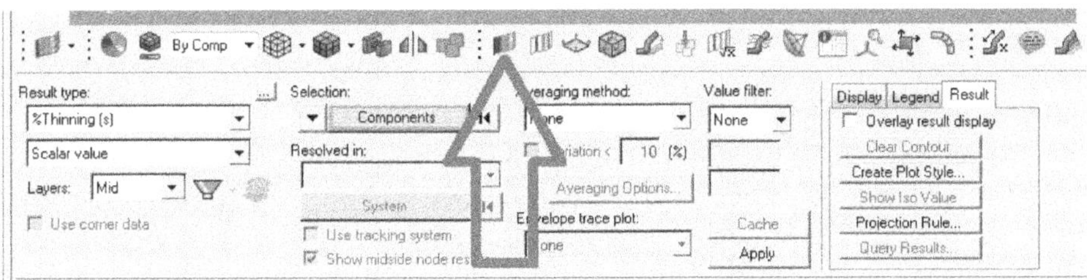

5.4B Result type: Select thinning from the drop down menu.

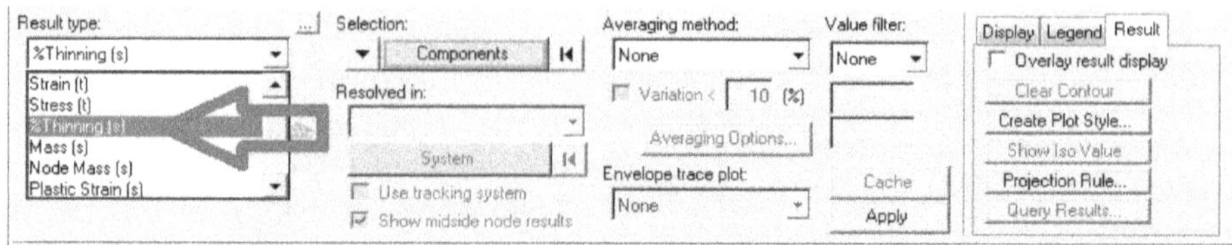

5.4C Selection: Before plotting the results, you must pick one or more components from the model. You can do this by picking entities directly from the screen, using the quick window selection.

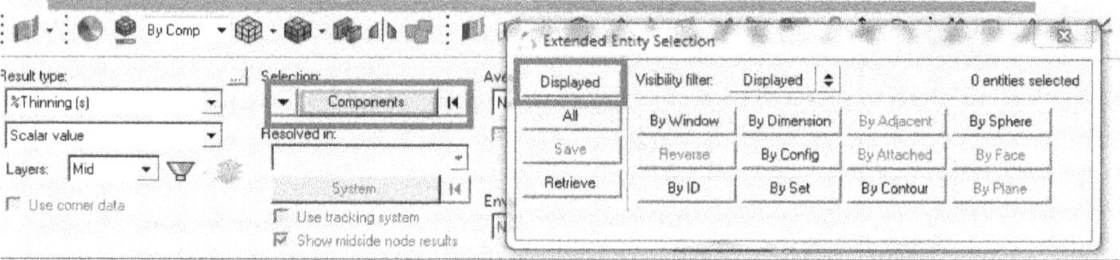

5.4E Applying the settings: Apply the settings as shown, keep all other options as default.

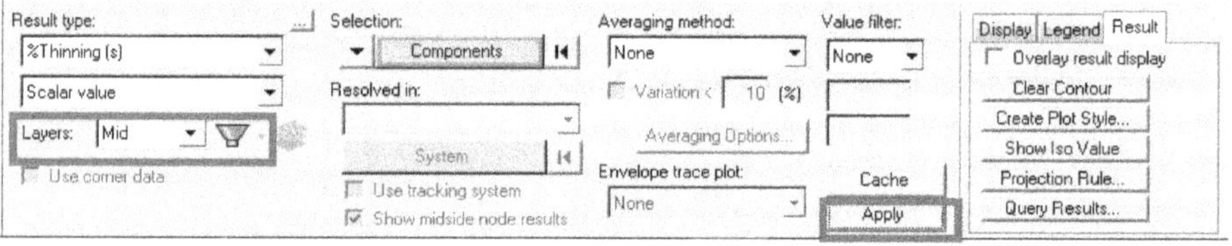

5.4F Changing the scale values: Right click the scale, as shown. Pick "Edit legend" and the control box will appear, then change the values as shown and precision is how many decimal places, you need for the thinning values and Click apply.

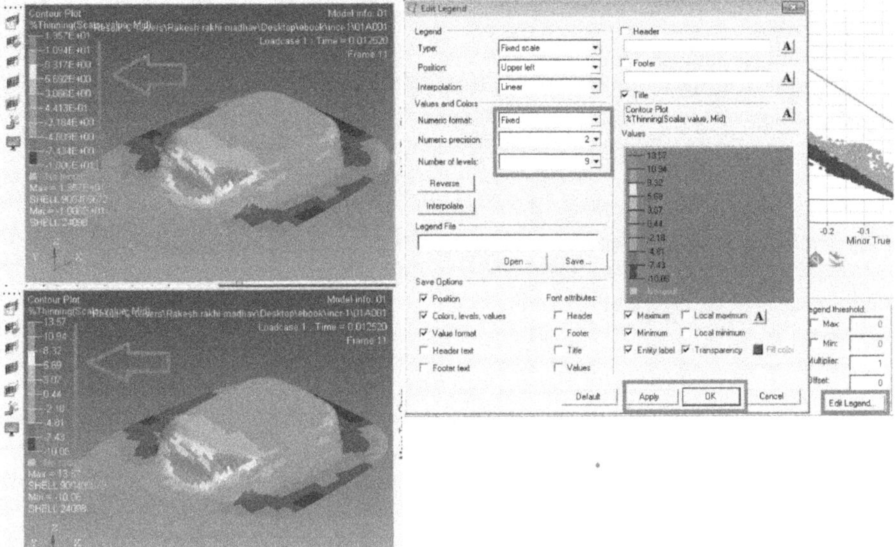

5.4G View results: The color coded contour plot is showing the thinning areas (Red) and thickening areas (blue), the % values are marked on the scale.

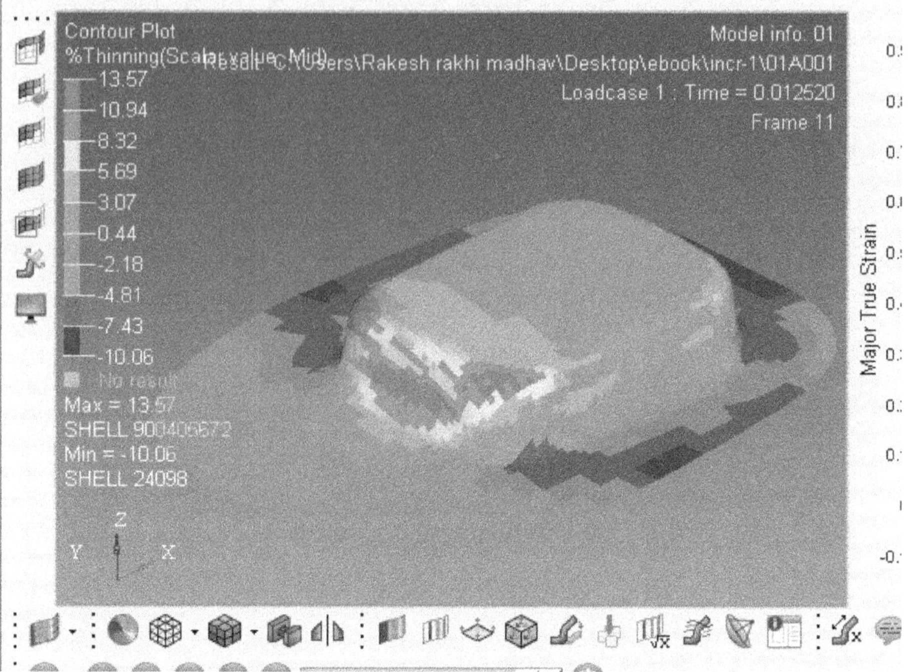

5.5 Animation control: with this control you can shape formed in each step, it can be played automatically or manually.

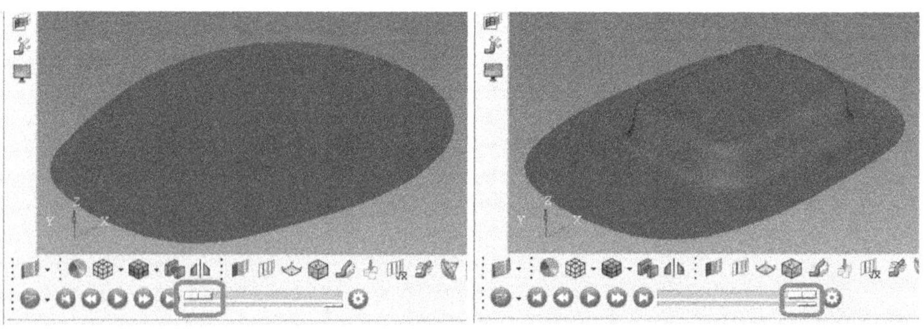

5.6Elemental contour: Elemental contour will facilitate to visualize the thinning at local regions.

Select the "measure" option, elemental contour from the drop down menu and the value will appear after selecting the element as shown.

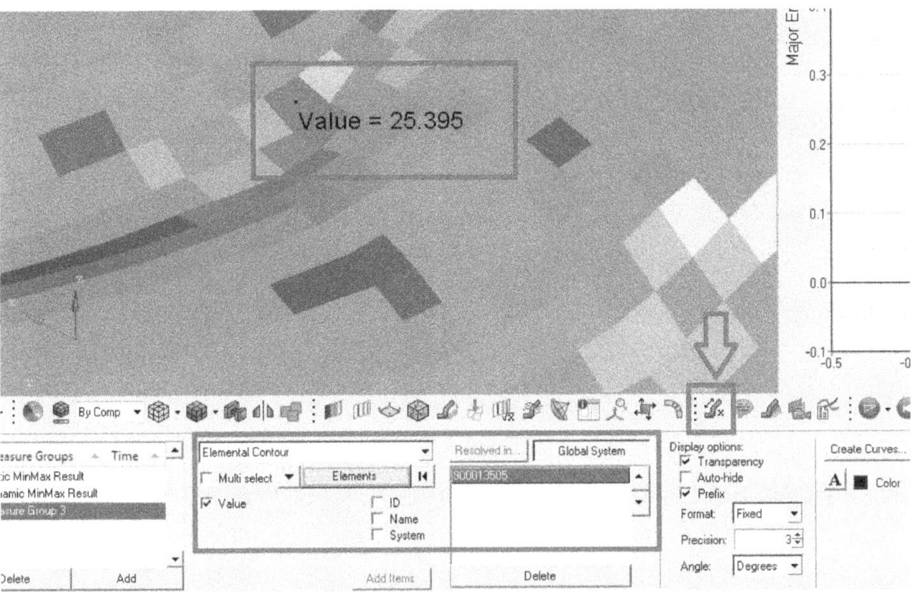

You can also edit the test colour, type and size from the "edit text" option as shown.

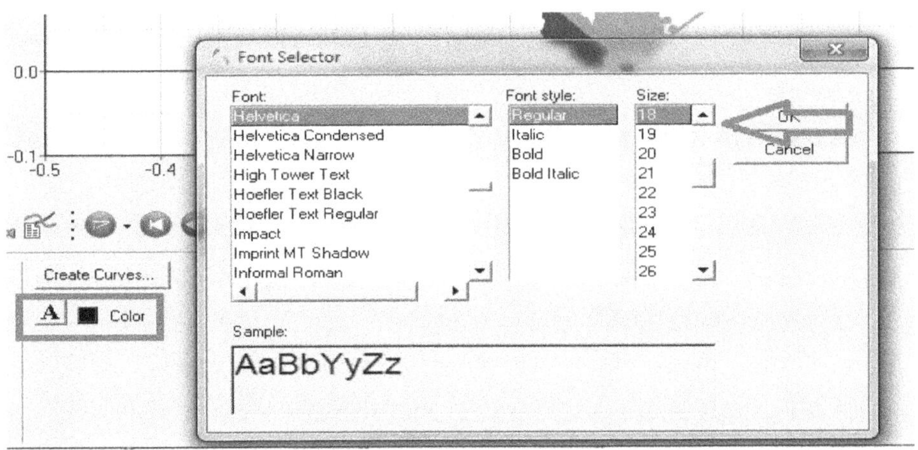

9. Calculate the Draw force

What are the forces acting during forming a sheet metal

During the process of forming sheet metal, various forces come into play, shaping the material into the desired geometry. These forces are essential for achieving the desired deformation while ensuring the structural integrity of the formed part. Here are the primary forces involved in sheet metal forming:

1. **Forming Force**: The forming force is the primary force applied to deform the sheet metal into the desired shape. It is typically exerted by a forming tool, such as a punch or die, and acts to stretch, bend, or compress the material. The magnitude and distribution of the forming force depend on factors such as the material properties, thickness, and geometry of the part being formed.

2. **Blank holding Force**: In many sheet metal forming processes, a blankholder is used to hold the sheet in place and prevent it from wrinkling or folding during deformation. The blankholder force applies pressure to the periphery of the sheet, ensuring uniform deformation and maintaining contact between the sheet and the forming tool. Adjusting the blankholder force is crucial for controlling material flow and preventing defects such as wrinkles or tears.

3. **Frictional Force**: Friction between the sheet metal and the forming tool surfaces influences the deformation process significantly. Frictional force opposes the motion of the sheet metal relative to the forming tool and affects the distribution of stress and strain during forming. Proper lubrication or surface treatments are often employed to reduce friction and improve material flow, minimizing the risk of defects such as galling or scoring.

4. **Bending Force**: In processes involving bending or folding of the sheet metal, a bending force is applied to induce plastic deformation and shape the material around a bending radius. This force acts

perpendicular to the surface of the sheet, causing it to bend or flex according to the desired geometry. The magnitude of the bending force depends on factors such as the material properties, thickness, and bend radius.

5. **Tensile Force**: Tensile forces arise in regions of the sheet metal subjected to stretching or elongation during forming. These forces act to pull the material apart along its longitudinal axis, causing it to thin and elongate. Managing tensile forces is essential for controlling material flow and preventing defects such as necking or tearing.

Overall, a combination of these forces is applied and carefully controlled during sheet metal forming processes to achieve the desired shape while ensuring dimensional accuracy and structural integrity. Understanding the interplay between these forces is crucial for optimizing forming parameters and producing high-quality formed parts.

How to calculate the force required to form a sheet metal part

Calculating the force required to form a sheet metal part is crucial for designing efficient and effective forming processes. The force required depends on various factors, including the material properties, geometry of the part, and the forming process itself. Here's a general overview of how to calculate the force required for sheet metal forming:

1. **Material Properties**: The material's mechanical properties, such as its yield strength, tensile strength, and strain hardening behaviour, significantly influence the force required for forming. These properties determine how much force is needed to induce plastic deformation in the material. Material data can be obtained from material testing or literature sources.

2. **Geometry of the Part**: The shape and complexity of the part being formed also affect the required forming force. Parts with sharper bends or more intricate features typically require higher forming forces. Calculating the surface area of the part and analyzing the

distribution of material thickness can provide insights into the force requirements for different regions of the part.

3. **Forming Process**: Different forming processes, such as bending, stretching, or deep drawing, require specific force calculations. For example:

- **Bending**: The force required for bending can be calculated using formulas such as the Air Bending Force Formula or the Barlow's Formula, which take into account parameters such as material thickness, bend radius, and material properties.

- **Stretching**: For stretching operations, the force required depends on factors such as the initial and final part dimensions, material thickness, and the extent of deformation. Formulas such as the stretching force equation can be used to estimate the required force.

- **Deep Drawing**: In deep drawing, the force required depends on the blank holder pressure, coefficient of friction, material properties, and the drawing ratio. Complex analytical and numerical methods, such as finite element analysis (FEA), are often employed to accurately predict the forming forces in deep drawing processes.

4. **Friction**: Friction between the sheet metal and the forming tool surfaces also influences the forming force. Higher frictional forces require more significant forming forces to overcome resistance. The coefficient of friction between the sheet metal and the tool surfaces must be considered in force calculations.

5. **Safety Factors**: It's essential to consider safety factors and potential variations in material properties or process conditions when calculating forming forces. Applying appropriate safety margins ensures that the forming process remains reliable and produces parts within acceptable tolerances.

In summary, calculating the force required to form a sheet metal part involves considering factors such as material properties, part geometry, forming process, friction, and safety factors. By accurately estimating forming forces, engineers can optimize process parameters, select appropriate equipment, and ensure the successful production of high-quality sheet metal components.

How the press tonnage is calculated by the finite element analysis software

Finite element analysis (FEA) software is widely used in the manufacturing industry to simulate and analyze the behavior of materials and components under various loading conditions, including sheet metal forming processes. Press tonnage, which represents the force exerted by the forming press during the forming operation, is a crucial parameter in sheet metal forming simulations. Here's how press tonnage is calculated using FEA software:

1. **Mesh Generation**: The first step in the FEA process is to create a finite element mesh of the sheet metal part geometry. The part is discretized into a finite number of small elements, typically triangular or quadrilateral in shape, to represent its geometry accurately. The density and quality of the mesh play a significant role in the accuracy of the simulation results.

2. **Material Modeling**: FEA software allows engineers to define material properties for the sheet metal being formed. Material models such as isotropic, kinematic, or combined isotropic-kinematic hardening models are used to describe the material's behavior under loading conditions. These models consider factors such as elastic modulus, yield strength, strain hardening, and Poisson's ratio to accurately simulate material deformation.

3. **Contact and Boundary Conditions**: Contact interactions between the sheet metal and forming tools are defined in the FEA model. Boundary conditions, such as fixed supports or prescribed displacements, are applied to simulate the forming process accurately. The interaction between the blankholder, forming tools, and the sheet metal is crucial for accurately predicting press tonnage.

4. **Incremental Forming Simulation**: The forming process is simulated incrementally using FEA software. Each incremental step represents a small deformation applied to the sheet metal. During each step, the FEA software calculates the distribution of stresses, strains, and displacements within the sheet metal part.

5. **Tonnage Calculation**: Press tonnage is calculated based on the reaction forces exerted by the forming tools on the sheet metal during the simulation. These reaction forces are computed by the FEA software as a result of the deformation and contact interactions between the sheet metal and the forming tools. The cumulative reaction forces obtained throughout the simulation represent the total press tonnage required to form the part.

6. **Analysis and Optimization**: Once the simulation is complete, engineers analyze the results to evaluate the quality of the formed part and identify potential forming defects such as wrinkling, thinning, or tearing. The press tonnage calculated by the FEA software is used to optimize the forming process parameters, such as blankholder force, tool geometry, or lubrication conditions, to achieve the desired part quality while minimizing manufacturing costs.

In summary, press tonnage in sheet metal forming simulations is calculated by FEA software based on the distribution of stresses, strains, and contact interactions between the sheet metal and forming tools. Accurate press tonnage prediction is essential for optimizing forming processes, ensuring part quality, and reducing manufacturing costs.

Practice Exercise

Get free video tutorials along with CAD files on Author's website

https://sharmarakesh.co.in/index.php/tutorials/

Password : Forming2025

8.1 Hypergraph 2D:

HyperGraph 2D supplies design, test, and analysis engineers with an intuitive plotting and data analysis package. HyperGraph 2D's combination of an easy-to-use interface and robust suite of automation tools enables engineers to view and analyze data more efficiently.

Benefits:

- Minimizes the manual effort and time required to generate plots. The automatic plot builder generates a family of fully labelled plots from data file(s), using file header and channel information.
- Eliminates repetitive tasks. Plot macros capture and automate common math expressions.
- Eliminates repetitive plot generation. Report templates can capture and automate the building of entire pages of data plots.
- A fully customizable interface. Customize the interface and the tools to fit any engineering environment.

- A customizable library of mathematical functions. You can add custom defined math functions to Altair's robust math library.
- Provides automation tools for efficient data analysis and report generation.
- Overlays sequential test and simulation results for visualization and analysis.
- Directly exports active session reports to HTML or PowerPoint XML.

Main components:

- **XY Plot**
  The XY Plot toolbar is displayed when you select HyperGraph 2D from the application menu and the active window is set to the XY Plot mode, ⏞.
- **Bar Chart**
  The Bar Chart toolbar is displayed when you select HyperGraph 2D from the application menu and the active window is set to the Bar Chart mode, ⅲ .
- **Complex Plot**
  The Complex Plot toolbar is displayed when you select HyperGraph 2D from the application menu and set the active window to Complex Plot mode, ⏠.
- **Polar Plot**
  Polar plots allow you to plot complex data and are very similar to HyperGraph 2D complex plots. The polar plot toolbar is displayed when you select HyperGraph 2D from the application menu and the active window is set to the Polar Plot mode, ⊛ .

8.2 Procedure to calculate the draw force:

8.2A Open a file:

Press the open tab "marked as 1st

Select the File with T01 and press open, marked as 2nd

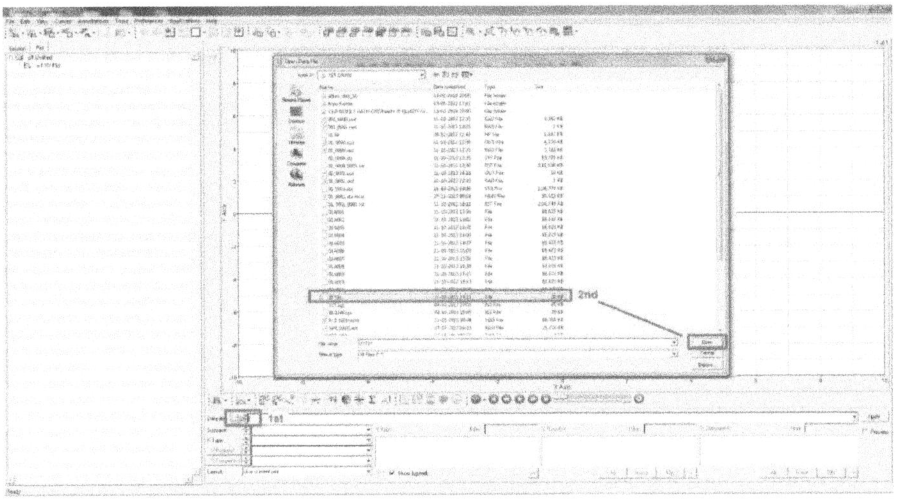

8.2B Apply settings for plotting die force graph:

Select the 1st marked option **Interface/TH_INTER**

Select the 2ndmarked option **1 DIE_BLANK_Contact**

Select the 3rd marked option **FNZ-Z NORMAL FORCE**

Click preview-4th and apply-5th marking.

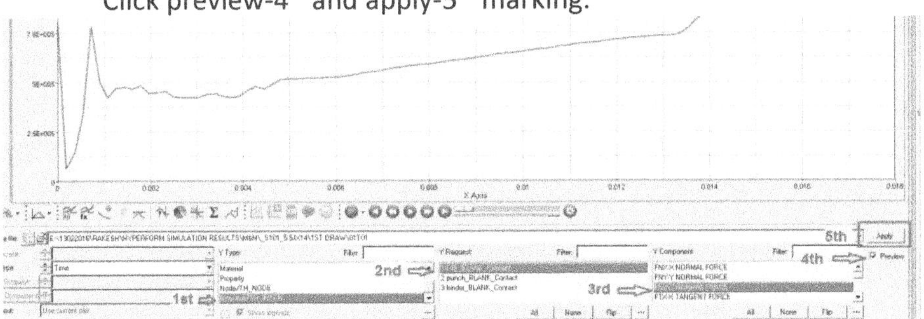

8.2C Apply settings for plotting binder force graph:

Select the 1st marked option **Interface/TH_INTER**

Select the 2nd marked option **3 binder_BLANK_Contact**

Select the 3rd marked option **FNZ-Z NORMAL FORCE**

Click preview and apply-4th marking.

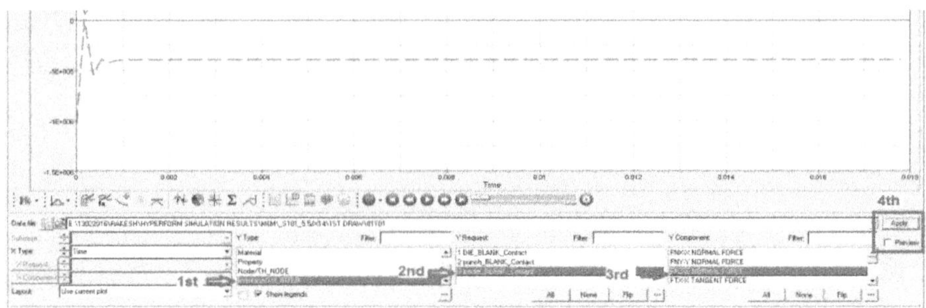

8.2D Edit the graph units:

Right click on the graph area.

Select the force units as shown.

Click ok to apply.

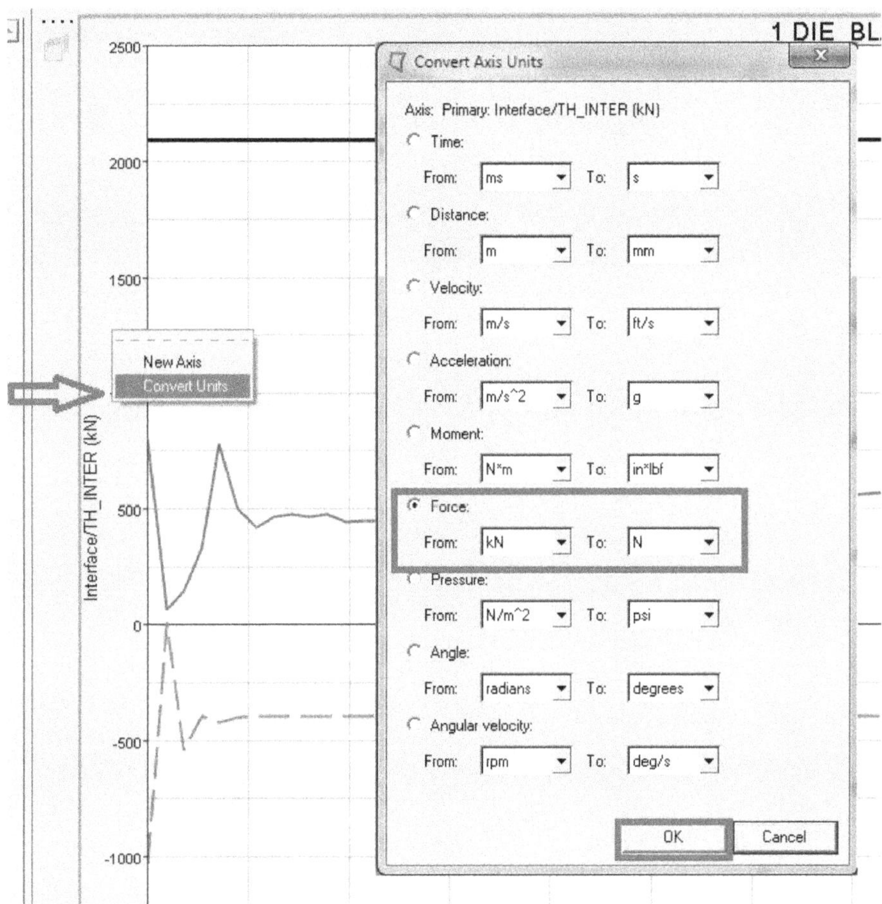

8.2E Measuring the values:

Calculating the Draw force:

Select the coordinate information marked as 1st

Select the peak point marked as 2nd and see the value.

The value 2090 KN (kilo-newton) can be further translated into Tons (2090/9.8) = 213 tons.

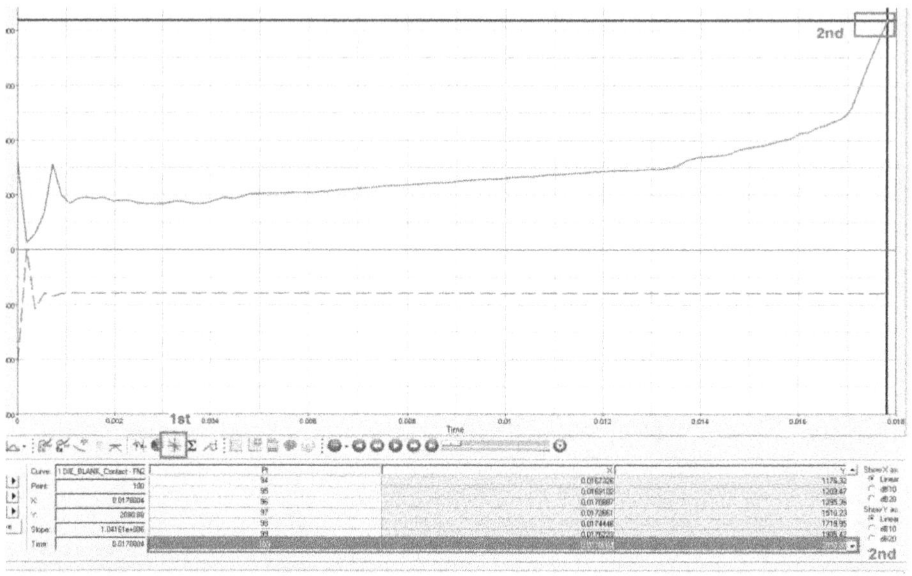

8.3 Calculating the Binder force:

Select the coordinate information 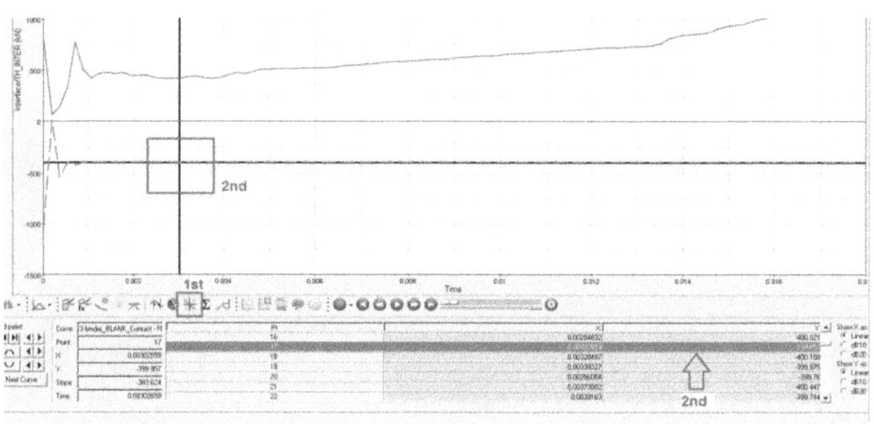 marked as 1st

Select the Average constant line and pick any point marked as 2nd and see the value.

The value 399 KN (kilo-newton) can be further translated into Tons (399/9.8) = 40.7 tons.

10. Springback analysis

Springback or Elastic recovery

During the forming process, springback occurs in every sheet metal part, even the simplest parts. In determining the magnitude and severity of springback, the main factors are the combination of the material's young's modulus of elasticity, Yield Strength (YS) , ratio of die radius to thickness, design of geometry and design of die. Often, complex sheet metal parts using high strength material exhibit extreme amounts of springback. During the design phase, if it is not accounted for, unexpected problems will arise.

Springback is the recovery of the elastic stresses induced during the metal forming process. Once a sheet of metal plastically deforms to a given shape by a forming tool, the final shape of the sheet is subject to change as soon as the forming tool is removed. The sheet of metal, having just been formed to the desired shape, relaxes to a new shape as soon as the forming force is removed. This is the equalization of elastic stresses and strains which occurs as soon as the forming force is removed.

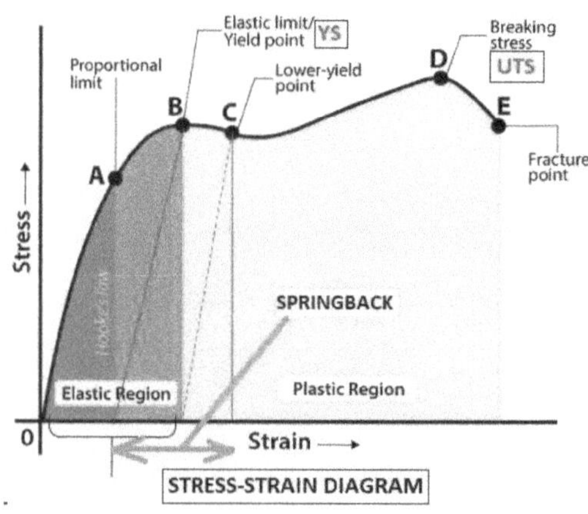

From the above basic stress strain curve, we are able to understand the main points.

A = Stress is directely proportional to strain and follows Hooks law

B = Yield point, after that plastic deformation starts

C = Lower yield point, theoratical point

D = UTS, ultimate tensile stregth, after which material straining even after reduction in stress

E = breakge point of material

Even after crossing the yield point, certain elastic recovery happens and shift the deformation from point B or C to point A, after the removal of forces.

As desired, stresses and strains in the plastic region deform, however, elastic stresses and strains attempt to return to their original state. As the majority of the sheet is permanently deformed by plastic stresses and strains, any residual elastic stresses twist and distort the sheet metal shape. Materials with high Yield Strength (e.g. YS = 410MPa) tend to springback in a more severe manner. Although, the key factor is not solely the Yield Strength, but also the Young's modulus of elasticity. Specifically, while moving towards higher value of YS and not raising the TS, the reduced gap between YS and TS (e.g. YS = 420MPa, TS = 540MPa) are potentially producing the worse magnitude of springback. Furthermore, the part's geometry, the forming process, and other factors determine the severity and lead to an uncalculated problem.

Negative, or positive, springback refers to the direction. Negative springback values may indicate the sheet's deformation in the -Z direction, while positive may indicate deformation in the +Z direction. Springback is a vector; therefore, a direction must be specified alongside its magnitude in reports.

To perform a calculation, the elastic properties of the given material such as Ys, Young's modulus E, bend radius, bend angle, type of process (air beding, forming, restriking) and material thickness are required. For the simplest straight line bending operations, springback may be calculated by hand. For complex operations, sheet metal forming simulation is required.

In overcoming springback in sheet metal parts, there are numerous techniques. For basic straight line bends (e.g. folded part on a brake press), overbidding is a valid technique. However, for the rest, especially complex 3D parts, sheet metal forming simulation is necessary to determine and adjust springback.

Through there are many advanced simulation software available such as Hyperform, AutoForm or Pamstamp, with the predicted springback shape calculation, the software helps us to compensates the affected areas in the opposite direction. Although, the shape required to fully correct for springback, is usually not 1:1. Bending the part, often in 3D, by more than the original amount of springback is required to attain the desired result.

Aside from springback compensation of overbending, stretching the entire part as much as possible during metal forming processes is another technique. The method work "hardens" or "strengthens" the entire surface area. Therefore, it holds the desired shape due to the increased plastic deformation induced by a stretch forming process.

Springback is a common phenomenon in metal forming processes characterized by the elastic recovery of a material after it has been subjected to deformation. When a metal part is formed through processes like bending, stretching, or deep drawing, it undergoes plastic deformation, meaning it permanently changes shape. However, upon the removal of the forming forces, the material tends to spring back slightly towards its original shape due to its elastic properties. This tendency of the material to return to its pre-deformed state is known as springback.

Several factors contribute to springback during metal forming processes:

1.**Material Properties**: The young's or elastic modulus **E** , yield strength **Ys,** and strain hardening exponent **n** , are the few characteristics of the material which significantly influence its spring back behavior.

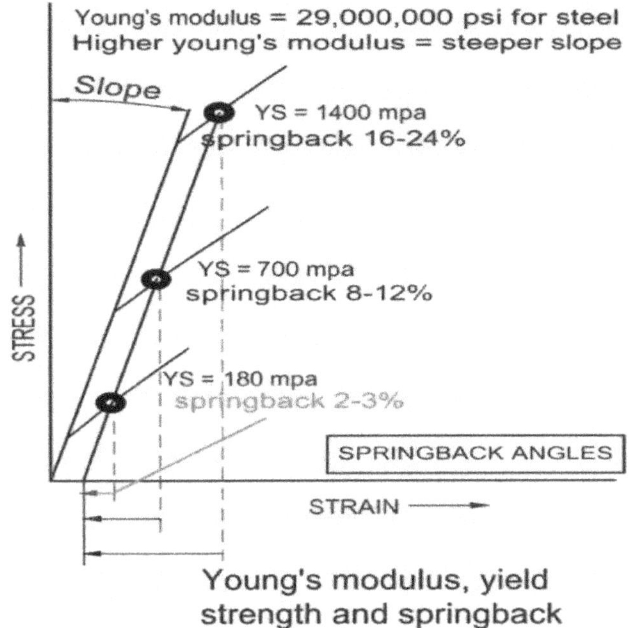

Young's modulus, yield
strength and springback

In the above picture, the relationship between young's modulus, yield strength and sprinback has been derived from the experimental data.

For example, for steel E = 29,000,000 psi, therefore have a steeper slope than non-ferrous metals such as aluminium.

The Ys is 180mpa for low carbon steel, whereas it rises to 700mpa for high strength and 1400mpa for ultra high strength Boron steels. The general acceptacne for elastic recovery point is 10% offset of the length of curve follow the limit of proportionality. It will meet at the yield points marked with dots for all 3 types of steels. If you drop the straight line from yield points and measure the springback at the base of the curve, you will come to know about why the elastic recovery angle increases with the increase in Ys of the material.

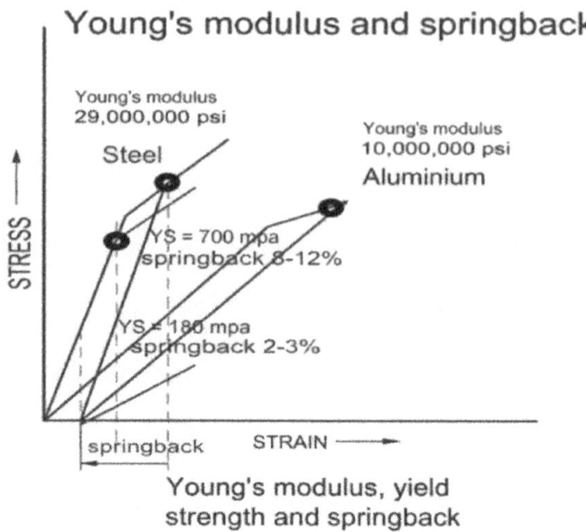

Young's modulus, yield
strength and springback

In the above picture, the relationship between young's modulus and sprinback has been shown. The steel has a steeper curve due to more value of E than Aluminium. If I am going to derive a 10% offset curve from the original curve to reach at yield points and drop the vertical lines to strain graaph, I will be able to calculate the impact of young's modulus on the amount of elastic recovery or springback. From the above curve, I think you can understand why Aluminium has much higher springback than steel.

Conclusion : Materials with higher elastic moduli exhibit greater resistance to deformation and consequently, higher springback tendencies.
Additionally, materials with higher yield strengths are more susceptible to springback due to their higher levels of elastic recovery.

2. **Forming Process :** The type of forming process employed also affects the magnitude of springback. Processes that involve high levels of plastic deformation, such as deep drawing, tend to result in more significant springback compared to processes with lower deformation levels. The complexity of the part geometry and the extent of deformation also influence spring back behavior.

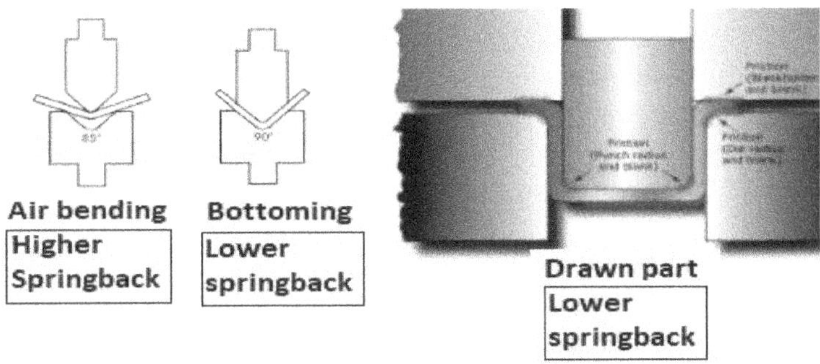

For example, air bending has more springback than bottoming dies or drawn parts.

3. **Tooling and Die Design** : The design and condition of the forming tools and dies play a crucial role in controlling springback. Factors such as die radii, punch angles, and blankholder forces can be optimized to minimize springback tendencies. Additionally, the surface finish and lubrication of the forming tools can affect frictional forces and, consequently, spring back behavior.

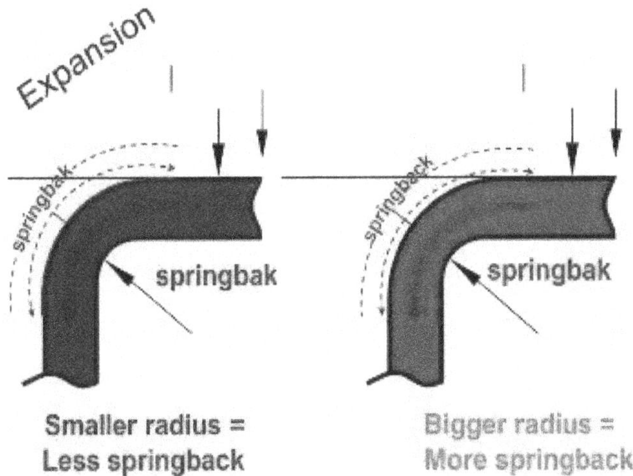

For example, choosing the smaller radius compared to thickness resuls in less amount of springback. The secret lies in changes occurs in atomic structure of material during bending or forming.

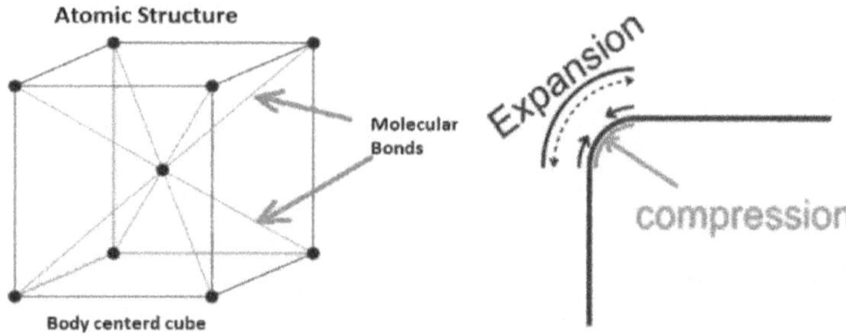

Molecular bonds of the atoms breaks during plastic deformation, Smaller the radius wrt thickness, more number of molecular bonds break, thus less springback. The inner wall of the material got under compression and outer wall remain under tension, the outer wall under tension is the portion where molecular bonds not fully broken. Thus tends to recover back, however inner area under compression limit it's movement. Hence reduce the springback.

4.**Process Parameters** :Process parameters such as forming speed, temperature, and lubrication conditions can influence springback tendencies. For example, higher forming speeds may result in reduced springback due to decreased elastic recovery time, while proper lubrication can minimize frictional forces and help control springback.

Controlling springback is essential for achieving dimensional accuracy and meeting tight tolerance requirements in metal forming applications. Strategies for mitigating springback include:

- Compensation techniques, such as overbending or preforming, involve intentionally deforming the part beyond the desired shape to account for springback.

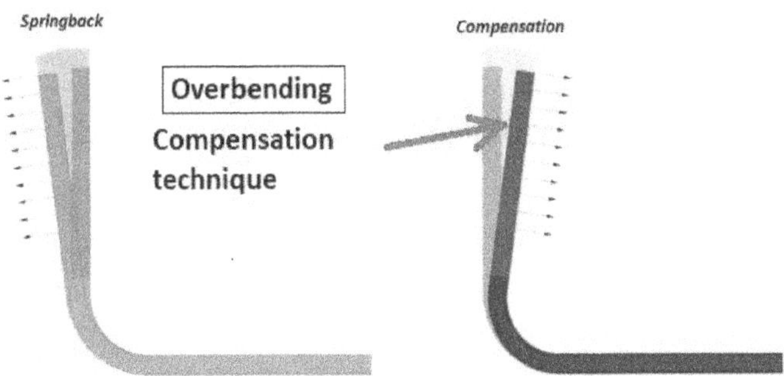

- Iterative process adjustments based on trial-and-error testing can help optimize forming parameters to minimize springback.

Trial and error method (old skool)

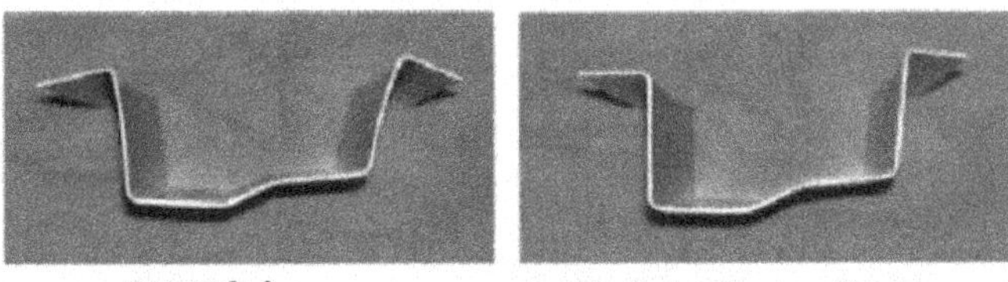

- Advanced numerical simulations, such as finite element analysis (FEA), can be used to predict and control springback behavior during the design and optimization of forming processes.

Advanced Finite element analysis technique

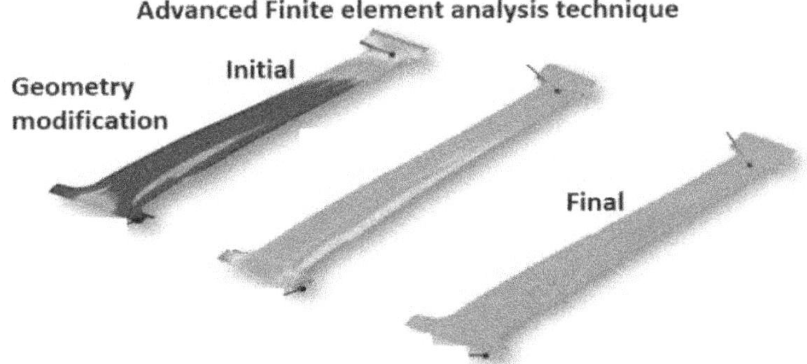

Overall, understanding the factors influencing springback and implementing appropriate mitigation strategies are essential for achieving precise and reliable metal forming operations.

169

Common methods to control springback in metal forming

Controlling springback is crucial in metal forming processes to achieve accurate dimensional tolerances and ensure the final part's quality. Several methods are commonly employed to mitigate springback effects and maintain the desired shape of the formed component:

1. Overbending: Overbending involves intentionally deforming the part beyond the target shape during the forming process. By overcompensating for the anticipated springback, the final part returns to the desired dimensions once the forming forces are removed. Overbending is often used in conjunction with iterative testing and analysis to determine the appropriate amount of overbend required.

2. Pre-Bending or Pre-Forming: Pre-bending or pre-forming techniques involve partially forming the material before the final forming operation. This pre-deformation helps to pre-distribute stresses in the material, reducing the amount of springback experienced during the final forming stage. Pre-bending is particularly effective for parts with complex geometries or tight tolerance requirements.

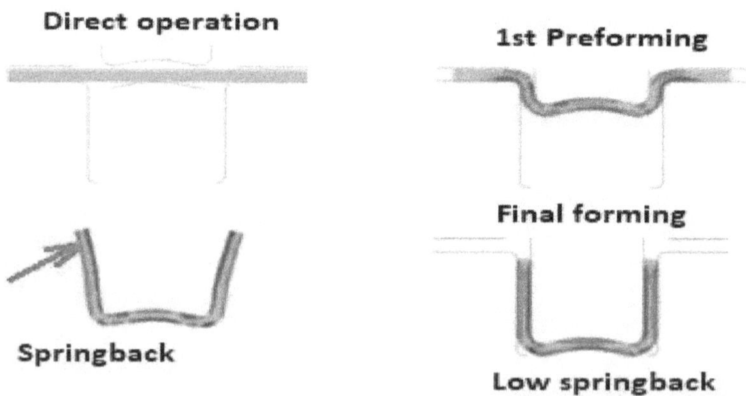

3. **Material Selection and Heat Treatment**: Choosing materials with specific mechanical properties or subjecting the material to heat treatment processes can influence its spring back behavior. Materials with higher yield strengths or enhanced ductility exhibit reduced springback tendencies. Additionally, heat treatment processes such as annealing or

stress relieving can help stabilize the material's microstructure and minimize springback.

4. Optimized Tooling Design: The design of forming tools and dies can significantly impact springback control. By optimizing die radii, punch angles, and blankholder forces, tooling designs can help distribute stresses more evenly throughout the material and reduce springback tendencies. Additionally, incorporating features such as draw beads or stretch forming can help control material flow and minimize springback in specific regions of the part.

5. Incremental Forming Techniques: Incremental forming techniques, such as stretch forming or incremental sheet forming (ISF), involve deforming the material in small, localized increments. This gradual deformation process allows for better control over material flow and reduces the accumulation of residual stresses, thereby minimizing springback effects.

6. Process Optimization: Adjusting process parameters such as forming speed, lubrication conditions, and tool temperatures can also influence springback behavior. For example, reducing forming speeds or optimizing lubrication can help minimize frictional forces and improve material flow, leading to reduced springback.

7. Simulation and Analysis: Advanced numerical simulations, such as finite element analysis (FEA), can be used to predict and optimize springback behavior during the design and development stages of metal forming processes. By simulating various process parameters and tooling configurations, engineers can identify optimal strategies for controlling springback and achieve desired part geometry.

By employing these methods in combination with each other and considering the specific requirements of the forming application, manufacturers can effectively control springback and produce high-quality, dimensionally accurate metal components.

How finite element analysis software calculates springback during forming analysis:

Finite Element Analysis (FEA) software plays a crucial role in predicting and analyzing springback during metal forming processes. Here's how FEA software calculates springback:

1. Material Modeling: FEA software allows engineers to define material properties for the sheet metal being formed. Material models, such as isotropic, kinematic, or combined isotropic-kinematic hardening models, are used to describe the material's behavior under loading conditions. These models consider factors such as elastic modulus, yield strength, strain hardening, and Poisson's ratio to accurately simulate material deformation.

2. Initial Forming Simulation: The forming process is simulated initially without considering springback effects. During this simulation, the FEA software calculates the distribution of stresses, strains, and displacements within the sheet metal part as it undergoes plastic deformation. Reverse Unloading: After the initial forming simulation, the forming forces are removed, and the sheet metal is allowed to spring back towards its original shape. This reverse unloading process is simulated using FEA software, where the material's elastic behavior is taken into account. The software calculates the elastic recovery of the material based on its defined material properties.

3. Springback Calculation: The difference between the deformed shape obtained from the initial forming simulation and the shape after springback is calculated to determine the magnitude and direction of springback. FEA software quantifies springback as the displacement or distortion of specific points or regions on the formed part relative to their initial positions.

4. Iterative Analysis: In many cases, predicting springback accurately requires iterative analysis. Engineers adjust process parameters, such as tooling geometry, forming speed, or blankholder force, and re-run simulations to refine the prediction of spring back behavior. This iterative process helps optimize forming parameters to minimize springback tendencies and achieve the desired part geometry.

5. Validation and Optimization: Once the simulation accurately predicts spring back behavior, engineers validate the results by comparing them with experimental data obtained from physical forming tests. Discrepancies between the simulation and actual forming behavior are analyzed to refine the computational model and improve its accuracy for future simulations. Additionally, engineers use simulation results to optimize forming processes and tooling designs to minimize springback and improve part quality.

Overall, FEA software enables engineers to simulate the complex interplay between material behavior, forming processes, and tooling conditions to accurately predict springback during metal forming analysis. By leveraging FEA simulations, manufacturers can optimize forming processes, reduce springback effects, and produce high-quality formed components with tight dimensional tolerances.

Practice Exercise
Get free video tutorials along with CAD files on Author's website

https://sharmarakesh.co.in/index.php/tutorials/

Password : Forming2025

9.1 Procedure to setup springback analysis:

9.1A Setup the basic bending analysis:

Import the geometry as shown, same method to be used as described in the previous topics, marked as step 1st.

Rename the parts as marked in the step 2nd, refer previous chapters for details.

Meshing of the parts, R-mesh for rigid bodies and Automesh (F12 Quad only) for blank.

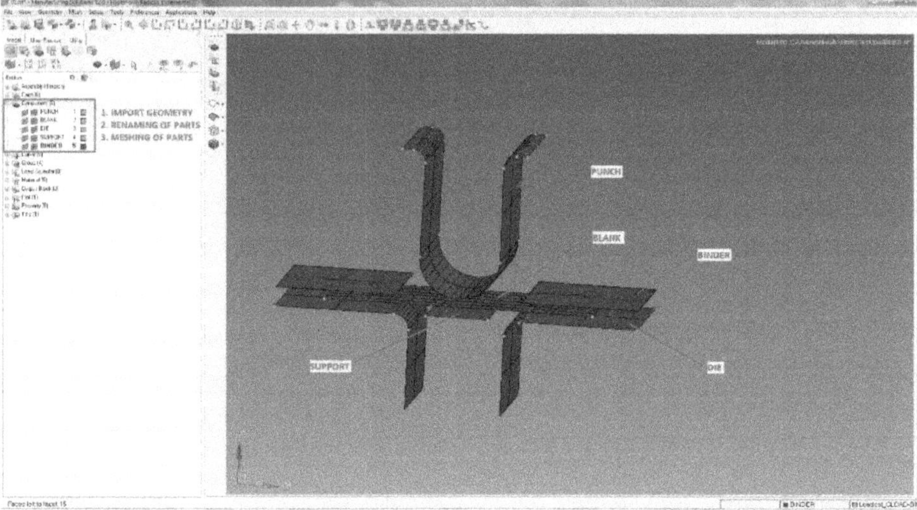

9.1BSpringback option in Autoprocess:

From the autopocess menu, select the "Setup Marked as 1st" in the below image.

Select the "Control marked as 2nd" in the below image, turn on the springback to yes "Marked as 3rd "

From the 4TH marking, you can customize the settings, however default is recommended.

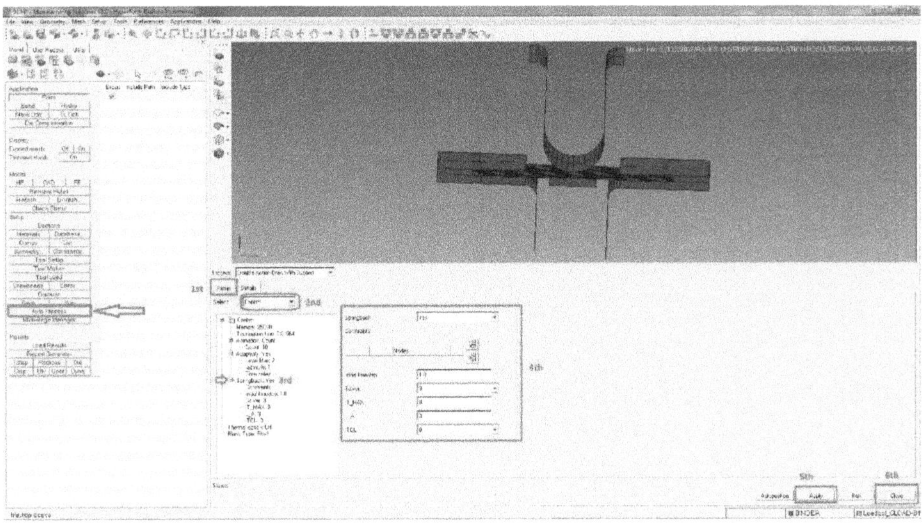

9.1C Run the analysis:

From the left pane under utility menu, select the "run option marked as 1st" in the below image.

You can see the animation and for final run press Run 2nd marking, the black window will appear showing the solving process by radioss solver.

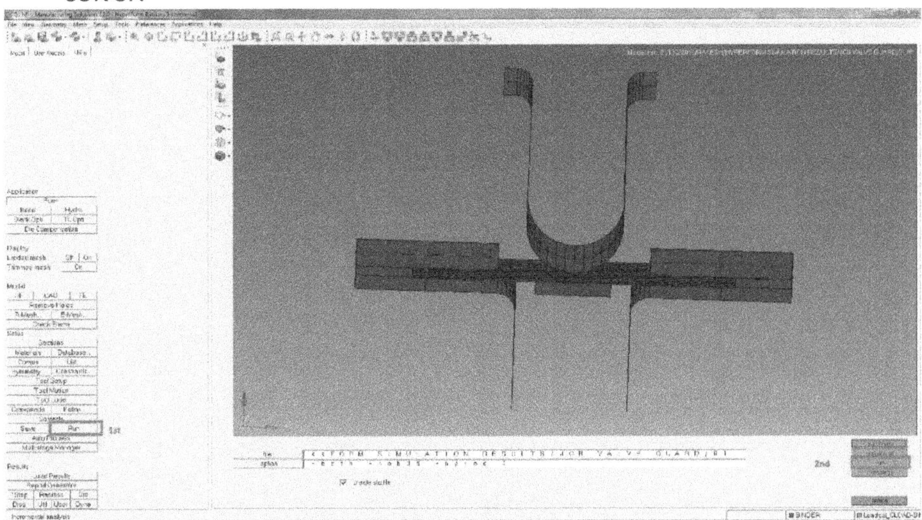

9.2 Setup Springback analysis:

From the left pane under utility menu, select the "Autoprocess option marked as 1st" in the below image.

In the Process menu, select the "Springback option marked as 2nd" in the below image.

Select the "Blank-1 as state file marked as 3rd" in the below image, followed by the path 4th marking. From the browser window select the ".sta file" marked as 5th and click open 6th.

On the 7th option assign material grade and thickness, 7th marking and click apply 8th.

The next window will appear after that, Pick the "nodes list 1st marking" and pick 3-random nodes 2nd marking, then press proceed 3rd marking.

The solver will run to process the inputs and create the result files.

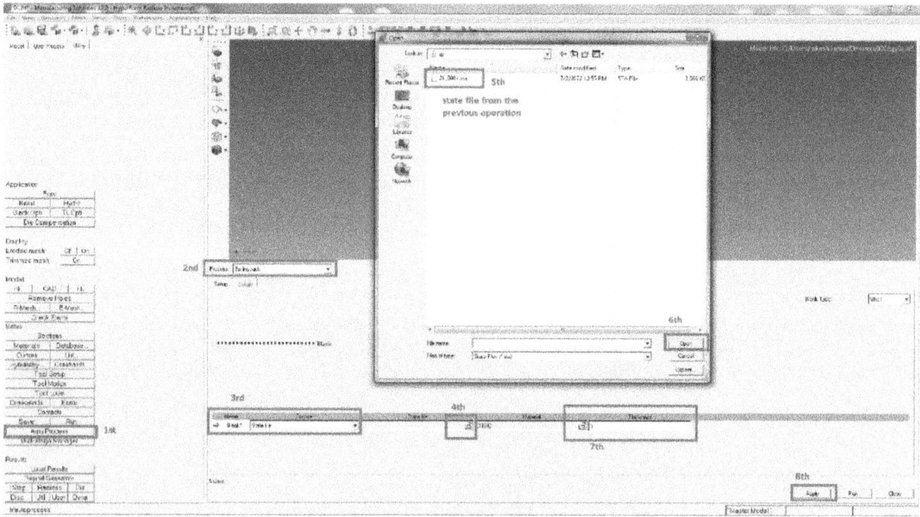

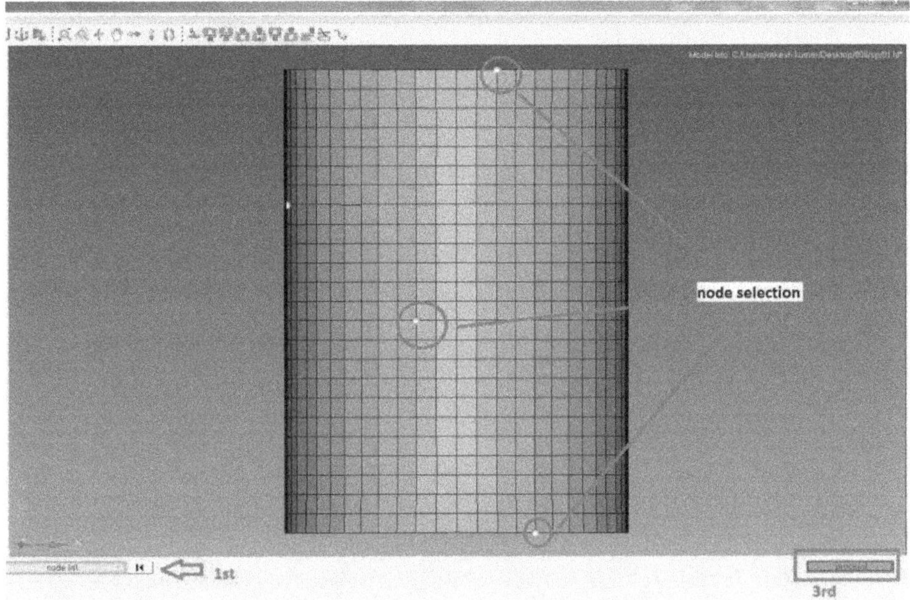

9.3 Load results:

Open the hyperview and browse the path 1ˢᵗ marking, select the
newly created file "A001 marked as 2ⁿᵈ"and click open marked as 3rd"
in the below image.

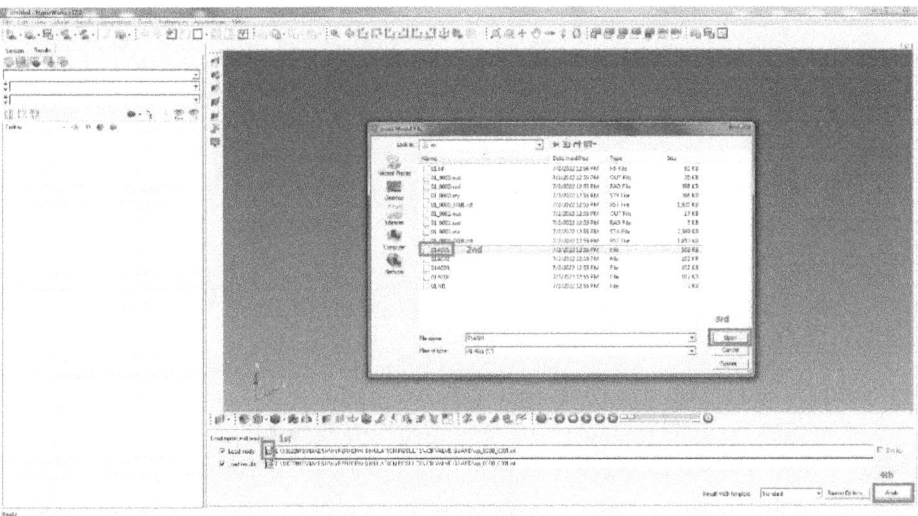

9.4 Displacement plot:

From the "contour plot 1st marking", select displacement 2nd marking in the below image.
From the component marked as 3rd ", the selection window will pop up, from there select the displayed 4th and click apply 5th.

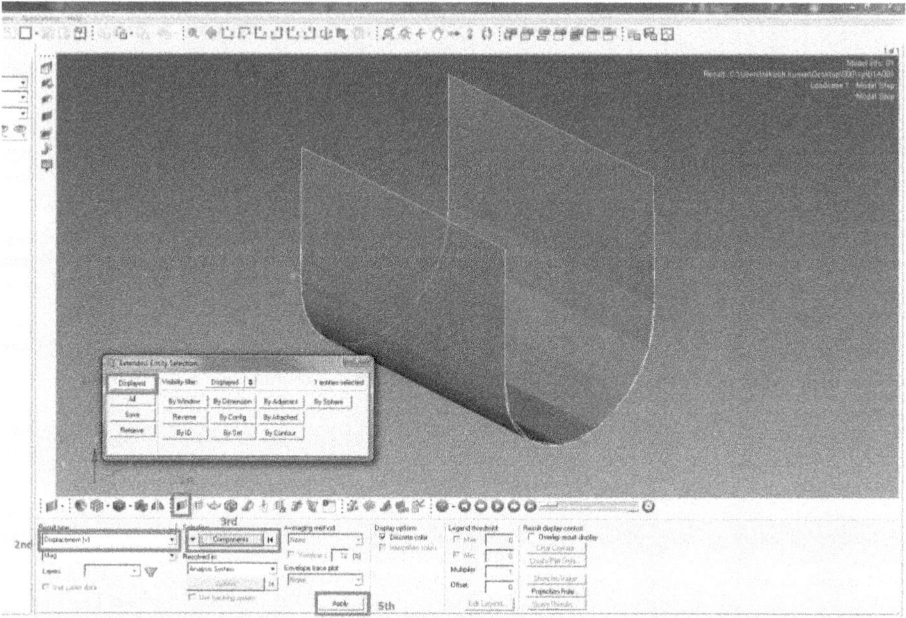

9.5 Plot results and edit the scale:

The displacement results appear to be color coded plot, where Red color predict the max. displacement or deflection and Blue as min. value. For changing the scale from engineering to metric values, just right click to Edit the legend and next window appears as shown.

In the Edit legend window, select the Numeric format 1st , then select the precision 2nd followed by apply 3rd and press ok marked as 4th.

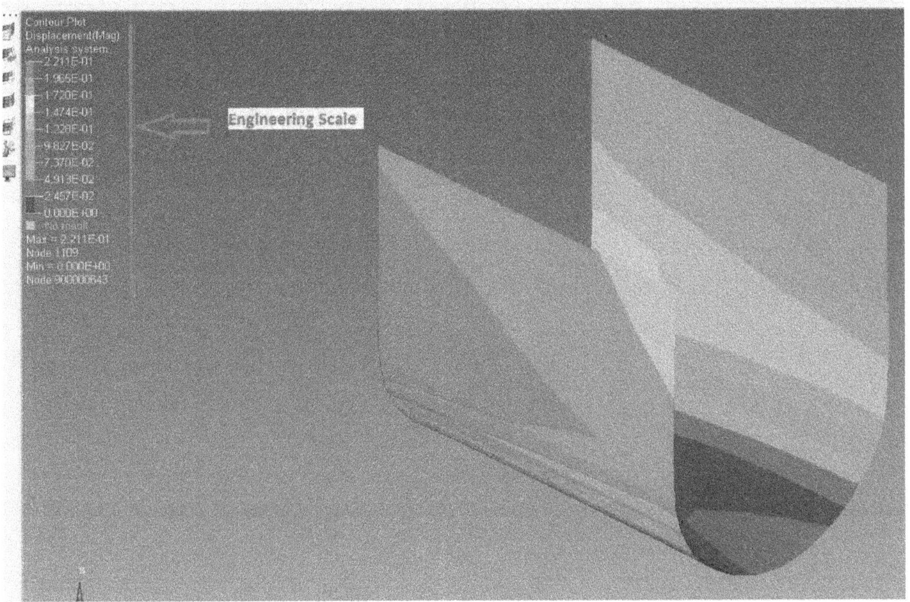

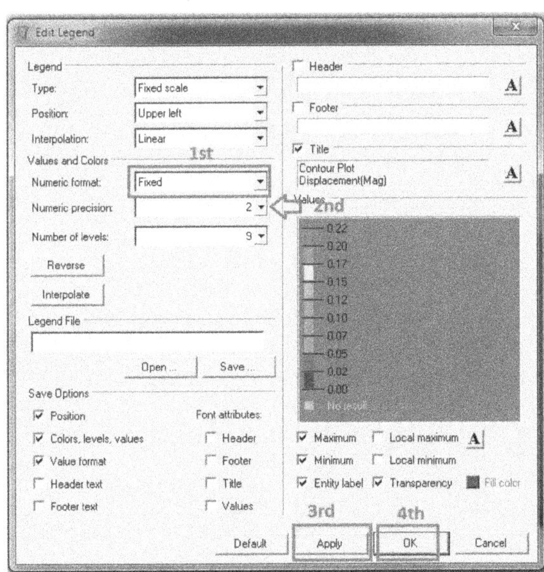

9.6 Compare with the original profile:

From the load model browser marked 1st , tick the overlay option marked as 2nd and turn off the load results option.

Pick the 000.rad file marked as 3rd in the browser window, press open 4th. and click apply 5th as shown in the below image. Next window will show both geometries.

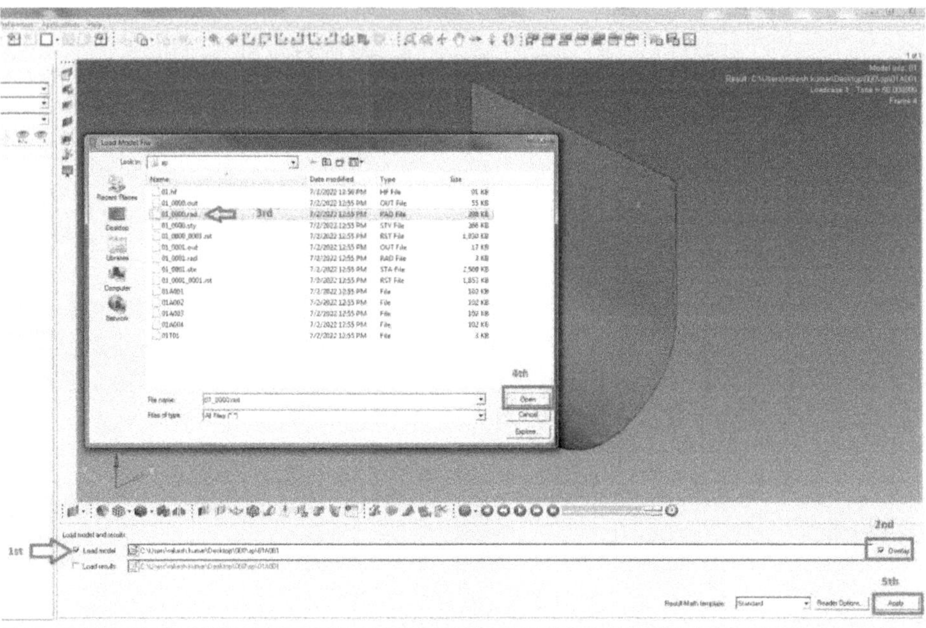

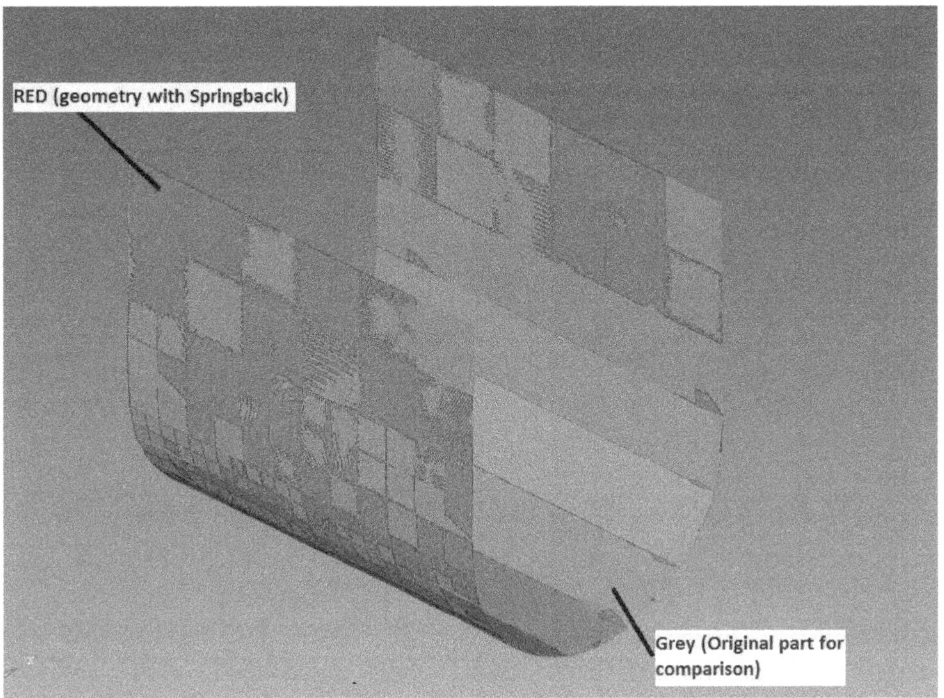

9.7 Cut Section for comparison:

Pick the section option marked 1st , Under the plane option marked as 2nd select the appropriate plane passing through and adjust the increment 3rd .

For cross section width adjust via 4th marking and adjust 5th for animation control and final shape.

In the next image you can see the section has been set to XZ plane marked as 1st with rest all settings as mentioned.

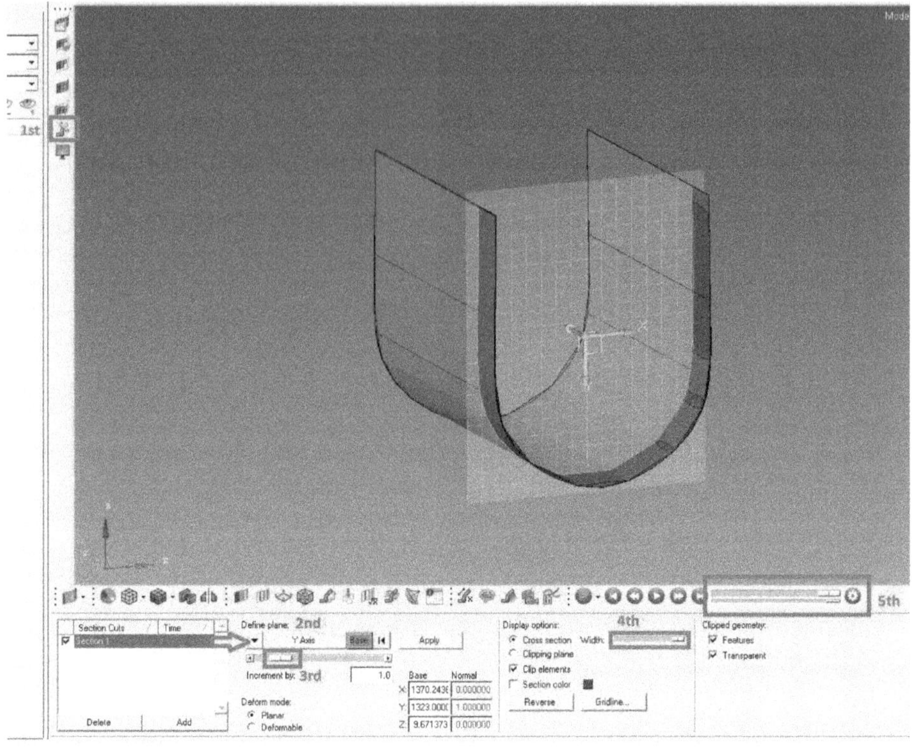

1st
2nd
3rd
4th
5th
Section Cuts
Time
Section 1
Define plane:
Y Axis
Base
Apply
Increment by:
1.0
Deform mode:
Planar
Deformable
Delete
Add
Base
Normal
X: 1370.243 0.000000
Y: 1323.000 1.000000
Z: 9.671373 0.000000
Display options:
Cross section   Width:
Clipping plane
Clip elements
Section color
Reverse
Gridline...
Clipped geometry:
Features
Transparent

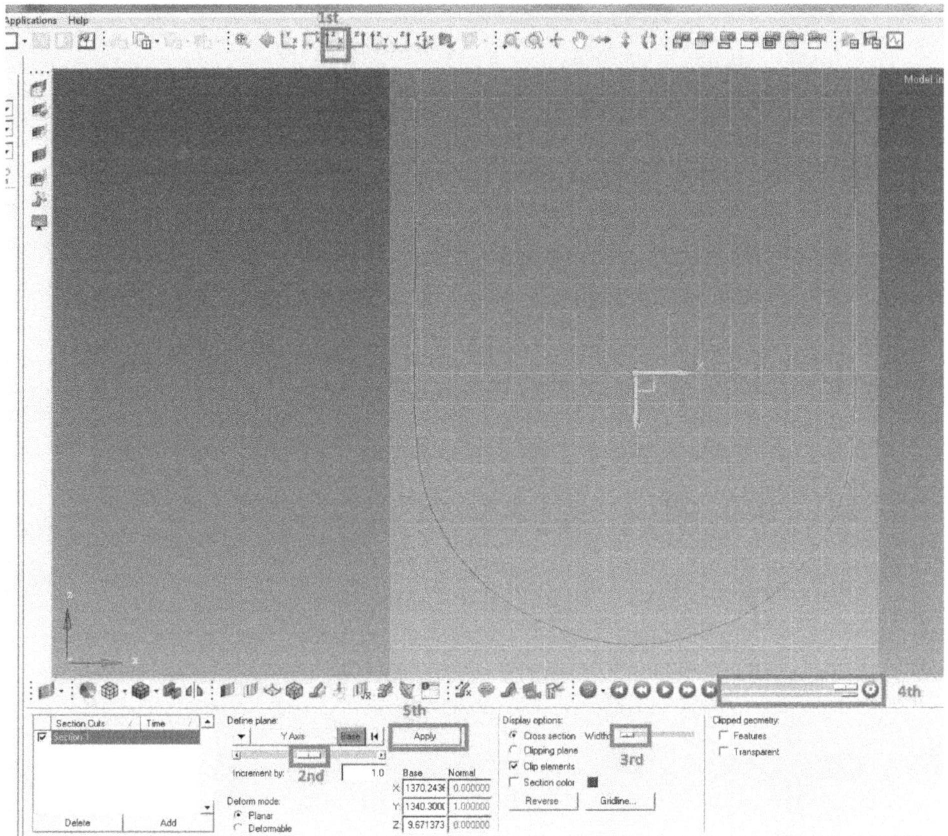

9.7 Measure the values:

Pick the measure option marked 1st , select option distance between marked as 2nd from the drop down menu, then select the nodes 3rd as shown and pick the appropriate option, like I have chosen X axis distance 4th marking.

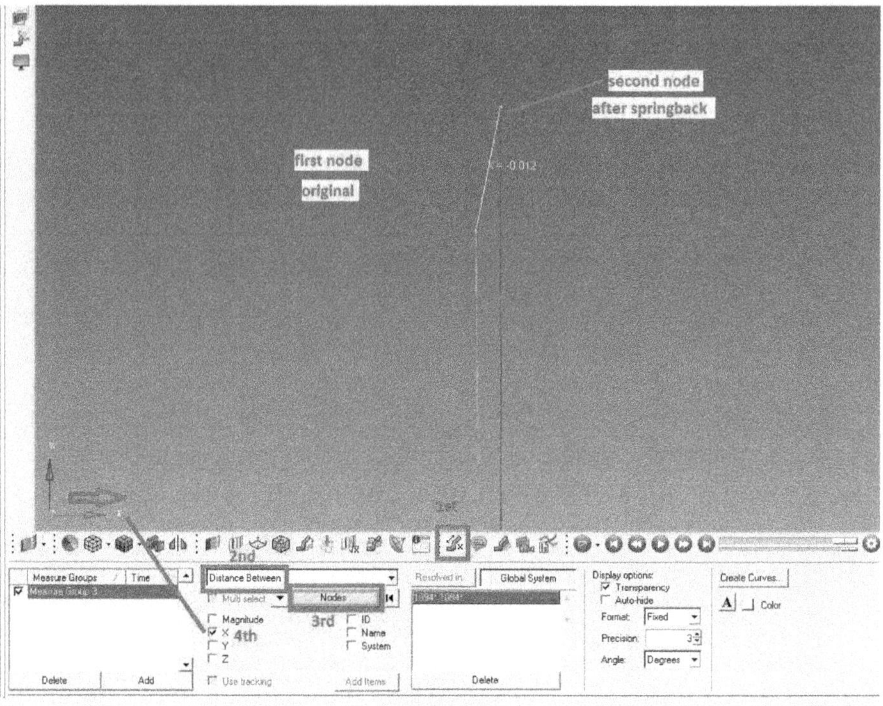
second node
after springback
first node
original
2nd
3rd
4th
1st
Measure Groups
Time
Measure Group 3
Multi select
Magnitude
X
Y
Z
Use tracking
Delete
Add
Distance Between
Nodes
ID
Name
System
Add Items
Resolved in
Global System
Delete
Display options:
Transparency
Auto-hide
Format: Fixed
Precision: 3
Angle: Degrees
Create Curves
Color

11. Gravity Analysis

Overview of Gravity analysis

In this chapter, you will learn about the effect of thin sheet metal blank placed on convex, concave or irregular surface, which is not flat. The metal blank tends to deform due to the effect of gravity, probably the area which are not supported, tend to deform or bent down. This process involves organizing, editing, and meshing the inputs, supported by the autoprocess of Gravity analysis. The three stages, preprocessing, post processing and view results later in hyperview player. You can not only visualize the results, but also measure the dimensions at deformed surface. The shapes thereafter can be imported into cad software in the form of elemental data for comparison with respect to the original one. It would help die designers to nest the deformed blank after the effect of gravity, which otherwise is nearly impossible to forecast or calculate.

Gravity analysis is being used to achieve the following objectives:

To measure the effect of gravity in the blank placed on irregular surface.

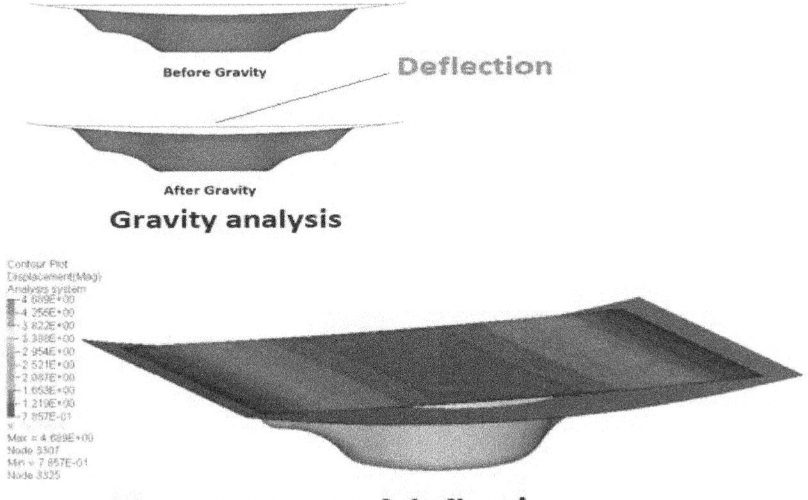

Gravity analysis

Measurement of deflection

Nesting of the deformed or bent blank on the blank holder.

To restudy the effect of blank deformation on the formability.

It would help to reduce the number of trials, to make the picture vivid during the design stage.

Gravity analysis also used to do anlysis on a sheet placed on a curved surface affects its deformation, stress distribution, and stability. The key impacts include:

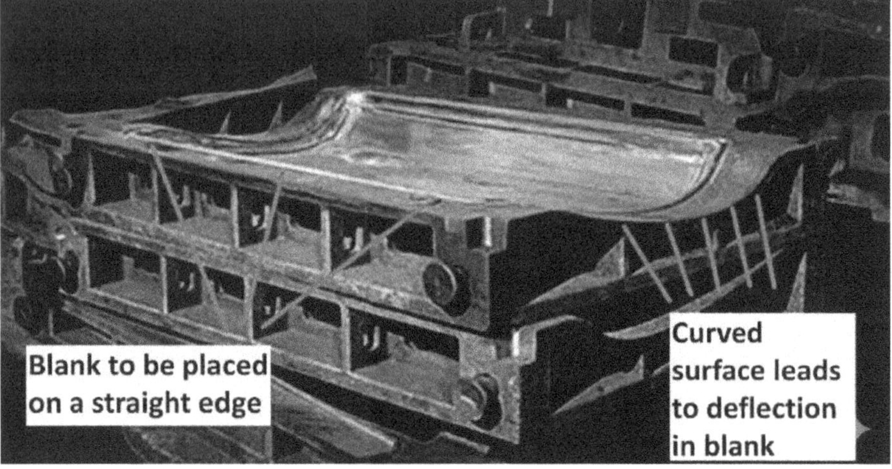

Potential troubles while ignoring the blank deflection :

1. Deformation (Sagging and Wrinkling)

The sheet will conform to the curvature due to its weight.

If the sheet is flexible, sagging occurs in areas unsupported by the curved surface.

Wrinkles may appear due to compressive forces in certain regions.

2. Stress Distribution

Tensile stresses develop along the sheet as it tries to stretch over the curve.

Compressive stresses may cause buckling in certain areas, especially for thin sheets.

Bending stresses occur due to the gravitational pull and surface contact.

3. Contact and Sliding Behavior

If the sheet is not constrained, gravity may cause it to slide down the curved surface.

Friction between the sheet and the surface plays a role in preventing or delaying movement.

Uneven contact may cause localized pressure points, leading to wear or damage.

4. Stability and Equilibrium

The final position of the sheet depends on gravity, friction, and material stiffness.

A sheet with higher stiffness will resist bending and maintain a flatter shape.

A sheet with low friction on the surface will tend to slide rather than deform.

Guidelines for die designers related to blank deflection :

For die designers, understanding the impact of gravity analysis on a sheet placed on a curved surface provides several benefits, especially in sheet metal forming, stamping, and deep drawing processes. Here's how it helps:

1. Predicting Material Behavior Before Forming

Helps designers understand how a sheet naturally conforms to the die surface due to gravity.

Identifies areas of potential sagging, wrinkles, or uneven contact before actual forming begins.

Allows adjustments to die curvature to improve material flow and reduce defects.

2. Optimizing Die Design for Better Forming

Ensures the sheet aligns properly with the die surface before pressing.

Helps in determining the best placement of blank holders to minimize sheet movement.

Reduces trial and error in prototype stages by predicting forming issues.

3. Reducing Wrinkles and Tearing

Shows how gravity affects the sheet's initial stress distribution before applying forming forces.

Helps adjust binder forces and clearances to prevent defects like wrinkling or tearing.

4. Improving Springback Compensation

Gravity analysis aids in understanding stress relaxation after forming.

Helps in compensating for springback effects, ensuring accurate final dimensions.

5. Enhancing Simulation Accuracy

Incorporating gravity in FEA simulations gives realistic predictions of how a sheet will behave in a die.

Reduces production errors, leading to cost savings and improved efficiency.

Case Study: Gravity Impact on Sheet Metal Forming for an Automotive Door Panel (The images haven't been displayed due to copyright issues)

Objective:

To analyze the effect of gravity on a sheet metal blank placed over a curved stamping die before forming. The goal is to identify potential sagging, wrinkling, and misalignment issues that could affect the final part quality.

Step 1: Initial Setup & Material Selection

Material: Aluminum Alloy 6061

Sheet Thickness: 1.2 mm

Die Surface: A curved surface with a complex shape (automotive door panel)

Gravity Direction: Acting downward (Z-axis)

Step 2: Gravity Analysis Before Forming

Using Finite Element Analysis (FEA) in AutoForm or Abaqus, the blank is placed on the die without any external forces applied, and gravity is simulated.

Key Observations:

The central region sags due to its weight.

Edges remain slightly elevated, not in full contact with the die.

Small compressive wrinkles appear at unsupported areas.

Step 3: Effects of Gravity on Forming

The sagging causes misalignment between the sheet and the die.

Increased risk of wrinkling when the press applies force.

Possible material thinning in areas that initially sagged more.

Step 4: Design Optimization

Modifications to Die & Process:

✓ Added blank holders to support edges and prevent sagging.

✓ Adjusted die curvature slightly to match the gravity-induced shape.

✓ Optimized binder force to reduce initial wrinkling.

New Simulation Results:

✓ Sheet maintains better contact with the die.

✓ Wrinkling and material thinning reduced.

✓ Improved accuracy of the final shape after springback.

Step 5: Practical Implementation & Benefits

✓ Reduced defects (wrinkles & misalignment) → Lower scrap rates.

✓ Better material flow → More consistent thickness after forming.

✓ Reduced springback → Less need for post-processing adjustments.

✓ Cost savings in die modifications & production efficiency.

Conclusion:

Gravity analysis before forming helps die designers:

◆ Predict issues like sagging & wrinkling early.

◆ Optimize die design for better material control.

◆ Reduce trial-and-error, saving costs and time.

Practice Exercise

Get free video tutorials along with CAD files on Author's website

https://sharmarakesh.co.in/index.php/tutorials/

Password : Forming2025

Set up a gravity analysis

11.1 Importing geometry:

First of all, import the geometry from the CAD file, as explained in the previous chapters.

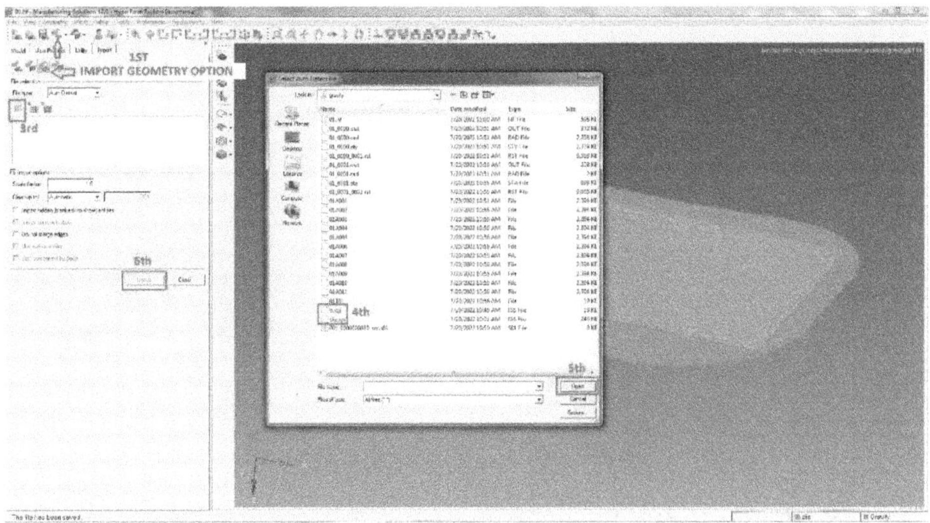

11.2 Renaming the parts:

Rename the parts under model tree, here we need only two parts, one is blank and other is binder or blank holder face, where it has to be places. Note that it is applicable only, where there is a convex, concave or irregular surface, that means only some area in under contact and rest are free and subjected to the effect of gravity.

11.3 Blank meshing:

For blank meshing, hide the die surface under the model tree as shown and make sure that the blank surface is visible, marked as 1st.

Under the Meshing dropdown menu, select the Automesh marked as 2nd in the below picture.

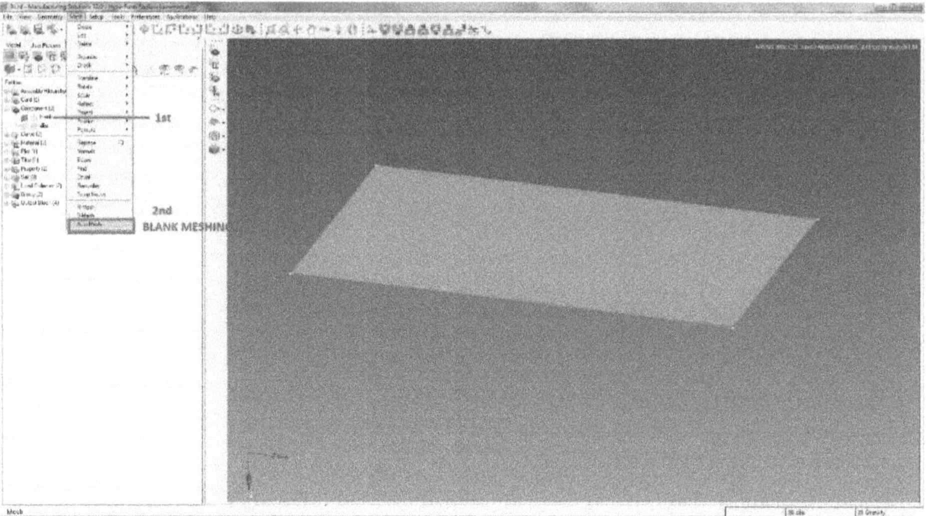

Show the blank under the model menu, marked as 1st in the below picture.

Select the element size, marked 2nd and select the mesh type to Quads only "3rd marking".

For the surface selection browsing window from 4th marking, refer the next steps.

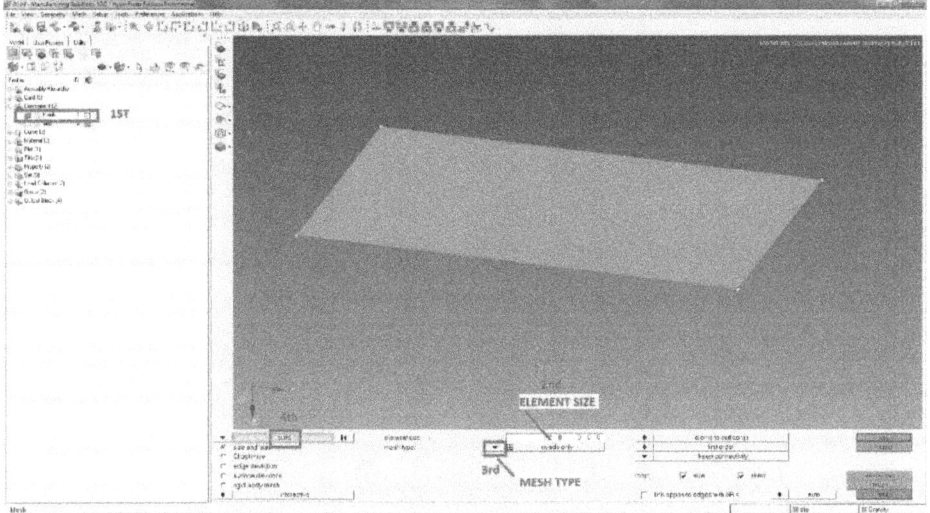

Under the surface window 4th , select the displayed option ''5th marking''
and select proceed ''6th marking'' as given in the below image.

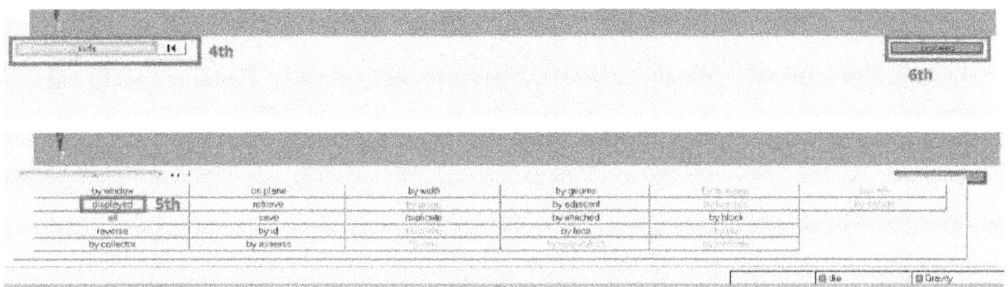

11.4 Tool meshing:

Select the R-mesh (Rigid mesh) marked as 1st under the utility menu.

For element setting, refer the same values, marked as 2nd and click mesh marked as 3rd.

For further selection of the surface, use same setting as mentioned in the above step of blank meshing.

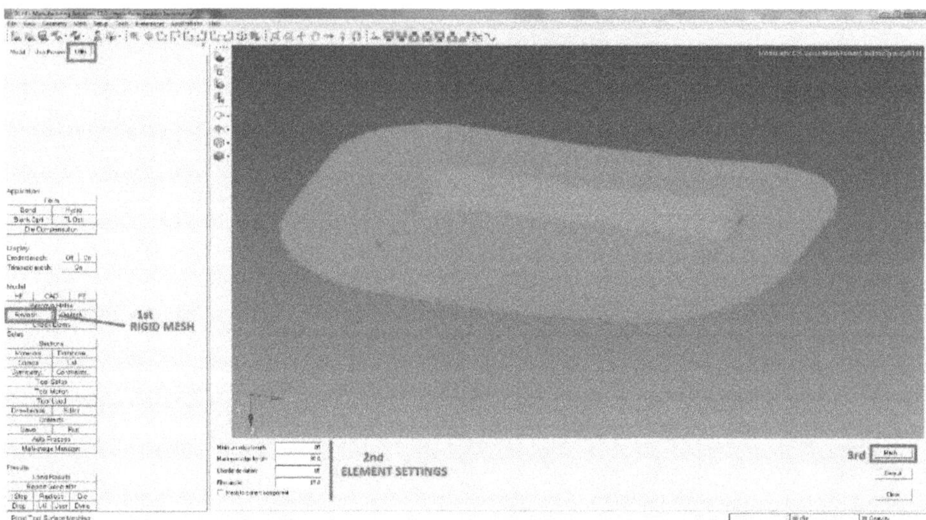

11.5 Auto process:

Select the Auto process option under the utility menu, marked as 1st.

Pick the Gravity option at 2nd marking, Draw direction as 3rd marking and put the material and thickness values, mentioned as 4th and 5th.

Select autoposition 6th followed by apply 7th and close from 8th marking.

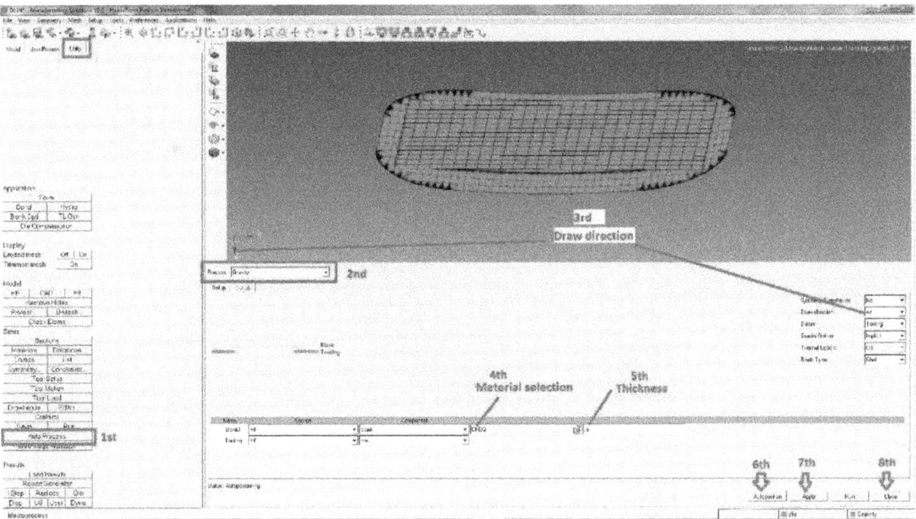

11.6 Save and run:

Pick the Save as from the file menu dropdown marked as 1st.

Save the file as shown 2nd marking and run the analysis from the 3rd and 4th.

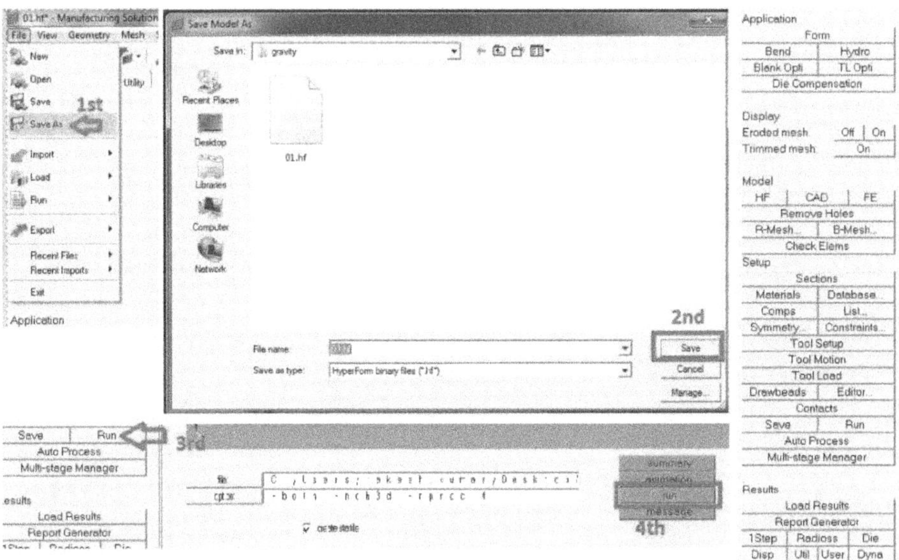

11.7 Load results:

After the post processing, load the results in to hyperview directly as shown in the trailing image.

To open the file, pick 1st and browse the path from the 2nd, pick the A001 file marked as 3rd and open 4thand apply 5th marked.

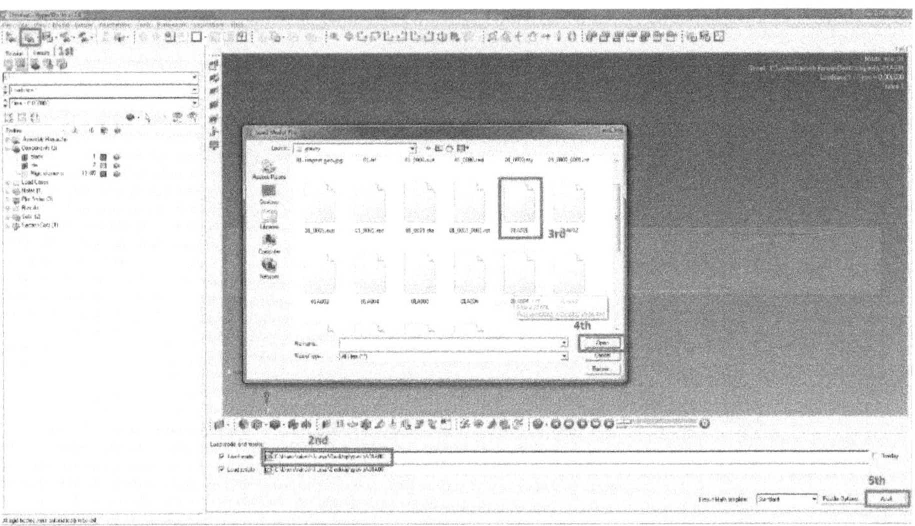

11.8Measure the deformation:

Pick the measure option marked as 1st, pick the axis of measurement 2nd.

Under the nodes selection 3rd, pick the start and end points 4th and 5th.

This measured value 6th is the initial position before gravity, marked at the 7th position as the start point of animation control.

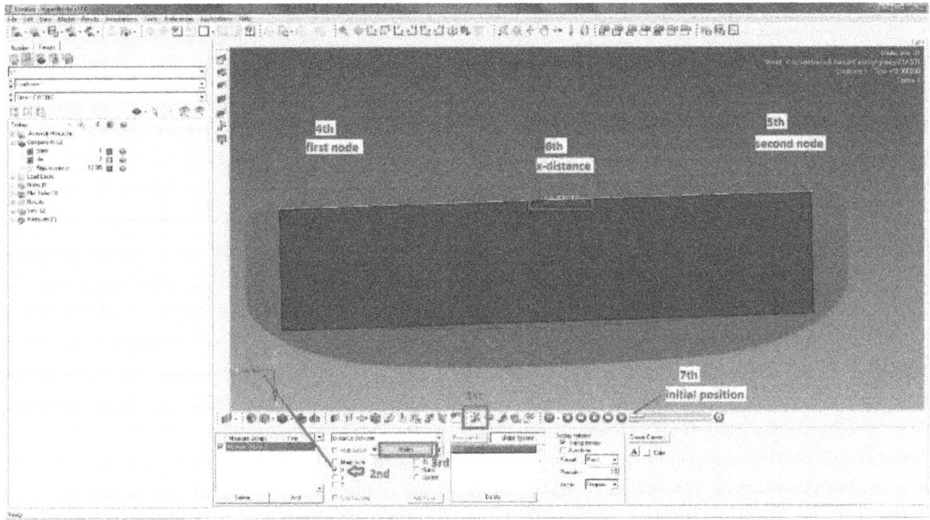

The measured value will change, as we move the slider of animation control to the final position. You can clearly see the bend in the blank due to the effect of gravity, which depend up on the blank size, metal thickness and depth of blank holder contour.

11.9 Compare with the original geometry:

To show the original part to compare with, press open from 1st, then untick the load results marked as 2nd and tick the overlay 3rd.

Open the file from 4th, pick the .0000.rad file 5th , open from 6th marking and click apply 7th, as shown in the below image.

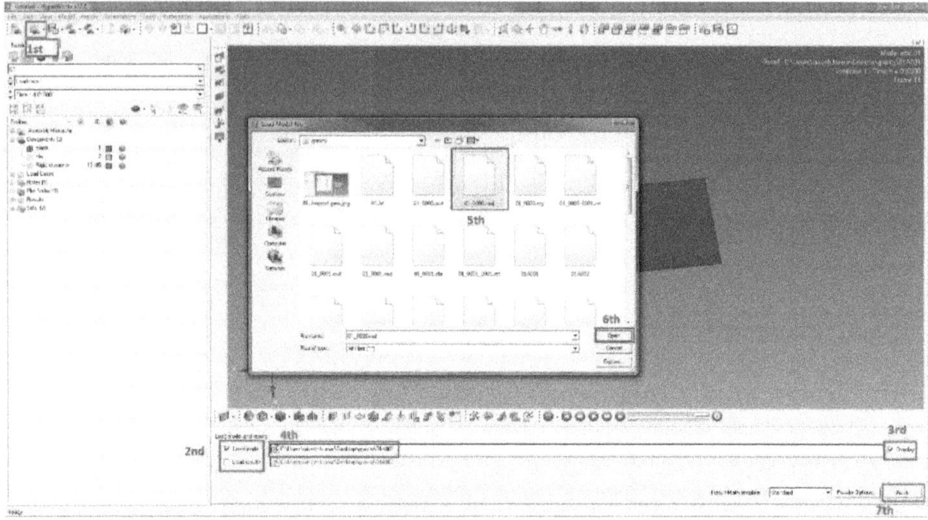

Grey is the original geometry 1st marking, while 2nd is the affected part at the animation position as initial, marked as 3rd.

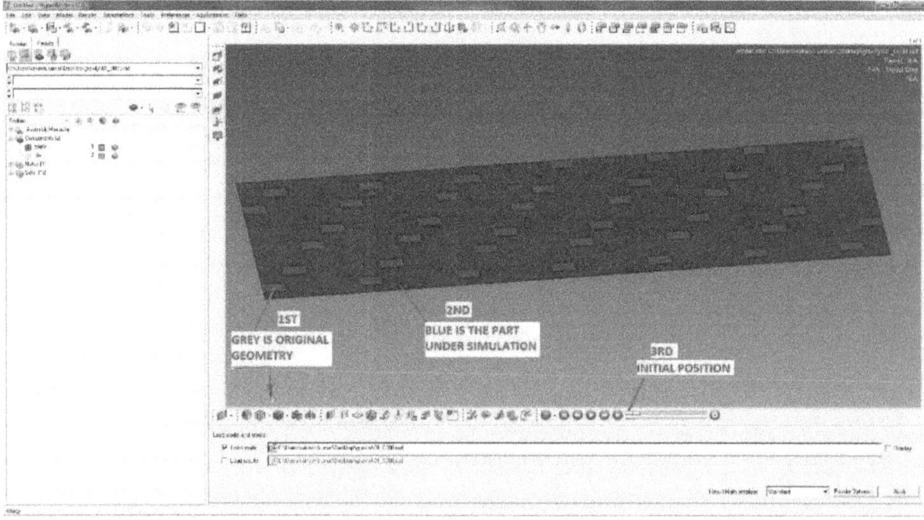

The difference among initial 1st and final 2nd is vivid at the final position 3rd of the animation control bar.

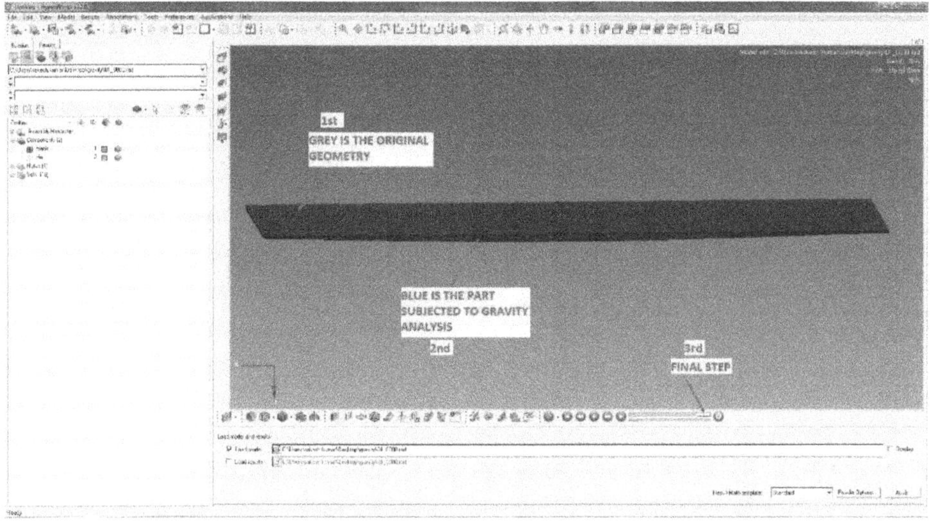
1st
GREY IS THE ORIGINAL GEOMETRY
BLUE IS THE PART SUBJECTED TO GRAVITY ANALYSIS
2nd
3rd
FINAL STEP

Rakesh Kumar is a Mechanical Engineer and Operations Management expert with over 18 years of specialized experience in the automotive industry. His core expertise lies in R&D, New Product Development (NPD), and Metal Forming Simulation.

An innovator by nature, Rakesh holds **3 Design Patents and 9 Utility Patents**, reflecting his commitment to pushing the boundaries of engineering design. Throughout his career, he has been instrumental in the development of over **200 complex sheet metal parts**, applying simulation techniques to predict and prevent real-world manufacturing failures. This profound hands-on experience shapes the content of this book, ensuring it remains a practical tool for solving industrial problems rather than just a theoretical text.

In addition to his corporate achievements, Rakesh is dedicated to engineering education. He developed the digital platform, <u>sharmarakesh.co.in</u>, to create a comprehensive learning ecosystem for his readers. By purchasing this book, engineers gain access to exclusive video tutorials and practice CAD files on the website, bridging the gap between reading about simulation and actually performing it.